Gordon Brown

The Biography

Gordon Brown

The
Biography

by

Paul Routledge

SIMON & SCHUSTER
A VIACOM COMPANY

First published in Great Britain by Simon & Schuster, 1998
An imprint of Simon & Schuster Ltd
A Viacom Company

Simon & Schuster Ltd
West Garden Place
Kendal Street
London
W2 2AQ

Simon & Schuster Australia
Sydney

A CIP catalogue record for this book is available from the British Library.

ISBN 0-684-81954-6

3 5 7 9 1 8 6 4

Where possible, permission to quote has been obtained from all
copyright holders.

Printed and bound in Great Britain by
Butler & Tanner Ltd, Frome and London

Contents

PREFACE

GORDON BROWN PROMISED TO 'HIT THE GROUND running' when Labour took power in May 1997. As Chancellor of the Exchequer, he kept his word. The reforms came thick and fast. For his biographer, the problem was keeping up. Sometimes it was impossible, and the interview had to be adjourned to a frantic car drive to Heathrow airport before his holiday flight to the USA. But Gordon Brown did make space in an overcrowded diary, even though there were areas of his life about which he preferred not to talk.

Accordingly, I am grateful to the friends of his childhood and youth, particularly Murray Elder, and of his days as a student politician, especially Jonathan Wills, and of his early political years, most notably Alex Falconer MEP, Bill Campbell, Dr Colin Currie, and David Stoddart, who was Gordon's agent for many years. Nick Brown, the Chief Whip, was particularly helpful on the Labour leadership period, and other MPs – including the ex-Chancellor Kenneth Clarke – gave generously of their time. Charlie Whelan, the Chancellor's Press Secretary, and Ed Balls, his Economic Adviser, were also of assistance. However, thanks are due most to Gordon's two brothers, John and Andrew, and to his parents. The help was all theirs. The faults are all mine.

I wish to thank Mainstream Publishing for permission to quote from Gordon's books, and my agent Jane Bradish-Ellames, together with Martin Fletcher and Jacquie Clare at

Simon and Schuster, who got the book together in record time. I must finally thank my wife Lynne for her patience and support in the face of demanding deadlines.

This biography is dedicated to the memory of Jimmy Airlie, the hero of the Upper Clyde Shipbuilders' work-in, who showed us all how not to fear the bosses.

Cowling
North Yorkshire
November 1997

CHAPTER 1

FIRST BUDGET

SMILING BROADLY, HE HELD THE NEW RED LEATHER BUDGET box aloft outside Number 11, Downing Street. It was a symbol of changing times. Instead of Gladstone's battered old brown briefcase with its worn royal crest, Chancellor Gordon Brown used one made by craft apprentices at the Rosyth shipyard in his Scottish constituency to take Labour's first budget for nearly two decades to the House of Commons. The young workers, Craig Miller, Leona Reid, Eileen Mullin and Eric Axford, gathered round him as the camera shutters clicked furiously. 'One on your own, Gordon,' cried the photographers. 'One on your own!' They wanted pictures of him isolated, alone with his plans for the future, but the Fife teenagers stuck by his side. It was a striking cameo of change: New Labour with the new generation. Of the following day's papers, only the churlish *Guardian* had the nerve to airbrush out the young men and women next to him, as though they were not part of political reality.

Brown stepped into his official car for the short ride across Whitehall. He had intended to go on foot, as he had arrived in Downing Street exactly two months earlier, but the press of the crowds on that hot July morning made walking impossible.

There was an air of high expectation as he swept round the corner of Parliament Square and into New Palace Yard beneath Big Ben. At last, after eighteen years of Conservative rule glorying in inequality, the people would see an alternative political vision: social justice, the moral purpose of a son of the manse who believed in 'the equal worth of every human being'.

His personal assistant, Sue Nye, was by his side as the chancellor made his way through the Members' entrance, up a series of back stairs into the chamber of the House of Commons. His budget statement on 2 July 1977 was due at 3.30 p.m., immediately after the weekly half-hour of Prime Minister's Questions. He was on the government front bench on the dot, a bottle of House of Commons mineral water – from a Scottish spring – by the despatch box to keep him going during the ordeal that lay ahead. Previous chancellors preferred something stronger. Kenneth Clarke allowed himself a smoky single-malt whisky. Gordon Brown enjoys a drink – indeed, he likes nothing more than a glass of champagne – but 'champers' would have been quite out of place on this occasion. It would come later.

There was plenty to toast in his statement, but the Tories were determined to spoil the show. Peter Lilley, looking uncomfortable on the Opposition benches as shadow chancellor, put down a private notice question complaining about advance leaks of the budget contents appearing in the press – chiefly the *Financial Times*, which has sources in the Treasury – ahead of the announcement in the Commons of tax changes. Essentially, Lilley's move, which required a ministerial response, was a try-on. All Oppositions try to wrong-foot the government on budget day. Normally, the Speaker simply rules such mischievous tricks out of order. On this occasion Betty Boothroyd had not, to the 'absolute rage' of the government's chief whip, Nick Brown, and business managers, who had not been consulted. Similar requests by Labour when it was in Opposition had been rejected, even in 1996 when practically the entire budget was leaked to the *Mirror* (which did not print it) and the *Sun* (which did). There was deep-seated hostility on the Labour benches, where Miss Boothroyd had sat for many years before ascending to the Speaker's chair. Even the new MPs sensed something was wrong, and became restive.

Ann Taylor, the combative Leader of the House and a rising star in the new government, knocked Lilley and his fellow bovver-boys round the field for fifteen minutes, while Gordon Brown sat patiently with the budget secrets on his knee, occasionally inspecting his well-polished black shoes. Only he knew everything. Brown turned to Tony Blair and murmured: 'We've waited eighteen years. We can wait another eighteen minutes.' Finally, at 3.46 p.m., Madam Speaker cut short the Whitehall farce and in accordance with parliamentary custom left the chair, handing over to her deputy, Sir Alan Haselhurst, who called the chancellor. Up in the gallery above the Opposition sat Kenneth Clarke, taking notes for his article in the *Independent*.

Brown gripped the despatch box as if it were the lectern in the kirk in Kirkcaldy where, as a boy, he heard his father preach so often, and launched into a fifty-nine-minute 'people's budget' speech that held the House in silent attention. The church-like calm sent Lucy, the guide dog sitting at the feet of the blind education secretary, David Blunkett, straight off to sleep.

The chancellor said his central purpose was to ensure that Britain was equipped to rise to the challenge of the new and fast-changing global economy, and 'not just a few of us, but every one of us'. Drawing on an old favourite, George Orwell's analysis of 'the British genius', he argued that this challenge offered a historic opportunity. 'The dynamic economies of the future will be those that unlock the talent of all their people, and our nation's creativity, adaptability and belief in hard work and self-improvement – the very qualities that made Britain lead the world in the eighteenth and nineteenth centuries – are precisely the qualities that we need to make Britain a strong economic power in the twenty-first century.'[1] To achieve that goal, however, the nation must address the four weaknesses that had held it back for too many years: instability, under-investment, unemployment and waste of talent.

He went through each in turn, listing the actions he had taken or intended to take. An Irishman would say that Gordon Brown is a terrible one for the lists. His friend the comedian Rory Bremner once hilariously mimicked him, growling, 'What the people of this country want is lists: long lists, short lists, depressing statistics, disturbing industry results and gloomy surveys.'[2] Now he could look on the bright side. Brown reminded MPs that, in the eight weeks since being elected on 1 May, he had brought in a wholly new framework for monetary stability. The government set the inflation target, and the Bank of England had been given unprecedented powers to set interest rates to meet that target. He would now do the same for the public finances. He pledged first to observe the 'golden rule' of borrowing only to invest, not to finance current spending, and second to keep public debt 'at a prudent and stable level' of national income. Against a background of rising anxiety about inflation, he disclosed a £10 billion tightening of fiscal policy – including £5.2 billion raised by his 'windfall tax' on the privatised utilities – over the ensuing two years.

The windfall tax had been perhaps the greatest issue of controversy in the run-up to the general election. The Conservatives criticised it as a tax on consumers, who would have to pay the price for Gordon Brown's 'welfare to work' programme, aimed at getting 250,000 jobless young people and the long-term unemployed off the dole. Industries most likely to have to pay the tax – gas, electricity, water, British Telecom and the like – squealed loudly about the raid on their excess profits. Sir Iain Vallance, chairman of BT, which was making profits of £90 a second, even threatened high-court action to have the tax declared unlawful. Brown's confidence that the cash-rich privatised utilities would pay up was undimmed. He knew, though MPs could not be told, that British Telecom had already thrown in the towel.

In a private letter to the chancellor on the day he took office,

2 May, Vallance – who is a personal friend of Tony Blair and who had lobbied hard to be excluded from the windfall net – said, 'I write to offer my warmest congratulations on your confirmation as Chancellor, and in what overwhelming circumstances. The tectonic plates have moved, in no small part due to your rigour on matters financial and economic. We are, of course, very aware that Labour has a clear mandate for the windfall levy, and I know from our conversation in March, that we fall within the scope of the tax.' He enclosed a paper prepared by BT experts on assessment and collection of the tax, to share with Brown and his team, and offered to meet again to pursue the matter, once the dust had settled. 'In the meantime, I hope you have some peace to savour the triumph,' Vallance added. 'Once more many congratulations – we very much look forward to working with you and your colleagues in bringing in a new era.' No court in the land would have ruled against Gordon Brown after that.

Turning to investment, the chancellor made clear that his aim was to concentrate on laying the foundations for 'tomorrow's wealth'. His two-year corporate tax review, begun in Opposition, would encourage personal savings, higher levels of investment and more long-term investment. 'Long-term' was a recurrent theme in his first budget. To stimulate investment, he abolished tax credits for pension funds, raising as much as a 5p hike in income tax would have done but also raising howls of anguish from the pension companies most affected by the change. He also announced a 2 per cent cut, to 31 per cent, in the rate of corporation tax, the lowest it has ever been – lower than in Britain's major competitors, Germany, France, America and Japan – and backdated it to April. He went further, slicing 2 per cent off the 23 per cent rate tax on small companies, and doubled the capital allowances on plant and machinery for small and medium-sized businesses for one year.

'This government will support the small businesses of Britain,' he declared. In another mouth, those words might have rung hollow. For years, Labour had been portrayed as hostile to business. Gordon Brown was neither an enemy of business nor a stranger to it. On the contrary, as he told the CBI conference in November 1996, 'Business is in my blood.' On his father's side, he comes from a family of farmers, and on his mother's from a family of builders and merchants. He once owned shares in the firm, of which his mother was a director. As an undergraduate in Edinburgh, he turned the Student Publications Board into a profitable business, and later he was briefly a director of the publishing company that brought out his books. As a television producer, he investigated the murkier side of business and politics in Scotland, and as a politician he had specialised in industry, commerce, jobs and economic affairs over the last decade and a half. For him, they were all part of the same mosaic, but one that needed a new artistic hand.

One industry in particular he singled out for encouragement: films. Brown is a serious film buff, and has been ever since the days when the whole family went to the pictures in Kirkcaldy for a treat. He was a member of the university film society, run by Linda Miles, who went on to become director of the Edinburgh Film Festival. One of his closest friends is Wilf Stevenson, director of the British Film Institute, who recalls that on one holiday 'We saw a movie every night for ten days.' Brown thought *Braveheart* was 'terrific' and he couldn't wait to see Billy Connolly and Dame Judi Dench in *Mrs Brown*, the story of Queen Victoria and the inseparable companion of her later years, Highland ghillie John Brown. So it was no very great surprise that his first budget rewarded the talents of British film-makers. Production and acquisition costs on UK films with budgets of £15 million or less would now qualify for 100 per cent tax write-off on completion. This £30 million measure should boost not only the number of British films but also British exports, he insisted.

Fiddling occasionally with his watchstrap, Brown moved on to his overriding passion: work. A true product of his Presbyterian upbringing, the chancellor is a convinced exponent of the Protestant work ethic. He honestly believes that work is good for the soul, which should mean that his own is in no danger. Colleagues describe him as a workaholic, first in to work and last home, often taking great bundles with him. Advisers at the Treasury dread the early-morning call at home. While they are thinking of getting up, Brown is already at his desk, working through his ministerial red boxes. One of his favourite new soundbites is 'I have seen the future. And it is work.' This is a play, albeit a serious one, on the remark made to the financier Bernard Baruch by an American journalist, Lincoln Steffens, on his return from Bolshevik Russia in 1919. He actually said, 'I have been over into the future, and it works',[3] though a diplomat who travelled with him believed that Steffens (in the finest journalistic tradition) rehearsed the comment even before he met Lenin.

In the new economy, Brown told MPs, in which capital, inventions and even raw materials were mobile, Britain had only one truly national resource: the talent and potential of its people. Yet one in five of working-age households had no one earning a wage. 'In place of welfare,' he declared, 'there should be work.' The welfare state 'was and remains' a great British achievement, but for millions out of work or suffering poverty, the welfare state denied rather than provided opportunity. It was time for the welfare state to put opportunity back into people's hands.

Getting out another little list, he said, 'First, everyone in need of work should have the opportunity to work. Secondly, we must ensure that work pays. Thirdly, everyone who seeks to advance through employment and education must be given the means to advance.' Labour would create a ladder of opportunity, allowing the many, by their own efforts, to benefit from opportunities once open only to a few. From 1998, young people would be offered four options: a job with an employer; work with a voluntary organisation; work on an environmental task force; and, for those without basic qualifications, the chance of full-time education or training.

However, the 'iron chancellor' did not flinch from the hard side of his New Deal. With these new opportunities for young people came new responsibilities, he told the House. 'There will be no fifth option – to stay at home on full benefit. So when they sign on for benefit, they will be signing up for work. Benefits will be cut if young people refuse to take up the opportunities.' In fact, they would face the loss of up to 40 per cent of benefits. This tough regime was not originally to the liking of many on the left of the party when it was first mooted. Even some Shadow Cabinet members recoiled from its 'coercive' nature. Labour Briefing, the hard-left grouping, denounced the scheme as intended to reassure the middle classes that a Labour government would respond to their anxieties about the development of an underclass of the long-term unemployed.

Such condemnation misses the point. Brown holds fast to the belief that no section of society – and no one – should suffer permanent exclusion. 'For too long, the United Kingdom has been united only in name,' he maintained. 'From today, ours is a country where everyone has a contribution to make.' Accordingly, he also addressed the needs of the one million lone parents bringing up two million children. They, too, should have employment opportunities. He allocated £200 million from the windfall fund for advice, training and day and after-school child care. He also gave tax breaks for the cost of child care, so that lone parents on benefit could earn up to £100 a week without losing in-work benefits. These measures, together with the abolition of the previous government's nursery-school vouchers and the offer of nursery-school places for all four-year-olds, represented 'the first step towards a national child care strategy for the UK', said the chancellor. He further announced £200 million of windfall cash to fund those who are disabled or on incapacity benefit, and who want training or work.

On income tax, Brown promised to introduce a bottom rate of 10p in the pound 'as soon as it is prudent to do so'. With the national minimum wage, set at a 'sensible' level, this would alleviate in-work poverty. But the non-driving, non-smoking chancellor also put up petrol by 4p a litre from six o'clock that evening, and a packet of twenty cigarettes by 19p from 1 December. He moved quickly on to honour his election pledge to cut VAT on domestic fuel and power from 8 per cent to 5 per cent – the lowest level permitted under EU rules – from 1 September, well in advance of winter bills. To pay for this measure, he abolished tax relief on private health insurance for the over-60s. He had no changes to make in the basic or top rates of income tax, and promised not to extend VAT to children's clothes, food, books, newspapers or public transport fares during Labour's first term of office. 'This is a government who keep their promises on tax,' he added, careless of grammar. *Hansard* recorded him thus, though the official Treasury version had him saying, 'This is a government that keeps its promises on tax.'

Brown turned to housing, promising an extra £900 million to councils for building and repairing homes, but for home-buyers, particularly the well-off, he had a shock. In the name of bringing stability to the volatile house market, he cut tax relief on mortgage interest from 15 per cent to 10 per cent, operative from 1 April 1998, and increased stamp duty to 1.5 per cent on sales above £250,000 and 2 per cent above £500,000. The House had been quiet up to this point, but his announcement brought forth subdued laughter on his side, and derisive jeers from the Opposition benches. Brown looked around in-quiringly. Tony Blair, who had just put his Islington home on the market for £650,000 after being told it was a security risk, was grinning ruefully. The penny dropped, and the *Yorkshire Post* sketch-writer noted a break in the chancellor's stern gaze: 'a brief, boyish smile lit up his face'.

A five-year deficit-reduction plan came next, committing the government to cutting the amount it owed. Borrowing was slashed by £6 billion in 1997/98, and by almost £7 billion in the next financial year. Beyond that, Brown published a range of projections based on different assumptions, but all below

those of the Major government. 'For this year, and the foresee-
able future, we are comfortably within the Maastricht criteria
for levels of both debt and borrowing.' Tantalisingly, he left the
subject there, prompting unease among Tory Eurosceptics that
Labour was positioning the UK so as to be able to be in the first
wave of EU countries joining the European single currency in
1999. Brown is in favour of the Euro, in principle, if it is in
Britain's interest to join and after Parliament has agreed and the
people have spoken through a referendum. It was a delicious
tease, no more.

The chancellor left until last his 'goodies' for the National
Health Service and education. He gave £1.2 billion from the
contingency reserves to the NHS, but only for 1998/99, and £1
billion for schools in the same year – plus a further £1.3 billion
of windfall cash to repair and upgrade school buildings and
equipment, for which schools would have to bid, on the basis
of a modernisation plan. Those measures had Labour backbenchers, who had been wondering when the 'meat' was coming, waving their order papers in pleasure. Brown allowed
himself a brief moment of self-congratulation about 'a people's
Budget for Britain's future', commended it to the House, and
sat down. The thunderous applause woke up Blunkett's dog.

The debate on the budget resolution that followed went on
for more than five hours. William Hague, the new leader of the
Conservative Party, was now thankful that the media speculation had been so accurate. He made a reasonable fist of his
response, tweaking Tony Blair – the stamp-duty hike would be
of interest only 'to rich people like the Prime Minister' – and
criticising it as a tax-raising budget. As indeed it was. The
abolition of tax credit for pension funds would yield more than
£5 billion a year by the turn of the century, noted Alex
Brummer in the *Guardian* the next day. 'This is the tax bombshell which was waiting to be exposed during the election, but
was never able to surface because of Labour's efficient spin-
doctoring,' he added. Removing the tax advantage ought to
persuade corporate Britain to invest more of its retained prof-

its, but occupational pension schemes would be hard hit. People would have to pay more to have the same pension income.

But the immediate reaction was not far short of euphoric. The Tory *Daily Mail* commented, 'Mr Brown, it must be said, has got down to business in fine style. He has inherited a boom, and he made clear he has no intention of letting it go bust.' On the same page, crusty right-winger Paul Johnson wrote, 'It would be churlish to deny that he has got it right so far.' Invoking another famous native of Kirkcaldy, the free-market economist author of *The Wealth of Nations*, he concluded, 'Long live Adam Smith, and his latest pupil, Gordon Brown.' The *Independent* thought he was 'prudent, managerial, responsible . . . a brilliant opening Budget', adding, 'Mr Blair, and his heavy-jawed but cheerfully confident friend, seem determined to say what they mean, and do what they say. If they're lucky, it might even succeed.' Kenneth Clarke stuck to the party line that this was 'tax now, spend later', but admitted that it was 'a very clever political Budget'.

With notices like that, mulled over when the first editions were delivered to a budget-night party in the formal rooms at Number 11, Brown might have been tempted to quit while he was ahead. Notoriously, a budget that is well received on the night falls out of favour within weeks, even days. Sure enough, by Friday morning the *Daily Mail* had reverted to type, with the screaming headline 'Who will pay for Brown's raid on pensions?' Under the headline 'Savers Browned Off', the *Daily Telegraph* accused the chancellor of a breach of pensioners' trust and predicted that his abolition of dividend tax credit would probably reduce investment. 'Mr Brown has simply made a grab for money where he thinks people will not notice it,' said the paper loftily. Malcolm Bruce, the Liberal Democrats' Treasury spokesman, was wittier: 'The Budget was the economic equivalent of a bottle of plonk – it may have seemed palatable on the night, but it's going to leave us all with a hangover tomorrow.'[4]

Chancellor Brown had other problems. A soaring pound –
catapulted to DM 2.96 – was hitting exporters hard, and a
surge in demand pointed towards an interest-rate rise.
However, the much-trumpeted slump in share prices of 400
points over the loss of pension-fund tax breaks failed to
materialise. In fact, the stock market rallied, rising by 200
points in three days after the budget, restoring most of the
'losses' suffered by the pension funds. Opinion began to swing
back his way. Even the 'City Comment' column of Saturday's
Daily Telegraph scoffed at the 'petulant' pension funds' com-
parison of Brown's actions to Robert Maxwell's theft. 'In truth,
they had it coming,' said the paper. 'The tax-exempt status of
pension funds encouraged all sorts of fiddles.' And a Gallup
poll in the *Telegraph* showed that voters backed the budget. The
government's approval rating was 74 per cent – almost twice as
high as John Major's best of 38 per cent. Labour's lead on
economic competence, a mere six points on the eve of polling
day, now stood at thirty points.[5]

When the budget debate wound up the following week, the
Liberal Democrats recaptured the headlines, with their assertion of a £5 billion 'black hole' in the budget arithmetic. They
pointed out that Brown had decided that inflation forecasts in
the budget 'red book' should be increased from 2 per cent to
2.75 per cent, but the government had not put up the spending totals of departments, leaving Whitehall with the unenvi-
able task of squaring the circle. Malcolm Bruce told the media
that the figures made 'an absolute mockery' of the chancellor's
promises of more money for schools and the NHS. Labour
officials accused him of being 'economically illiterate', but
failed to dispose of the charge.

More predictably, the Labour Party's left finally woke up and
fired off a few salvoes. Ken Livingstone MP chose the impecca-
bly right-wing *Sunday Telegraph* to denounce the budget as 'a
tragic lost opportunity for Britain'. He thought its 'errors' were
all the more surprising because the chancellor 'remains funda-
mentally a man of the left' and had correctly analysed the

nation's problems. 'Unfortunately, his half measures barely scratch the surface. Far from being the Iron Chancellor Britain needs, Mr Brown is more like a soft cuddly toy still eager to seduce the voters of Middle England.'[6] The crusty business commentator Bernard Dineen confided to his readers in the *Yorkshire Post*: 'This will prove to have been a cowardly Budget as well as a damaging Budget for British industry. Every real problem has been dodged in the interests of gimmickry.'[7]

When the Finance Bill implementing the budget went for its second reading in the Commons on 10 July, it had a majority of 135. It passed on to the statute book at the end of the month to the accompaniment of another celebration party. Critics still abounded. Brown had not done enough to curtail consumer spending, which was pushing up inflation and, by extension, interest rates, they said. He should have been bolder on mortgage-interest tax relief, and scrapped it altogether; he probably will, but in stages. Gavyn Davies, chief economist at Goldman Sachs merchant bank, and one of the City's most respected commentators, told the Treasury Select Committee that he was 'very comfortable' about the fiscal arithmetic. 'Still more taxes in the Budget would have represented overkill.'[8]

There seemed to be no quarter from which Gordon Brown could not expect support. The Prince of Wales agreed to a joint operation between his Prince's Trust volunteer scheme and the government. Speaking to employers in Glasgow, he said, 'I'm delighted that the government is considering some of the lessons learnt by my programme as it develops its New Deal for unemployed young people and also its plan for millennium volunteers.' Prince Charles attended a dinner with the chancellor hosted by Business in the Community on 15 July, when Brown called on employers to make 'welfare-to-work' a success. At this, his first official engagement with the prince, he said his aim was to make the unemployed employable, and to rebuild the welfare state around the work ethic. 'I want you all to feel part of a national crusade to tackle the threat of an underclass,' he urged.

The next day, David Sheppard, the Bishop of Liverpool, welcomed the budget as a step in the right direction. He told the Church of England General Synod that 'there could be enough good work for everyone' and urged private-sector bosses to take pride in expanding employment rather than cutting jobs to save costs. Unemployment was offensive to God, said the bishop, arguing that the government should alter the structure of taxes to make it less costly to employ people and more expensive to use other resources.

Between them, the prince, the bishop and the chancellor appeared to be brokering common ground in public policy on an issue close to Brown's heart. Ironically, that same day new unemployment figures showed the number out of work and claiming benefit at a seven-year low, at 5.7 per cent of the workforce.

The final seal of approval for Brown's first budget came from the International Monetary Fund (IMF) just a week before Parliament rose for the long summer recess. 'The new government has made an excellent start,' said the IMF. 'It has set a high standard for its economic policies, aiming to maintain stability and foster long-term growth while seeking fairness and developing human potential.'[9] (It would be difficult to imagine a sharper contrast to the IMF's verdict on Denis Healey in 1976, which demanded £2 billion spending cuts and sent Labour's political fortunes plunging.) Publication of the report coincided with the chancellor's first appearance before the Treasury Select Committee, when he rejected IMF advice to widen the VAT net to raise revenue. 'There are fairness issues here,' he declared. He promised a 'green budget' consultation paper in the autumn, ahead of his second budget in March 1998. To a heavyweight interview team from *The Times* he appealed, 'Judge me over a period of years, not weeks.' Then he jetted off to Cape Cod for a three-week holiday with his brothers, John and Andrew. More discreetly, he was joined by his girlfriend, Sarah Macaulay, a 34-year-old public affairs consultant.

In little over three months, Gordon Brown had set a course towards the objectives he had nurtured over fourteen years in public life. The idea of goals is a family trait. His father, the Rev. John E. Brown, once preached a sermon on Jeremiah 50:5, which says, 'Thou shall ask the way to Zion, with their faces thitherward.' He had been reading Lord Butler's latest volume, *The Art of Memory*, which had a chapter on Ernest Bevin, foreign secretary in Winston Churchill's wartime coalition government. The Rev. Brown has always had a sneaking interest in politics. He quoted Butler on Churchill and Bevin, 'the two most forceful ministers with whom I worked. On the surface they might seem to have been totally different in every way . . . But both were egotistical, both tried to control this fault, both were impatient and both determined on set objectives.' The Rev. Brown reflected on those words. 'That phrase, *determined on set objectives*, is worth wondering over. Should not all of us, like these two statesmen, have set objectives, which we are determined to attain?'[10] He need look no further than his own son to see these qualities in action.

CHAPTER 2

FIFE CHILDHOOD

THE KINGDOM OF FIFE IS A PLACE SET APART, EVEN IN HIGHLY individualistic Scotland. Its brooding hills and fertile valleys have nurtured a strong spirit, proud even. The Brown family can trace their roots back to the land there for almost two centuries. Gordon Brown's ancestors were tenant farmers at Inchgall Mill, near Ballingry, in what is now his parliamentary constituency of Dunfermline East. In the early nineteenth century they moved a few miles south to Easter and Wester Lochhead in the parish of Auchtertool, and members of the family continued to farm there on the Wemyss estate for more than a hundred years.

But Gordon's great-grandfather, John Brown, struck out on his own in 1878, taking over the tenancy of Brigghills Farm, land that had previously been farmed by his father-in-law, Sandy. The farm lay in the parish of Auchterderran, close by the town of Lochgelly, and was part of the Earl of Minto's estates. Although predominantly agricultural, the neighbourhood was very much part of the well-established Fife coalfield. The Minto colliery was situated at Brigghills, providing much-needed local employment but disfiguring the landscape. Nothing remains of it now.

John Brown farmed there for the next forty years, raising a family of eight children, six boys and two girls. Gordon's grandfather, Ebenezer Brown, was the fourth child to arrive, and the first after the family moved to Brigghills. He went to the village school in Auchterderran. The family worshipped at Churchmount, a United Presbyterian congregation, in nearby Lochgelly, where Ebenezer's father was an elder. John Brown evidently had a well-developed sense of social duty. He was also a parish councillor and a member of Kirkcaldy Burgh Council. When the boy Ebenezer left school, he left home to work on his father's cousin's farm in Lochhead, where almost twenty years later he met and married Rachel Mitchell Mavor, the daughter of a builder from Dysart, a village on the coast. The couple thought there was an 'understanding' that they would farm Lochhead. But there was a family disagreement, and Ebenezer and his new bride decamped twenty miles east to take over the tenancy of Peatieshill Farm, New Gilston, in the parish of Largo, the birthplace of Alexander Selkirk (the original for Defoe's Robinson Crusoe).

It was at Peatieshill Farm on 26 October 1914, that Gordon Brown's father, John Ebenezer, was born. World War I was about to break out. When baby John was only a few months old, his father gave up the farm tenancy and became a shepherd at Nisbet Field Farm, Letham, in the hills near Cupar. His work on the farm was classified as essential to the war effort, and he stayed with his sheep until the armistice of 1918. Thereafter, he worked on the Jeannestown farm, part of the Rankeillor estate owned by the Nairn family, a rich family of linoleum-manufacturers in Kirkcaldy. He was a shepherd there until going into semi-retirement at Kingskettle, in the mid-Fife valley of the River Eden, in 1929.

John Ebenezer Brown was an only child. He walked every day to the Cults Public School (a local authority school, not to be confused with an English public – i.e., private – school) in Pitlessie. He went on to Bell Baxter High School in Cupar in 1926, the year of the General Strike, which sorely affected the

Fife coalfield. He excelled academically, and at the age of eighteen won a place at St Andrews University, one of Scotland's most ancient seats of learning. With his strongly religious family background, it was not surprising that John chose to read for a degree in divinity in preparation for becoming a Church of Scotland minister. It was the practice to complete an arts degree first, which he did as a travel-in student, making the journey every day for three years by steam train from his parents' home in Kingskettle. Money was very tight. John's mother died from cancer during his second year at St Andrews. His father worked occasionally on the farms of relatives, particularly at harvest time, and he had some meagre savings. These he shared generously with his only son, taking immense pride that he had chosen the ministry for his career. It was (and, indeed, still is) a highly regarded profession.

At university, John made many close friends, none closer than Murdo Ewen Macdonald, a native of the Western Isles who became known as 'Padre Mac' through his wartime ministry as a PoW. He was later to gain prominence as professor of divinity at Glasgow University and some notoriety as an outspoken socialist. He shared much of Macdonald's view of the world, though not his strongly ideological stance, and developed a social concern rooted in his Christianity that was to have a profound influence on his son, Gordon Brown. Many years later, in a foreword to a collection of sermons published to celebrate John Brown's eightieth birthday, Murdo Ewen Macdonald cited the lesson of the philosopher Professor John MacMurray, that 'the self that thinks is the same self that acts', adding, 'I know of no one who has demonstrated this truth more fully than John E. Brown.'[1] John Brown graduated MA in 1935, with a 'liberal sprinkling' of merit certificates, and then moved on to St Mary's theological college where he acquired more first-class certificates and medals in Hebrew and systematic theology. After six years at St Andrews, he graduated Bachelor of Divinity in 1938, virtually on the eve of World War II.

John Brown's first post was as assistant minister at St Mary's

Church in Govan, the industrial heartland of the Clyde, where he served for only a year before moving on to St Cuthbert's Church at Dunoon, a seaside resort in Argyll on Scotland's west coast. He stayed there for four years until his formal ordination and induction as a minister, before returning to Govan in September 1943. He found St Mary's a changed place. German bombs had destroyed the fine windows, and services were constantly interrupted by the din of construction in the shipyards a stone's throw away. Yet there was a job to be done. 'It was a compelling call,' he said later.[2] John Brown was exempt from conscription, but joined the Home Guard. In wartime Govan, he had to come to terms with the appalling poverty and deprivation around him. The experience fortified his social concern, but his youngest son, Andrew, relates that it did not drive him into ideology. 'He was uncommitted to any political party. He believed that as a minister to a congregation with a wide variety of political views, he should be impartial. He did, however, believe that something should be done about the ravages of poverty, and that the levels of unemployment that he had witnessed in the 1930s should never be tolerated again. The Labour victory in 1945 was certainly one that he welcomed. He recalls now the hope and opportunity it seemed to herald, and remembers a member of his congregation saying "We're all socialists now".'[3]

Soon after the war, John Brown met Jessie Elizabeth Souter, the daughter of John Henderson and Jessie Riach Souter. He was a builder and ironmonger whose business was in Insch, in the hilly but fertile country of west Aberdeenshire. She was four years younger than her future husband, but had seen wider horizons, working as a wartime secretary in the bunkers below Whitehall during the Blitz. As a child, Elizabeth went to a local primary school and secondary school in Aberdeen, some twenty miles away on the coast. Her father, John, died when she was only eleven years old, and her brother, Gordon (after whom the chancellor was named), took over the family business. Her elder sister Gladys, to whom she was very close, was a talented pianist and organist, despite being left frail by a severe illness when still quite young. Had it not been for the war, Elizabeth might have gone to university, but instead, after a short time working for the family firm in Insch and nearby Inverurie, she joined the WRAF and rose to the rank of sergeant. She left rural Aberdeenshire for war duties in the Isle of Man and the south of England, but even now rarely talks of the experience. Service in the maze of tunnels and offices below the streets of London was a frightening experience.

The couple married in July 1947, while John Brown was still minister at St Mary's, Govan. Here, their first child, John Souter Brown, was born sixteen months later on 15 October 1948. More than two years were to pass before the future chancellor made his appearance. James Gordon Brown was born in a nursing home in Giffnock at 8.45 a.m. on 20 February 1951, weighing 'eight or nine pounds'. He came into a hectic world, on the brink of dramatic change. Govan was then a thriving industrial suburb, but it had not always been so. It had once been the fifth largest borough in Scotland, and was only incorporated into Glasgow in 1912 in the teeth of strong local opposition. Govan's origins are very old. Its ancient parish church occupies the site of a Celtic foundation, and boasts the largest collection of early Christian stones north of the border. The settlement was once famous for its salmon fishing, and before the Industrial Revolution was considered an idyllic resort on Glasgow's doorstep. But the development of the upper Clyde for shipping in the late eighteenth century brought a sharp increase in trade, particularly the transport of coal from local collieries. Shipbuilding, steel-fabrication and engineering had grown dramatically in the late nineteenth century. The Co-op employed 3,500 in a huge factory making everything from boots to coffins. Govan was busy, but it became a byword for teeming slums and hard living. Despite the hardness and the poverty, John Brown still recalls with affection the great warmth, friendship and sense of community he found there.

In turn, St Mary's, at Govan Cross overlooking the shipyards, became a touchstone for the social conscience of the Church of Scotland. It established a radical tradition, attracting progressive figures like the Rev. James Barr, a minister in the 1920s and also a Labour MP. But as the 1940s gave way to the 1950s, Govan started to slip into industrial decline, bringing a multitude of economic and social problems. Surprisingly, perhaps, for a boy who was to feel keenly the circumstances of those around him, Gordon Brown has no childhood memories of Govan. The family moved to the Fife coast when he was three years and two months old, when his father was called, in the custom of the Kirk, to St Brycedale Church, Kirkcaldy.

Gordon's childhood was spent in a town steeped in history, but heading for sharp decline. Kirkcaldy, the 'lang toun', was made a royal borough in 1644, its prosperity built on coal. Daniel Defoe, travelling through on his Grand Tour of Britain in the early eighteenth century, found it 'a very well built town, with clean and well-paved streets'.[4] It was a town of no small intellectual pedigree. Adam Smith, the philosophical originator of Thatcherism, lived here in the eighteenth century, and wrote his *Inquiry into the Nature and Causes of the Wealth of Nations* in a house in the High Street. Thomas Carlyle taught here in 1816–18. There was a textile-trade boom in the nineteenth century, when spinning, and the weaving of coarse linen and canvas led to the invention of linoleum, for long the town's staple industry. Its products graced the floors of St Brycedale, and the linoleum works dominated the town in both economic and olfactory terms, leading Mary Campbell-Smith to write in her 1913 poem 'The Boy in the Train', 'For I ken masel' by the queer-like smell/That the next stops Kirkcaldy.' The 1930s, when John Brown was studying a few miles up the coast, brought serious economic deterioration. Coal and textiles declined, and pottery-making – the highly collectable Wemyss ware came from here – collapsed. In the postwar years, new coal reserves were opened up, but in the 1950s the industry was concentrated in central Fife.

Before John Brown's induction in April 1954, there had been some controversy about the future of Kirkcaldy's churches, harking right back to the famous Disruption in the Church of Scotland in 1843. In May of that year, at the Church's ruling General Assembly, there was a long, disputatious argument over the rights of congregations to 'call' their own ministers, rather than having them 'intruded by patrons'. Essentially, it was a rank-and-file revolt against the powers of patronage wielded by rich and well-placed members of the church. A large body of ministers and elders withdrew from the Assembly and formed their own Free Church. In all, 474 ministers gave up their churches and manses. In Gordon Brown's own words, 'Ministers actually left the employment of the church, because they felt they were under the control of the gentry and the Lords. They refused to be bound by the Lords.'[5]

Nowhere was the rebellion more strongly evident than in Kirkcaldy. Three of the five churches in the locality joined the insurrection, and dissenting minister Mark Bryden boasted in 1869 that the Free Churches were attended by large congregations, whereas one established church was closed and the other commanded the loyalty of only 'a band of dejected and sorrowing, but not despairing men'. The Christians of Kirkcaldy were plainly an egalitarian fellowship, coming as they did from a town that worked hard to gain a living from the sea, the coal industry and textile factories. It was fifty years after the split before the rival religious traditions began a process of reconciliation, when members of St Brycedale's congregation worshipped in the established parish church while a new pipe organ was built in their own. The division was not finally healed until 1929 when the Rev. Dr Fairweather preached in Kirkcaldy that 'the cause of unity and brotherhood has triumphed over the bitterness of mere denominationalism'.

St Brycedale, the imposing church to which John Brown now came, was a product of the Disruption. It was built in 1881 by the congregation of Kirkcaldy Free Church, whose first church, a building 'plain to a degree and unpretentious', was built on a site in Tollbooth Street in the immediate after-math of the Disruption. St Brycedale Free Church (the 'Free' was dropped after 1929) was an altogether grander affair. With a spire soaring to 204 feet, it was built at a cost of £21,000 in the heart of the town, on a site gifted by the provost, and opened for worship in 1881. However, in the years after World War II, St Brycedale, in common with other town-centre churches, suffered a serious decline in attendances as the population moved out to new homes in the suburbs. Kirkcaldy Presbytery considered a merger of St Brycedale and the old parish church, arguing that it seemed desirable to create a union of 'the brethren whom some one hundred years since parted company'.

But dissent clearly dies hard in the Kingdom of Fife. The Presbytery concluded that while the time was ripe for such a union, the people were not, and the congregation was allowed to call a minister in the usual way. And so, eleven months after the departure of the Rev. E. Macdonald Ross, the Rev. John Brown was called to succeed him. On 25 April, he preached to his congregation for the first time, on 'The Contribution of the Church', basing his sermon on Acts 3:6: 'Then Peter said, silver and gold have I none; but such as I have give I thee.'

At first, the Brown family lived in South Fergus Place, Kirkcaldy, in a large house divided into two. After a few years, they moved to 6 East Fergus Place, a home 'essentially gifted by a member of the church'. Gordon did not want to go. He sat on the pavement and refused to budge, recollects his mother. 'He didn't like changes when he was little. Well, he has plenty of them now.'[6] One of young Gordon's earliest memories is of St Brycedale's fine peal of bells ringing out over the town. His father would probably have been at home with the Disrupters of 1843 who threw off the yoke of patronage. 'He was more of the dissenting tradition, lower in terms of ceremony,' he recalls, adding quickly, 'but there was music.' He also remembers his father's outlook. 'Our church was more social in its Christianity. My father was very good at helping people, dealing with their problems, visiting them when they were ill. That was what he was really most involved in.'[7] The Rev. Brown did not preach hellfire and damnation. 'My father was, and is, more a social Christian than a fundamentalist,' Gordon told interviewer Lynn Barber many years later. 'His sermons were about charity, good works.'[8] They made a deep impression on the growing boy. 'I was very impressed with my father. First, for speaking without notes in front of so many people in that vast church. But mostly, I have learned a great deal from what my father managed to do for other people. He taught me to treat everyone equally, and that is something I have not forgotten.'[9] And again: 'Personally, my religion is built on a far greater sense of people's importance and potential.'[10]

The manse was a dutiful household. The Rev. Brown, a teetotaller, worked all hours and welcomed parishioners with problems into the manse. They regularly turned up on his doorstep. Young Gordon once invited in for a cup of tea a man who turned out to be the local burglar. 'There was always a constant stream of people passing through our front door,' he recollected. 'In a place like Kirkcaldy, the church is very much at the centre of community life. And as a child growing up in a minister's family, you get to see all the hardships that are going on around you at first hand. Being a minister's wife was certainly a full-time job for my mother. Lots of people came knocking on the door, some begging for money or a cup of tea, others with psychological or social problems. All of them had been hit hard.'[11]

Gordon attended nursery school under the stern gaze of Miss Bogie. The nursery was accommodated in two rooms of her flat in Townsend Place. In the summer, the children played in her garden. Murray Elder, a classmate of Gordon's (and now a political adviser to Donald Dewar, the Scottish Secretary) remembers only that 'She was a bit of an institution in the town.' Gordon went on to Kirkcaldy West School, the local primary school, aged only four. 'I don't know how it happened,' he says. 'I was a year ahead.' His first teacher, Miss

Aileen Mason, was reluctant to take on the toddler from the
manse, because he was so much younger than the others. Five
was the normal starting age, but in Scotland then, with two
intakes in the spring and autumn of each year, some were five
and a half years old. The nineteenth-century school, since
rebuilt, had windows set very high up and was consequently
gloomy. Pupils made their way through the narrow streets of
central Kirkcaldy, still given over to linoleum manufacture.
From the high buildings came a strong smell of linseed oil given
off by the sheets of drying linoleum.

Kirkcaldy West was a traditional, old-fashioned Scottish
school, a place to learn, not a place to play. This may have been
the middle 1950s, but the boys and girls learned to write on
slates, with slate pencils. Murray Elder still flinches at the
memory of slate pencils scraping across slates, and the foul
smell of the wet rags that the pupils kept on their desks to wipe
off their work. Kirkcaldy was certainly an olfactory place. There
was much learning by rote: remorseless repetition of arithmeti-
cal tables and reading practice. 'Not very imaginative, but it
worked,' says Elder. 'They taught us to read and write, in the
rigorous old way that Scottish schools did quite well before
they got trendy.'[12]

In Miss Mason's class there were three streams, separated by
six months in age and at varying levels in the learning process.
Miss Mason quickly discovered that Gordon found his first
stage too easy. He graduated to the second stage, and then the
third, within weeks, and was soon doing schoolwork that
children a year older had only just begun to master. The future
chancellor was particularly quick at sums. Eventually, she had
to set even more difficult work to keep pace with his appetite
for learning. Another of his primary-school teachers, Miss
MacDonald, recollected to John and Elizabeth Brown that she
'couldn't keep Gordon in work. I was always having to give him
more to do.' At home, as an infant, Gordon was enthralled by
the adventures of Thomas the Tank Engine. His parents
noticed that he knew it by heart when he was still only four,

and could be heard reciting it in bed, in the room he shared with his elder brother, John. His precocity was already being noticed, but at that age he was chiefly interested in kicking a football about on Volunteer Green in the local park. He was encouraged by his father, who took him to Starks Park, Raith Rovers' stadium. The first match he saw, on a New Year's Day, was East Fife v. Raith Rovers.

Kirkcaldy had its fair share of natural calamities. In April 1958, strong winds blew for three days, and eighty-foot waves crashed over the town's sea walls, flooding side-streets to a depth of three feet. The fire brigade could not cope. The YWCA was cut off, and people were evacuated from their submerged homes. The Rev. Brown was with them in their hour of need, and so was seven-year-old Gordon. These were not scenes that a small boy would see under normal circumstances. It was a very quick education in what was really going on out there 'and it taught me that collective responsibility goes beyond the garden gate,' he remembered. Even as a child, he was aware of the contrast between the hardships others faced and his own comparatively comfortable circumstances. 'I don't remember opulence, but we never went without.'[13]

The young Brown came early to politics, encouraged in his almost childlike concern for other people by his father's example. 'I think my father was very concerned about seeing people in difficulties, and helping them, and certainly that had a big influence on me. Growing up in Kirkcaldy, in Fife, when the mining and textile industries were under great pressure, made you aware of social problems. What I saw and what I read made me aware of social problems and influenced me. I grew up and became politically aware in the early Sixties when the Tory government was failing, and the idea of change – even for a twelve-year-old – was an important thing.'[14]

His first accurate political memory actually dates from 1959, when as an eight-year-old he was allowed to stay up late listening to the general election results on the radio. When he and his brother John were sent off to bed at 1.30 a.m., it was quite clear that Hugh Gaitskell and the Labour Party had lost.

In the late autumn of 1963, he was holidaying with his parents on his cousin's farm at Crieff, Perthshire. Sir Alec Douglas-Home, formerly Earl Home, had just become prime minister in succession to Harold Macmillan, who resigned the premiership on grounds of ill-health. After signing away his title and leaving the House of Lords, Home was in need of a seat in the Commons. The Tory Party gifted him Kinross and West Perthshire, a safe constituency in the Scottish Lowlands, largely made up of small towns and villages spread thinly in rich farming country famous for its fruit-growing and cattle-breeding. It was a celebrated by-election. Labour's choice was schoolteacher Andrew Forrester from Glasgow. Christopher Grieve, better known as the Scots poet Hugh MacDiarmid, stood for the Communists – having rejoined the party when others were leaving in 1956, the year of the Hungarian upris-ing. Arthur Donaldson, a journalist, stood for the SNP, while the comedian Willie Rushton offered himself as an Inde-pendent candidate. This was not Labour country, and the out-come was never in doubt. Douglas-Home swept in with 57 per cent of the vote; Labour came third with only 15 per cent.

Gordon, only just into his teens, followed the progress of the poll avidly. 'I remember very clearly hearing [Home] speak,' he later recalled. 'The meetings generated such excitement that I decided to follow him as his speaking tour circulated through the villages. It amazed and appalled me – although it wouldn't surprise me now – to hear [him] making the same speech every-where he went. I soon saw through the tricks that the politi-cians got up to. I thought it was awful.'[15] He was also shocked when Douglas-Home was asked the routine question: would he be buying a home in the constituency if he won? No, replied the former fourteenth earl, he had too many houses already.

Young Brown offered his services to Labour's Andrew Forrester – who at twenty-six was not so much older than his would-be helper. 'But I was too young to be of any use.' Murray Elder was also in the neighbourhood on holiday during the campaign. On his return home, he showed young Brown – he is a year younger – that he had got Alec Douglas-Home's autograph. Gordon was unimpressed. He pulled out a grubby piece of paper bearing the autographs of all the candidates.

He was writing 'political' articles by this stage. In fact, his journalistic career began at the age of nine, when he contributed to a news item on the annual sports festival in Ravenscraig Park to his brother's first attempt at newspaper production in May 1960, *Local News*, a cyclostyled handwritten sheet that sold for three old pennies 'in aid of refugees'. In the third edition, now typed on the minister's typewriter and printed on his duplicator, Gordon had progressed to reporting on the Scotland v. Hungary football international. *Local News* also reported on the Brown boys' tuck-shop event in the family garage, which realised £2 11s 0d (£2.55) from the sale of food, including Mrs Brown's much-liked 'tablet', a Scottish soft toffee. The front-page lead was a report of Socialist Party demonstrations in Tokyo against the Japan–USA Security Treaty.

Later forays into the publishing field were even more professional, bringing the Brown brothers to the attention of the Scottish national press. On 5 April 1962, the *Daily Record* and the *Scottish Daily Mail* carried stories about six Kirkcaldy High School pupils raising £6 3s 9d (approximately £6.20) for charity from the sale of 500 copies of the *Gazette*, four stencilled pages stapled together. John Brown was joint editor, and Gordon was sports editor. The first edition of the *Gazette* led its front page with a story on unemployment and the impact of threatened pit closures on 'poor doomed miners'. Gordon's report on Raith Rovers was on the back page. The second edition, on 7 April, carried a lead on Selwyn Lloyd's third budget. And in addition to his report on Scotland's chances in the football match against England at Hampden Park ('I think Scotland have a good chance of regaining their "Lost Glory"'), he had two small items on page one. The first disclosed that the Liberal Party was opening three new local branches, and commented, 'Surely the Liberals are Prospering.' The second, headlined 'Buy Time against Drink', recorded the local Presbytery's campaign to cut down on television advertisements for drink, and a proposal that the Church buy air time to denounce alcohol. 'Let us hope this plan will be a success and that the sale of drink and cigarettes to the younger and older generation will fall when these against-drink & cigarettes are show[sic],' wrote eleven-year-old Gordon. By the third edition, he had his own sports page, and two staff.

The following year, 'Scotland's Only Newspaper In Aid of the Freedom From Hunger Campaign' reappeared with a proper masthead. Edition number four, dated 4 April 1963, ran to ten pages of local and national news, and carried a lead on Reginald Maudling's 'expansion without inflation' budget. Gordon shared the by-line honours on page one with Stephen Salmond, on a story about the closure of Barry, Ostlers and Shepherd's linoleum factory, with the loss of six hundred jobs. He also wrote a post mortem on Tory by-election losses (without mentioning the results, or where the polls were), offering a prescient analysis: 'They must face the fact that this year may be their last in office for a long time.' He suggested that Prime Minister Harold Macmillan, aged 69, was too old 'for this responsible job' and the trend pointed to younger men like Harold Wilson, Jo Grimond and Edward Heath. Gordon, aged twelve, wrote, 'We should and must have a strong and reliable government, to promote our interests in Europe and the world. In Britain, too, we must have a less casual government that must take drastic measures in solving our unemployment, economic, transport and local government problems. Not long ago, we were looked upon as a strong country; now our only hope of survival, in an age dominated by nuclear power, is to link up with our stronger Western allies. So as you can see our status in the world today leaves much to be desired. I conclude, we can and indeed must have a more dynamic government.' Around this time, the Brown brothers were avid watchers of the late-night TV satirical show *That Was the Week That Was*, which often pilloried Macmillan for his languid ('too casual') style. Their father, who rather liked political gossip (he was a keen reader of the 'Crossbencher' column from Westminster in the *Sunday Express*) allowed them to stay up late for the Saturday night programme, though he was worried about some of the sexual innuendo.

The *Gazette* of 5 July 1963 went even further in its political coverage, carrying a full page – 'Labour Triumphs' – by Gordon, with a brief overnight report of two Labour by-election victories in West Bromwich and Deptford, and a long article by Harold Wilson, the Labour leader, headlined 'The Battle Against Poverty'. It was a remarkable coup for the boys to have persuaded the party to give them the article, which was 'balanced' by shorter pieces further inside from the Tories, the SNP and the Liberals. On the back page, Gordon appealed for support for Raith Rovers. 'I am sure that this season you will not be let down,' he promised readers. They would certainly find him there every Saturday with his brother John, selling programmes. They earned 1s 6d (7p) for every hundred sold, and the bonus was free admission to the match. They also earned extra pocket money distributing and sometimes selling the sports papers on Saturday nights.

Another article that has survived is from the Christmas 1963 issue of *Zeal*, the cyclostyled parish magazine put together by the youth fellowship of St Brycedale, and sold for one shilling (5p), the proceeds going to charity. Gordon wrote a four-hundred-word piece entitled 'Persecution'. It was a paean of praise for the Jewish people, a mixture of religiosity and politics. 'Persecution – this is the pernicious eclipse under which the Jewish people have always existed,' he wrote. 'Ever since Biblical times there have been controversies between the Jews and other nations.' Recalling 'Adolf Hitler and his blood-thirsty regime', he said the Jews had now subdued part of the Holy Land to make a national home. 'The new state of Israel is, however, not recognised by the United Arab Republic, which comprises Egypt, Syria and other Arab countries.' The controversy between Arabs and Jews 'is perhaps best illustrated by the recent event of Lord Mancroft, a Jew, being forced to resign from a board of directors because of pressure from ambassadors belonging to the UAR'.

On considering these historical facts, continued the twelve-year-old portentously, 'The question we may now ask ourselves is: "Why did God allow these other nations to persecute His Chosen People?" Could He not have allowed this to happen in order to correct the Jews hoping that they might become a perfect people? They seem to have had a lot of suffering and persecution to endure. Is there a Divine purpose for them and the world in all this?' He did not answer his own rhetorical question, but said that, despite all their persecutions, the Jews had made a valuable contribution to the world. He cited Einstein, Epstein, Mendelsshon (sic) and Yehudi Menuhin. 'Perhaps their greatest contribution has been in the realm of religion. The Old Testament gives us names of the prophets. Nor should we forget that our own Christian faith came to us through the Jews. The Holy Child of Bethlehem, who we remember especially at this time, was a Jew. Jesus who came to be the saviour of the world belonged to this persecuted people. Truly, our debt to the Jews is very great.' This mixture of religious and social concern, politics and a dash of current affairs suggests an extraordinary maturity – an unduly serious outlook, even – for a boy of twelve. Just why he chose this subject is not known, though his father's great interest in the Holy Land is well attested. John Ebenezer Brown visited Israel several times during the 1960s, 1970s and 1980s, initially as a representative of the Church of Scotland, and later as a guide leading tour groups of Church people.

Gordon was 'a very shy boy, a trait that he retains to this day', according to his younger brother, Andrew. 'His father recalls how he would always seek out the back row at any meeting he attended. He particularly recalls how he would take a back seat at the Sunday meetings of the Youth Fellowship.'[16] His older brother, John, by contrast, was always keen to adopt a leading role, and took the chair as president of the Fellowship. Yet Brown himself prefers to remembers his schooldays as 'football, football, rugby, tennis, running and then football again'. He saw the great Jim Baxter play for the local team before his transfer to Rangers. Jock Stein, manager of Dunfermline, then Hibernian and Celtic, was his hero, and he was prone to the typical schoolboy fantasy of becoming a professional footballer. 'Right from the time I was very young, it was always less classrooms than playgrounds, less books than football matches.'[17]

His cleverness had already come to the notice of the education authorities. Fife education chiefs were worried by the high failure rate of High School students, particularly those from homes affected by unemployment or low income. The answer, introduced by the county's progressive chief education officer, Dr Douglas Mackintosh, was the 'E-Stream' experiment, which singled out intelligent boys and girls for rapid development, bypassing the 11-plus intelligence test then required to get into selective secondary education. Reputedly, an IQ of 130 was required to get into the stream. Gordon was chosen to join the experiment at Kirkcaldy High School, along with Murray Elder, his classmate at primary school. The High had around 1,200 pupils. It had effectively been a comprehensive school before moving into new buildings in the late 1950s, when it became highly selective.

Gordon enrolled there at the age of ten, a year younger than most of the 'E' class of eleven boys and twenty-five girls. Murray Elder remembers that for the first two years they were 'separate, and slightly cocooned' from other pupils. The teaching was intensive. A few years later, Brown was to write his own, damning verdict on the experiment, which ended in failure for many of his friends, and thrust himself into university at too early an age.

But for now, it was nothing but excitement. Gordon, following his brother by tradition, was put in Raith House. The preponderance of girls in his year was 'quite a good experience'. That is to say, it made him even more keen on sport. 'I think

we believed that showing prowess at sports made us more popular with the girls,' he told *The Times*. His first girlfriend
excelled at tennis, and 'for at least a month I dreamt of being a
Wimbledon champion, but I only got as far as the Kirkcaldy
Boys' Cup'. Here he is economical with the self-praise. He was
junior champion at the town's tennis club. A lanky boy with
fashionably long hair, the young Brown also showed a turn of
speed that took him to the Fife County Schoolboys Athletics
Championships. His sports master, Harry Moultrie, reckoned
him 'a super all-round athlete'. At the age of fifteen, he won the
400-yard sprint against all comers from other schools in the
county – but was disqualified for wearing a jersey over his shirt,
which obscured his competitor's number. The incident upset
him, but his real passion was rugby. That year, his sprinting
abilities won him a place as a wing three-quarter in the school
First XV rugby team. He scored the winning try in his first
game, securing an injury in the process. 'I was more keen to get
into the rugby team than bothering about exams. We were
unbeaten for a season and a half.'[18]

His passion for sport was not allowed to eclipse class work.
Kirkcaldy High (where Gordon's father was school chaplain)
may have been a big-hitter on the sports field, but under its
stern headmaster, Robert Adam (known to the boys as 'the
Bod'), the school was determinedly academic. 'His great thing
was getting more and more people to do more and more
Highers,' Brown recalled. 'He was a very tough disciplinarian,
a great traditionalist who inculcated the standards of the public school into state schools.'[19] He had the good fortune to be
taught by some outstanding teachers: Sid Smith, the English
teacher, was very popular. History was his passion, but the
history teacher, Tam Dunn, lectured walking from one side of
the room to another as if he was giving dictation. 'If you
learned the notes, you got a "B" in history,' remembers Murray
Elder. For Gordon, blessed and cursed with an inquiring mind,
this was not enough. He read widely beyond the set notes.

Dr Mackintosh's 'E' experiment was not a complete success.

'A lot of people fell by the wayside. It was quite difficult, to begin with,' recollects Brown. Murray Elder's gut feeling is also that 'it didn't quite work. If you are to be good at English, you need to have read and written more than you can at that age. And at sport, you need to be playing against children your own age, not people who are older and bigger.'[20] But for the son of the manse, it gradually worked out. Gordon took his O-levels at fourteen, and passed 'eight or nine', and his Highers – the equivalent of A-levels – a year later, just after his fifteenth birthday. He scored five straight As, and was an obvious candidate for early entry into university. He also played the violin in the school orchestra, and took part in the literary and debating society activities. The annual magazine for 1966 records him speaking in a debate on 'Whether the [Ian] Smith regime in Rhodesia should be crushed'. And there were political influences at school. Tam Dunn, Gordon's history teacher was regarded as left-wing. 'There's little doubt that Tam Dunn's teaching played a formative part in the shaping of Murray and Gordon's views,' argues Andrew Brown.[21]

In his final year, Gordon was a prefect, along with Murray Elder, who was later to become a leading official of the Scottish Labour Party and an adviser to John Smith, Tony Blair and Scottish Secretary Donald Dewar. His brother John organised a mixed-sex Youth Fellowship trip to Sweden that year (his first trip abroad). Gordon was also one of eight sixth-formers who jointly edited the school magazine in 1967. The eight announced their intention to write a serious editorial. It was entitled 'We're fired . . .' and continued in small print 'with enthusiasm' at the response from the junior school to a call for contributions. Young Brown's offering was not exactly serious: 'Suggested Additions to Your Book List', a cod review of two imaginary books, *Communist Theory Today* by Professor Erasmus Wosjig, and *I Was a Red Guard*, by Sir Hubert Slash. Gordon's schoolboy sense of humour was a little laboured, strewn with references to Mao Tse Tung and Joseph Stalin and assuming some knowledge of life 'behind the iron curtain' as it was still known. 'Especially revealing are the accumulative figures Wosjig gives us of the voting behaviour of the totalitarian states of Europe,' burbled the would-be satirist. 'Equally revealing are the mini-skirts which party members are forced to wear. Of special interest to our unemployed readers will be the Professor's report that there are vacancies for experienced dustmen and red guards in Berlin and Peking respectively.' There is a mild dig at the prime minister – 'Wosjig reveals news of the condemnation of images, especially Harold Wilson, and the condemnation of relics, including Great Britain and democracy.' He rounds off with a quotation showing that communist unity is near, which turns out to be the first four lines of 'Should Auld Acquaintance Be Forgot' written backwards. It is difficult to believe he raised many laughs with this effort. Far better, on the same page, was a short lyric poem on the tribulations of an American soldier in Vietnam by fellow-editor Fiona Buchan.

Gordon's literary efforts were not always so banal. Later, he won first prize in a newspaper competition organised by the *Scottish Daily Express* for an essay describing Britain in the year 2000. He beat off nine hundred hopefuls to lift the £200 prize. Only a brief fragment survives, but it is enough to give a glimpse of the teenager with a vision. 'A new generation is being born,' he wrote. 'By 2000, Scotland can, for the first time in history, have found her feet as a society which has bridged the gaps between rich and poor, young and old, intellectual and labourer. The inheritance of a respect for every individual's freedom and identity, and the age-long quality of caring, both transmitted through our national religion, law and educational system and evident in the lives of countless generations of our people, makes Scotland ideal for pioneering the society which transcends political systems.'[22] The language is interesting. He is already talking of 'our people' like a politician, while rejecting political systems. In his emphasis on individual freedom and identity, he anticipates the values of the 1980s. In talking of 'caring', he both picks up the social conscience of his father and reflects the sentiments that were later to come to the fore in a Labour Party still dominated by ideology.

Ten Kirkcaldy High School pupils distinguished themselves in the university entrance bursary competitions during their final year, among them Gordon. He was first in the history section of the Edinburgh Competition, where two girls and three other boys also gained a mention in the merit list. The 'E' experiment had yielded some results, but Brown today has his doubts about the forcing of young talent. 'The trouble was, they pushed people too hard, and many didn't get even near university. Maybe only a third, or a half.'[23] Still only sixteen, and loaded with examination honours, Gordon himself was clearly on the brink of a brilliant academic career. He could have stayed on for another year at the High School, where he was Dux – the leading scholar – of his year.

Among the papers of his elder brother John, Gordon's own unpublished critique of the 'E' experiment, written when he was only sixteen, was found during research for this biography. The typewritten essay, dated May 1967, opens: 'I was a guinea pig, the victim of a totally unsighted [sic] and ludicrous exper-iment in education, the result of which was to harm materially and mentally the guinea pigs.' He describes the 'year early' entry system, designed to give them an extra year at secondary school to prepare for university. 'At ten years with nothing but anticipation I began my course of senior education. At sixteen, I had more problems than I had years.

'I watched as each year one of two of my friends would fail under the strain. I saw one girl who every now and then would disappear for a while with a nervous breakdown. I stood by as a friend of mine, who I knew was intelligent enough, left school in despair after five years of strain with no university/higher qualifications. I though continually of how it could have been for these young guinea pigs, how the strain of work, the ignominy and rejection of failure could have been avoided. All this, I thought I saw better than any educationalist in his ivory tower.'

At the age of twelve, he had been faced with 'a next to impossible task' – to decide for all time in what subject he should specialise. He chose history. 'I know my choice was wrong, but what could I do?' he lamented. 'The mistakes made with materials are revocable, but the mistakes made with people cannot be altered.'

At the ages of fourteen and fifteen, he sat his leaving certificate examinations. 'I was lucky and passed,' he wrote. 'But many of my friends met with dismal failure, despair and a sense of uselessness. I cannot emphasise too much the demoralisation I saw in some of these guinea pigs.' He was surprised that none of them broke down completely. For the failures, there could be sympathy 'but nothing else. They had failed and there was nothing anyone could do about it.' Young Gordon had watched as, every year, another class of eager children embarked on the great experiment. 'It is now that I see that it is not the idea that is the victim of the experiment,' he reasoned. 'The victims are us, the guinea pigs.'

At sixteen, he went on, he had to make an even bigger decision: whether to stay at school for the proposed extra year, or go to university with his friends, or do something else. The last choice, doing voluntary service or something similar, was out because of his age. To his horror, he discovered that a seventh year at school would simply be a repeat of the sixth, without university conditions or transitional work. Even his teachers advised him to go straight to university. From the planners of 'E', there came little advice, encouragement or planning. The preparations for Edinburgh he had envisaged were negligible. Six years of strain had been pointless. 'Against my wishes, I was forced by circumstance to proceed to university.'

Behind him, Gordon left 'a track of failure, disappointment and resentment'. Instead of carrying out the original purpose of averting failure by extra time at school, the 'projectors' had effected a far more grievous crime. They were responsible for the failure of the twenty pupils who had to suffer the ignominy of repeating years, and for the few who left school without qualifications for university. 'One question sticks in my mind,' he concluded. 'Surely it is better for children to succeed at school, and leave with some qualifications for work, rather than endure failure, ignominy, rejection and at the least, strain, for the ironic reason of averting failure at university?'

This sombre little essay, with its tortured *cri de coeur* for those less able than himself and its withering assessment of the ivory-tower 'projectors', offers an insight into the developing social outlook of the young Brown. Other boys would simply have gone off to university, only too thankful to have succeeded academically and to have escaped from the apron-strings of home. Gordon went, but reluctantly, and evidently burdened with guilt at the fate of his fellow-students, forced to take part in an experiment that had pushed them further and faster than they could go at that age. If the sea-floods and the beggars at his father's door opened his eyes to conditions around him, the 'E' clearly quickened his acquisition of a social conscience. The guiding idea of 'fairness' took root early.

On the eve of Brown's first budget in 1997, the Glasgow-based *Sunday Mail* tracked down his schoolmates at Kirkcaldy High. The class of 1967 is scattered far and wide, but they remember him well. Jamie Millar, who also went to Edinburgh University and is now a commercial lawyer, recalled, 'Gordon was one of a group of boys who hung around together. We all knew he was going to do very well. He was, by far, the most gifted student in our class.' Murray Elder had memories of a 'gregarious and jolly' lad who was 'ferociously bright. He was never a swot. I am not saying that his academic success was effortless but he didn't make a great song and dance about it. He always seemed more interested in Raith Rovers.' Ian Smith, who became chief executive of Dumfries and Galloway Council, said, 'The whole school was an intellectual hothouse at that time. But in our class, it was Gordon who set the pace, and the rest of us would do our best to keep up . . . socially, as well as academically. He was so sharp. The banter and wise-cracking that would go on between the boys was great. Gordon was always the quickest to come out with a funny line and would soon have the rest of us doubled over in laughter.' Michael Lamont, today an architect with a rail company in Hong Kong, agreed. 'He was simply great fun to be around. He was always wise-cracking, but in a very clever way, using puns and a play on words.' The boy who sat beside him, Russell Sharp, who became head of history at Kirkcaldy High, remembered Gordon's 'fascination' with a history lesson on Lloyd George's budget. He added, 'To be honest, I don't remember him being interested in politics but, with his father being a minister and the school chaplain, he always had a social conscience.' Fiona Buchan, who works for an overseas education charity, recollects Gordon as 'a brilliant debater', but always 'good fun'. 'I remember him always smiling. People nowadays describe him as too serious and remark on the fact that he actually smiled on election night. But he was never as po-faced as he sometimes can be now.' Marie Maxwell, running a travel business in Fife, also recalls Gordon and his brother John 'in the thick of things', always organising dances. Shirley Halley remembered half a dozen of his fellow-pupils talking in the last week of term about who in the class would make it to the top. 'Everyone voted for Gordon.'[24] Even then, it was clear in which direction he was heading.

CHAPTER 3

RADICAL STUDENT

EDINBURGH UNIVERSITY IS THE ACADEMIC GOAL OF THE clever Scot. Its architecturally delightful scatter of buildings tumbles down the hill south of the castle on to the Meadows, facing Holyrood Park. Some were designed by Robert Adam and William Playfair in the late eighteenth and early nineteenth centuries, but the university was founded by the town council in 1583, under a charter granted the previous year by King James VI of Scotland. Scotland then had four such seats of learning, while England had but two. The 'tounis college' expanded over the centuries, as did the city around it, making Edinburgh truly 'the university in the city', a setting that brought its undergraduates into close contact with the people – and, in Brown's case, their problems. It was at the centre of the Scottish Enlightenment, offering intellectual direction to the Western world. The roll of those who studied or taught there is stuffed with the names of the great, the good and the celebrated: James Boswell, Charles Darwin, David Hume, Thomas Carlyle and Arthur Conan Doyle – joined in more modern times by Dr Julius Nyerere and Stella Rimington, the first woman head of MI5. The university now formally recognises a number of leading political figures, such as Malcolm Rifkind,

David Steel and Gordon Brown among its alumni. The inclusion of Brown in this list of distinguished contemporaries was a little tardy. He did not exactly leave the university under a cloud, but the authorities had good reason to be glad to see the back of him. As a student politician, he turned their world upside down.

All that was in the future when he went up to the university in October 1967. As a prize scholar in the bursary competition, he was marked out as a potential high-flyer before he even took his first tutorial. The then principal, Michael Swann, had already reported that the university had recruited the youngest student – he was sixteen – of the postwar era. Gordon took the train to Edinburgh one Tuesday morning full of hope and expectation. However, there was one nagging problem. In the months succeeding a particularly 'physical' incident during a rugby match between the school First XV and the Kirkcaldy High School Former Pupils six months previously, he had experienced serious problems with his eyesight. 'I knew something was wrong, but I couldn't quite place what it was. It was like getting reflections from the sun in your eye all day,' he explained later. Three days after he went up to university, he went to see a doctor, who referred him immediately to a specialist. 'He just flashed a mirror in front of me and said I had retinal detachment.'[1]

Brown the fresher was just getting into the swim of things, going to parties and meeting people. Now he faced the very real prospect of blindness. The pitch incident is seared on his memory. 'I was playing wing forward for the school's first team against the former pupils, and some of them must have been about three times our weight. I remember the game had just started when I went down on the ball in a loose scrum and they all came piling in on top of me. I felt a kick on the side of my head. When I came round, I knew something was wrong, but I couldn't figure out what it was, so I went back on the field. That was the last game of rugby I ever played.'[2]

It was also the last time he was able to see properly. He was taken into the Edinburgh Royal Infirmary on the Sunday before the university autumn term formally opened, and missed the whole of the first term. Gordon almost immediately had an operation to save the sight in his left eye. 'It was really too late. That eye was dying. The detachment was too complete for it to be properly mended. It was old treatment, not like the lasers they have now. The operation took four hours – quite massive. They have to get to the back of your eye.' Two more operations were to follow in 1968 and 1969 to save what was left of the sight of his right eye, entailing long stays in hospital when his eyes were completely covered. 'I was actually blinded for weeks.' When he was allowed home, the impatient scholar was instructed not to read. 'It was very frustrating. You have to avoid reading, and the eye is patched. I couldn't go back to university. I couldn't read. I was getting the talking book service, but you can't do very much. I fell behind quite a bit.'[3]

Yet, when he finally began his studies in the spring term of 1968, Gordon made an immediate impact. Professor Henry Drucker, then a newly arrived politics lecturer, describes him as 'an important figure, even as an undergraduate. He was hugely popular, a natural politician: totally self-assured. He was good to everybody, and everyone wanted to know Gordon Brown. He was a bit like a Bill Clinton figure.'[4]

Some contemporaries have less starry-eyed recollections. Jonathan Wills, a flatmate and close political ally, remembers that 'He led a quiet life for his first two years in Edinburgh – the archetypal tweed-jacketed and grey-flannelled Scots lad o' pairts studying hard in a university which even in the late Sixties was becoming a refuge for flighty Oxbridge rejects from wealthy middle England.'[5] Others recall that Brown could be a little dour. He was one of the few activists of his time who never grew a beard, and he invariably wore a tie, often a long one that hung unfashionably below his waist. When Wills – later to become Scottish correspondent for *The Times* – first met Brown, he was living in 'a filthy, chaotic tenement flat' in the Grassmarket, a cobbled street just behind the castle and now one of the most

sought-after parts of the city. Then, it was full of slums and
vagrants emerged from the Grassmarket mission every morning
to beg. Gordon's flat, he recalled, 'was disgusting even by
students standards.'[6] Brown had rented it for £6 a week.

Like other universities, Edinburgh was experiencing student
unrest, though not on a very big scale. As Gordon lay in bed listening to his talking books, the biggest issue on campus was a
'great debate' on whether women students should have access
to the contraceptive pill. The argument was settled in favour of
the women. In April 1968, the campus newspaper, *Student*,
reported that university ex-rector James Robertson Justice, the
bearded, circumferential actor, had just returned from a trip to
Moscow, where he found that students had 'no say whatsoever'
in the running of their university. 'We are more socialist in this
respect than they are . . . At least we have a rector and he can
do a great deal if he does his job properly.'[7]

Justice was touching on a sensitive point: student power, an
issue that was to dominate much of Gordon Brown's stay at the
university. Edinburgh had a long tradition of students electing
a rector, who technically chaired the university's ruling body,
the Court, but generally also spoke up for the undergraduate
body. The post usually went to a public figure from the arts,
politics or journalism. Some radical elements suggested that a
student in the university, rather than an outside nominee of the
students, should stand. Others argued that there should be
direct student representation on the Court, the body with ultimate executive responsibility for the university's £13 million
annual budget and £50 million assets. Such a step was
anathema to the principal (or vice-chancellor), Professor
Michael Swann, an administrator of impeccable right-wing
credentials, who had written the right-wing 'Black Papers' on
education earlier in the decade. He did not share the view,
which he regarded as modish, that students had a right to
participate in the decisions governing their lives.

Brown's first direct involvement on campus was in the
students' rag week, known in Edinburgh simply as 'Charities'.

In April 1969, he was busy demanding a twenty-four-hour, round-the-clock jamboree of show stunts, dances and café collections, all aimed at raising £30,000 for good causes. 'And what about coming to grips with television?' he asked in the campus newspaper. 'There's thousands to be made in selling an hour's show. And what about offering a weekend at Buckingham Palace, or a trip on the royal yacht with Prince Philip at the helm, as prizes,' he added irreverently.[8] He was to return to the subject of the royal yacht nearly thirty years later, though not in jest.

At the beginning of the autumn term, he interviewed the university principal, who said loftily that he was not worried by student radicals. Later that year, around a hundred students occupied the campus appointments office in protest at the policies of Barclays Bank, then on a recruiting tour. The bank was accused of investing heavily in Ian Smith's breakaway Rhodesia. Gordon Brown was not to be found among those sitting-in. 'Among the student body, he was the only person who ever showed me that he really understood what it was all about,' remembered Professor Drucker. 'What the various weapons were, how to use them, and how not. He was miles ahead, not just in Edinburgh. I remember him saying to me that a sit-in would not work, and telling me why. He got it absolutely right. His line, in retrospect an act of considerable political perception, was that a sit-in only worked when the students had already won.'[9]

Brown the politico-journalist was also getting into his stride. In late 1970, a 'mole' in the administration gave the campus paper a set of documents detailing the university's investments in South Africa. It was devastating stuff. Principal Swann was a leading office-holder in the Anti-Apartheid Movement in Edinburgh. He had only recently reassured the university Court and student leaders that the university did not invest in companies known to be active in support of apartheid. Only five people had access to a stockbroker's report giving details of the true picture, which showed deep financial involvement in apartheid South Africa. One of them was so disgusted by the deception being practised that he left a copy of the secret report in a toilet deep inside the old college building. Then he rang the Student Publications Board and suggested they take a look.

At first, 'Boredom Beaver Brown' (as he was known, to differentiate him from his elder brother John, who was a couple of years ahead of him) and his radical pals did not grasp the significance of the complicated tables of figures and names. 'Brown and his team pored over them in their cramped office in Buccleuch Place and soon realised what they had. There would not normally have been another issue of the newspaper until January but waiting was unthinkable,' said a later account.[10] Jonathan Wills, a geography student, who chaired the Student Publications Board, sanctioned the printing of a special edition of *Student* – for which he had no budget. 'The leaked documents showed they had half a million pounds in shares of some of the most notoriously oppressive, white-supremacist mining corporations, most of them linked to the shadowy Broederbond organisation. This was heady stuff in Edinburgh, where there was a vociferous community of South African exiles – many of them linked with the Kirk of Scotland.'[11]

A four-page *Student Special* was distributed around the campus. 'They knew their story was dynamite,' according to a later press report. 'But not even Brown realised that for the next five years he would be caught up in its shockwaves.'[12] Brown campaigned for months to call the university to account. 'Sell the Shares' stickers and posters appeared everywhere. A petition signed by 2,500 students and 300 staff carried the same message. The campus was in ferment. The Anti-Apartheid Movement demanded Swann's resignation, and he was forced to agree to change stockbrokers and liquidate the shares.

It was a famous victory. Gordon and his friends on *Student* were the heroes of the campus broad left. He still reflects with pleasure on the outcome: 'The university wrongly claimed they had no shares in South African companies like de Beers. We forced them to sell. It was exposure that got results. You didn't need a sit-in. It was so embarrassing for them to be caught not telling the truth.'[13]

Life was not always so serious. Brown also tried out his talents in a new direction: gossip columnist. *Student* gave him the whole of its back page to write an occasional diary. He reported on such weighty matters as the lack of sherry for VIPs at a new refectory opening, and the nickname workmen had given to the health centre which would dispense the contraceptive pill: the 'fornication room'. He also disclosed, in the best tabloid 'I can reveal' fashion that the university was to appoint, for the first time, an information officer. He was already getting the passion for well-aimed publicity that would mark his ambitious political career. The job of PRO for the university, he said, would go to John Dundas, a principal information officer at the Scottish Office, and he would be paid £4,000 a year – comparable with Fleet Street journalistic rates. In the same edition, Brown wrote a feature on student housing, a worthy but dull effort. He was more value on the gossip front, though later that month he and fellow-undergraduate Allan Drummond contributed the splash story on 'Six Theses Lost', a tale of missing dissertations. The article was somewhat portentously by-lined 'Student Insight', after the manner of the highly successful *Sunday Times* Insight team. He picked his models well, even if the subject matter was infinitely less weighty.

Under Gordon Brown's editorship, the paper was often quite louche: plenty of sexy women undergraduates and the occasional bare breasts. The Conservatives' ill-fated Industrial Relations Bill aimed at curbing the power of the trade unions, going through parliament at this time, came under attack, but Gordon seemed to have other things on his mind. In his gossip column, now on page two and renamed 'Back Inside', he lamented that the billiards bar would remain an all-male preserve. 'But what of the freedom to get drunk and make a fool of yourself and to gamble away a term's grant in an afternoon with the imminent threat of women upstairs?'[14]

It was not until late April 1971 that Brown began to play serious student politics. At a meeting of the Students' Representative Council, he proposed a three-part motion whose impact would reverberate through university life for years to come. Speaking as chairman of the publications board, he proposed that all future rectors should take the chair at meetings of the university's Court; that students should accept in principle the desirability of a duly elected student performing the duties of lord rector; and full student membership of the Court.

The idea of a student rector was not new. It was first mooted in 1968, when campuses across Britain were in ferment in the wake of the student uprising in Paris. Activists at Edinburgh exploited the loophole in the Universities (Scotland) Act, which laid down that the students should elect a rector to preside over the Court. In the past, it had been a largely honorific post, though it attracted leading politicians of the day: Gladstone, Disraeli, Churchill, Loyd George and Baldwin had all been rectors. But in more recent times, the poll was invariably regarded as an occasion for campus merriment. The candidates were usually drawn from showbiz or the media, and the winner did not take the job too seriously. This absentee-rector situation suited the authorities admirably. The principal presided over a group of establishment yes-men, who simply rubber-stamped his wishes.

In February 1968, however, the rector, broadcaster Malcolm Muggeridge, quit after denouncing from the pulpit of St Giles Cathedral the students' decadent 'pot and pills' morality. In the ensuing brouhaha, politics student Steve Morrison, later to become managing director of London Weekend Television, stood against a wide field: comic actor Alastair Sim, educationalist A. S. Neill, left-wing journalist and writer Claud Cockburn and broadcaster Kenneth Allsop. The student campaign failed. Essentially, it came too soon, and was not properly organised. Allsop won, but later said that the three years of his rectorship were 'the most unhappy of my life', not least because of the 'contempt' with which he was treated by the principal.[15] He died early in 1973.

Brown was not about to repeat in 1971 the early radicals' mistake. He couched his appeal for radical reform in cautious terms. Now was the time, he argued, for serious consideration of the rectorship, and its role in the reform of university government. The rector was not merely a man for speech days, nor a man to make famous for being famous. He was, by statute, chairman of the university Court, and his potential power existed not because of his views, but because – unlike other members of the Court – he was directly and democratically elected. 'A student would be in a far better position to represent student interests than anyone else,' he insisted. 'He will be in Edinburgh, and should be in touch with student demands. He has neither the fame nor the faith to deify himself in St Giles, and cannot disappear to London or the Holy Land at vital times.'[16]

If a student took the chair at Court meetings, Brown argued, there would be an immediate change in the way it functioned. Attacking the idea that a general demand for more student power would somehow be enough, he continued, 'It is useless to think of increasing student representation, only to find that students being bound by unsatisfactory procedures of the court, the confidentiality which precludes him from telling students what is happening or criticising court policy in public, or the lack of information, access to which is given primarily to the chairman. Allsop's power rests not only on his obvious ability, but on his access to information and his control of procedure at court meetings. A student chairman would claim the same advantages. In addition, he would be able to articulate decisions taken elsewhere.' A new style of rectorship, he maintained would be 'a catalyst for change' in making members of the university Court realise how undemocratic the university government had become. The rectorship was 'potentially an extremely powerful institution', which could speed reform in the university.[17] Disingenuously, Brown did not offer himself as a candidate in the rectorial election due that autumn. Now was the time for discussing ideas. Personalities could come later. They did, including his own.

Brown's first and third proposals were approved unanimously. They were uncontroversial, or vague. The idea of a student rector was not, and it was no coincidence that Gordon devoted almost all his persuasive speech to this issue. His proposal passed by only sixteen votes to thirteen, indicating substantial reservations in the student body about giving up 'celebrity rectors', but the idea had been sown on fertile ground. A groundswell of support grew in favour of Jonathan Wills, and Brown played a considerable role in the campaign.

Yet he was still capable of youthful disillusion with the system. Only two weeks after he dragged the student body with him, Brown wrote a short, sceptical essay, 'Empty Pipe Dreams', subtitled 'On Student Politicians', for the campus paper. He contended that 'sooner or later' the student politician must come face to face with 'the terrible truth that the realities of power are that he doesn't have any'. So the promises and pledges – 'words so devalued by Harold Wilson' – made today would mean little tomorrow. Can the politician achieve anything? he asked, replying to his own rhetorical question, 'I believe he can, only by first realising the limits of the possible. That his actual power is minimal, and that his real power lies as a propagandist, in providing the ideas and policies for change.'[18]

For 'he', read Gordon Brown, the twenty-year-old student mulling over the prospects of ever being able to change a world he found so unsatisfactory. He was concerned for the community of Edinburgh, cut off from the university in its midst by a sense of social inferiority; for the campus blue- and white-collar employees, whose views were ignored until they went on strike; and for the ten thousand students treated by the authorities as so many widgets on a conveyor. An editorial in the same issue of *Student*, bearing all the hallmarks of Brown's style, offered a more optimistic attitude. 'The present system implies that students are not capable of participating effectively in the university's government – but actors, journalists and comedians are. We don't believe this.'

Brown spent some of the 1971 summer vacation examining the most remarkable industrial upheaval of postwar Scotland taking place at the time, in his native Govan. In late July, Edward Heath's Conservative government announced it would not give further financial assistance to the ailing, state-owned Upper Clyde Shipbuilders (UCS) group. The company would go into liquidation, with the loss of thousands of skilled jobs on Clydeside. The workers, under the charismatic leadership of two communist shop stewards, Jimmy Airlie and Jimmy Reid, rejected the ultimatum, and organised a work-in to keep the yards open. Heath's biographer admits that 'they turned UCS into a potent symbol of working-class self-help in defiance of hard-faced capitalism, winning considerable sympathy and popular support.'[19] Brown, whose interest in the potent myth of 'the Red Clyde' was already more than academic, travelled to Glasgow to investigate conditions at first hand.

His report appeared as a two-page centrefold in the first edition of *Student* in the autumn term, headlined 'The Guts of UCS'. He was clearly impressed by what he saw – strong leadership of the rank and file and the discipline of the men who were trying to keep the yard at work until public pressure forced the government into a policy U-turn. But he could not suspend his political disbelief. He identified a 'powerful and infectious determination' among the workers, accompanied by a strong sense of moral indignation. However, he argued that 'in ideological terms, the Clyde has been pink rather than red'. Brown's verdict was that in the longer perspective, the UCS work-in was 'doomed to both success and failure'.[20]

He explained this apparent contradiction by the observation that 'whatever happens, the Clyde workers will have made the point that the right to work forged in Beveridge's time must be restated in Wilson's super-efficient managerial society and Heath's laissez-faire individualist nation'. Demanding the right to work, he went on, remained an important – 'even revolutionary' – idea. 'It is a new challenge to the pre-eminence of economic over social planning, and it may lead to a complete re-think of the managerial society with positive policies for workers' control and participation.' From looking at Clydeside, Brown could see no reason why stewards elected from the floor could not run the yards. Presumably, he also had in mind the prospect of a student rector participating in the running of the university.

'But the UCS work-in is also doomed to failure,' opined the young politico. 'Whatever happens, the old men of Clydeside will look back at the might-have-beens of 1971.' He compared the situation at Govan with the riots in George Square in 1919, recalling the words of the communist leader of the time, Willie Gallacher, who said, 'We were planning a strike. We should have been planning a revolution.' And he asked, 'What will Jimmy Reid be saying ten years from now?' In fact, Gordon was wrong. The work-in succeeded in turning the government. In February 1972, Heath conceded defeat and pumped £35 million into a rescue operation, and marine construction still goes on at Govan, though privatised and on a much smaller scale. Jimmy Reid went on to become a full-time official of the engineering workers' union, a parliamentary candidate for the Communist Party and then, like Gordon, a television journalist. But Brown's article on the work-in still has the ability to arouse curiosity, because it shows a mature refusal to accept the Red Clyde myth at face value, alongside a fanciful belief in the role of shop stewards. Its main conclusion, about the paramount need to restate the right to work, stayed with him down the years.

UCS quickly faded into the background as the campus battle for a student rector hotted up. The contest in November 1971 was between Brown's candidate, Jonathan Wills, campaigning on a platform to 'end this badly scripted farce', and the satirist Willie Rushton. The Edinburgh University Labour Club (chairman: Gordon Brown) came out in favour of Wills. Brown said in a statement, 'We are supporting the student rectorial candidate because of the principle involved. But we want an end to elitism, paternalism and confidentiality in the government of the university, and its replacement by an open, democratic and responsive system.'[21] Gordon was still only twenty, yet he appears even then to have been preoccupied with the notion of 'government'. One can only speculate about how many other undergraduates shared his obsession. In the event, Wills was elected, and the authorities agreed that he could chair meetings of the Court. The president of the Students' Representative Council, Allan Drummond, later to become a key adviser to Brown, was initially allowed into the meetings by invitation. He was later excluded for leading a student sit-in in the Senate Room in February 1972, described in best po-faced manner as 'an attempted confrontation with the authorities' in the university's annual report.

Surveying the field, Brown was satisfied that he had got most of what he wanted, at this stage. He was popular, and respected. Students listened to him, and acted on his policies. 'You could go and talk to Gordon for hours,' said a junior academic of the period. 'He had no sense of his own time being precious.' And socially, life was good. The parties he threw, first in the Grassmarket and later in his top-floor flat at 48 Marchmont Street, hard by the campus, were legendary. 'He used to have the most wonderful parties,' said one partygoer. 'If you were "in" in Edinburgh, you got invited.' His New Year bash was particularly sought-after. The flat spread over two floors, so there was ample room for partying. According to Jon Wills, the new address rapidly became as untidy as his Grassmarket lodgings, 'but never quite so dirty'. He lived there for another fifteen years, long after he became an MP, and eventually bought the flat as a sitting tenant for £12,000.

The new academic year opened in October 1972, with a row over files held by the authorities on 'militant activists', a hardy annual in student politics. It is sometimes difficult to work out who is more obsessive on this score: the students, or the administrators with their mania for controlling their charges by filling buff folders with information – much of it wrong. Brown did not get involved. He was busy relaunching *Student* as a racy tabloid. One of his stories exposed a professor of French for trying to get his son a first-class honours degree. Academic tenure ruled out dismissal for the wayward professor: he was shunted sideways into romance linguistics. Gordon was also back on the gossip circuit, explaining to freshers the pitfalls of party time. The previous year, he recalled, one student had had to have his stomach pumped, there were drunks in the quad and someone insulted the principal. Worse, indecent suggestions were made to the waitresses. Back in his favourite slot, 'Inside Page', he advised on the Edinburgh pub-crawl. In one bar, he reported, a toper had been thrown out for explaining how to bugger a cat without getting scratched. There were other references to sex being banned 'because of the noise of creaking beds'. He had not lost his mildly salacious touch.

But politics were swiftly back on the agenda. A secret caucus of leading student politicians on the campus met to decide who should succeed Jon Wills, who was leaving after serving only one year of his three-year rectorial term. Gordon Brown had just graduated with first-class honours in history. One of his tutors said his was the best collection of papers the department had ever seen. Brown's first (ordinary) degree had been awarded in 1970, when he was still only nineteen. Now, *Student* reported, he was about to begin a three-year PhD research course at Edinburgh. His credentials for the rectorship were undeniable. He was ex-president of the Labour Club, and a student member of the university Court-appointed Constitution and Structure Committee, which was about to recommend modest reform of the university government. Furthermore, *Student* went on, Gordon was 'known to have clear ideas of his own about how more effective student representation could be achieved'. He was 'the most likely choice' of the student caucus.

The news item read like a Brown press briefing, which it

undoubtedly was. Embarrassingly, he faced the prospect of a challenge from the left, that is, left of his own position. A communist postgraduate and a challenger from the ultra-left Socialist Action appeared briefly on the scene, before vacating the ground amid calls for unity. The eccentric astronomer Patrick Moore was mooted as an outside candidate, together with Matthew Lygate, a Scottish republican revolutionary currently serving a jail sentence for armed robbery. But the Prison Department ruled that, as he was a category-A prisoner, he could not be released to take part in the hustings. David Steel, the brilliant young Liberal MP who had won the Roxburgh by-election in the Scottish borders in 1965, was also nominated.

In the end, however, it was a straight fight between Gordon Brown and Sir Fred Catherwood, a surprise last-minute nomination. Sir Fred, a Shrewsbury and Cambridge educated captain of industry – he was head of Laing's, the construction group – could offer a varied career. Knighted in 1971, he had been chief industrial adviser to George Brown's Department of Industrial Affairs in the Labour government of Harold Wilson, and director-general of 'Neddy', the National Economic Development Council, a forum for consultation between ministers, industrialists and trade-union leaders. A committed Christian, he also served on Lord Longford's Committee on Pornography. One way and another, he was the ideal establishment candidate.

That proved to be his undoing. Brown claimed that at least seven hundred students had signed his nomination forms. Not only had the rival lefties pulled out, but even the Tory Club president, Rory Mcleod, signalled his support. Brown introduced a carnival atmosphere into the election, dishing out T-shirts emblazoned 'Gordon For Me'. The mini-skirted girls wearing them were known as 'Brown's Sugars', after a current pop song. A picture of three of them appeared on page one of *Student*, pouting alongside Gordon, who, with his shoulder-length wavy hair, cut a passable facsimile of Che Guevara.

Brown dwelt on his rival's business background, arguing

(justifiably) that the court already had more than its fair share of business and professional men and Oxbridge graduates. He also dug up the dirt, disclosing that Catherwood had an undeclared business interest: his company was involved in a number of building projects on the campus. Sir Fred, wrong-footed by this revelation, accused Brown of being unable to handle university bureaucrats. 'To chair any business meeting, let alone a high-powered university court, needs skill and experience, and to get a bureaucratic machine to change direction requires training and experience in a tough school,' he said loftily. He would go for one reform a year. 'I am an idealist, a radical and a reformer,' he wrote in his manifesto. 'Society's problems today are not technical but social and moral. I believe the university must play a leading role in setting social and moral standards in a civilised society.'[22]

This was not quite what the students wanted to hear. They warmed more to Brown's rallying cry that this was the most important contest in the 112-year history of the rectorship, a 'turning point in the students' struggle for self-representation'. He did not shrink from playing the nationalist card. This was a fight between a student living in Edinburgh and 'a visitor from London'. A student rector would begin to redress the balance of power. He would keep students informed through a regular column in the campus paper. He would inject fresh thinking. He would be at once practical and idealist. He would raise the grievances of university technicians over pay. Indeed, he would say practically anything to get elected, but he was sure the voters understood. 'There is no convincing argument against a student rector,' he declared.[23]

The electorate concurred. On polling day, 10 November 1972, Gordon Brown, aged 21, thrashed the captain of industry, taking 2,264 votes to Sir Fred's 1,308, a majority of 956. The turnout was 36.45 per cent, slightly down on the previous poll. In their dismay at the result, the authorities sought to make much of this. Principal Swann, who three months before had predicted that, after Jon Wills, the students were looking for 'a more traditional type of rector', was officially the returning officer. But such was his disgust that he delegated the task of announcing the result to an underling, who attempted to read some significance into the lower turnout. Brown pointed out quickly that he had received two hundred more votes than Wills, and took more than 60 per cent of the votes cast – the equivalent of President Nixon's 'landslide' in the US presidential election.

Brown took the job immensely seriously, setting up a virtual cabinet of 'ministers' charged with looking after various aspects of university life. They were mainly final-year politics, history and law students, with one postgraduate zoology man and a second-year English undergraduate member of the Students' Representative Council executive. This team of eight assessors was supplemented by a raft of six planning groups charged with getting the university more involved in the life of the city. It was as though Gordon Brown had been elected prime minister in a Scottish parliament, rather than spokesman for ten thousand students. There is little evidence that these new bureaucracies functioned effectively, or even at all in some cases.

Nevertheless, Gordon the politician was launched. His first act was to seek the support of the university authorities for the National Union of Students' pay demand, for a rise in grants from £455 to £510 a year. This was at a time when students did not pay academic fees, and had a reasonably generous means-tested living allowance from the public purse. With a clear nod towards Labour's wages policy, Brown said, 'We are not asking that students have a greater right to an increase than other low-paid groups – but we all have. If students and universities don't push their own claim, nobody else will.'[24] Quite so, but the university Court, memorably described as 'Edinburgh's version of the House of Lords, full of used-up members of the establishment who went there after they had made their contribution to the world – not the people who ran the city, but those who used to run it',[25] was an unlikely ally in this battle. The Conservative government was in no mood to be generous.

William van Straubenzee, Under-Secretary at the Department
of Education, expostulated that students did not deserve a rise,
because they had helped inflation by supporting strikes.

The pay campaign was quietly forgotten in the excitement
that ensued very soon after Brown's accession to the rectorial
chair. Principal Swann announced that he was to quit
Edinburgh University to take up the less nerve-racking role of
chairman of the governors of the BBC. His appointment was
made public in December 1972, a month after Brown had been
elected to his three-year rectorial term. Negotiations for such a
sensitive post must have been going on for several months, but
there are those who believe to this day that Swann went because
he saw the writing on the wall – and it was Brown's. Professor
Drucker maintains that 'Swann left Edinburgh because of
Gordon. He looked around. He was very open about it. He
couldn't stand Gordon. None of the older generation knew
how to cope with him. Gordon was constantly taking over the
agenda at Court meetings. He forced senior people to consider
issues that students took seriously.'[26]

One issue is of interest. The university had a century-old
bequest of paintings that were on loan to the Scottish National
Gallery. The Heath government wanted to charge entrance fees
to public galleries, and the Court might have turned a blind
eye. But Brown pointed out that the university had gifted the
paintings on condition that they were shown free to the people
of Scotland. There was a furore over the suggestion of charging
to see them. Demonstrations involved all Scotland's leading
figures in the arts world. The Court was embarrassed, and
Brown won his point.

Swann's departure was greeted with some amusement by
Brown. In his new 'Feedback' column for *Student*, he observed,
'Cynics will say that principals come and principles go.' But the
real power of the principal was to divide and rule. He by-passed
the university Court in the interests of the Senate, and vice
versa, to play off dons and faculties against one another 'and
then get [his] own decision through the committee of [his] own

choosing'. Rector Brown suggested that the post be radically changed. He wanted a fixed five-year term of office, 'and ideally one wants the principal elected directly from the staff and students of the university. It is a representative job, and if someone wants it, he should be prepared to submit himself to election.' He demanded student involvement in the process of choosing a successor to Swann, claiming that any other method would 'prolong trouble'.

This was a bootless quest, as was his next manoeuvre, a campaign to compel withdrawal of South Africa and Rhodesia from the Commonwealth Universities Conference being held in Edinburgh in 1973. The Court rejected his appeals for solidarity with the downtrodden of southern Africa, and further dismissed his suggestion that the university give works contracts to a local, community-based consortium. The ideas never stopped coming. Brown suggested an all-night radio programme, put together and broadcast by the students themselves. It came to nothing, but his interest in broadcast journalism dates from this period. Within a few years, he was a leading figure in the Scottish electronic media.

Rector Brown seized an opportunity in February 1973 to open up the membership of the Court to a more broad-based democracy. Two vacancies occurred in the body he was busy denouncing as 'a coterie that would not have disgraced the Russian Czars'. Indeed, the Court was like something out of Tolstoy. Apart from the rector and his assessor, it was made up of the city's lord provost, five professors, two lecturers, two high-court judges, a civil servant, an accountant, a doctor, a banker, an insurance broker, an industrialist and the headmaster of a fee-paying school. To remedy this establishment imbalance, Brown nominated Mrs Helen Crummy, secretary of Craigmillar tenants' group and Ray Wolff, president of Edinburgh Trades Council, the city's trade union 'parliament'. Reject these two, he maintained, 'and we can be sure that the court does not have within itself the capacity for change'. The establishment did not disappoint him. His candidates attracted risible support.

He allowed no let-up in his campaign for a more open society in university government, rejecting the vetting of his press releases by the authorities, and ridiculing attempts to impose confidentiality on what he learned at Court meetings as 'political censorship of the crudest and most despicable sort'. Most of what happened at the monthly meetings was 'no more secret than the six o'clock News'. Not when he was present, certainly.

In April 1973, matters came to a head. The establishment moved decisively against their 22-year-old tormentor. Lord Cameron, one of Scotland's most senior high-court judges, proposed a rule change to end the rector's right to chair Court meetings. Lord Robertson, another senior judge, supported him. Only Gordon voted against the move. Encouraged by this mobilisation of their voting power, the Court went on to exclude Allan Drummond, Brown's excitable assessor, on the grounds that he had led an occupation of his old college. Brown was on his own. The weight of votes was stacked against him on issue after issue. It was a genuine crisis. Students picketed the Court meetings. *Student* ran the splash headline 'Political Assassination'. The rector fulminated against the 'arrogant, brutal and reactionary way' the authorities were behaving. It was a tense time. Campus patrols were stepped up for fear of a sit-in. Brown had to force his way through a pack of security men to get to a protest meeting where he told students, 'Much more information than before has been made available about the running of the university, due to the Rector's access as chairman [of the Court] to the administration's dark and secret files.'

Brown refused to be beaten. He went back to his flat and researched his case in the university's rules. It was clear to him that the judges were acting *ultra vires*. So he would take the judges to court. Brown sought an interdict (a legal injunction under Scottish law) to restore his assessor to attendance at the Court. It wasn't easy. Two lawyers declined to handle the case, 'because of pressure from the old boy network', in the rector's view. The authorities sought a retaliatory caveat allowing them to carry on as they now deemed normal. Brown's case against the establishment was 'the talk of the legal community', according to a well-sourced newspaper profile. 'It was most unusual for one judge to sit in judgment over two of his colleagues. Brown was so nervous that he left the case to his counsel and retired to his flat in Marchmont Road with fingers crossed.'[27]

Brown proved to be right. In the Court of Session, Lord Keith ruled that the rector had correctly interpreted the university's constitution. He had the right to choose his own assessor, who could not be arbitrarily excluded. All business transacted in his absence was null and void.

Balked of their prey, the 'incandescent' Swann and his ruling elite tried another route. If they could demonstrate that their rule changes had wide support, the consent of the Privy Council could be sought to implement them. Brown and his allies frustrated this initiative, packing meetings of the General Council of Graduates and even winning supportive resolutions from academics in the Senate. The campaign went as high as Buckingham Palace. The Duke of Edinburgh was the university's chancellor. This was an entirely ceremonial role; he did not stoop to campus politics. But when his view was sought on the rector's role, he sided with Gordon Brown: the rector had the right to chair the Court. Without the duke's backing, Swann and his establishment friends could not look to the Privy Council for salvation. They conceded defeat. Just how a student agitator could invoke royal intervention is still something of a mystery. He had not spoken to anyone at Buckingham Palace, but it was clear that someone had lobbied Prince Philip. Then it dawned on his friends. There was a royal connection: the Duke of Edinburgh was godfather to Gordon's girlfriend, Princess Margarita of Romania.

With the settling of this dispute, and Swann's departure to Broadcasting House in September 1973, the authorities and Brown moved uneasily from confrontation to accommodation. The rector persuaded the university to become more involved with the life of the city. Students were given their own seat on the university Court, as of right rather than by invitation. In return, Brown conceded a rule change that students would no long stand for the rectorship. They were now inextricably linked into the government of the university, and their voice could no longer be ignored.

His term of office came to an end in the early summer of 1975. It had been a remarkable collision of cultures: the stuffy self-assurance of bourgeois Edinburgh versus the scintillating intellect and social passion of arguably the university's most brilliant student of modern times. He changed the political landscape of his university, but today he is ambivalent about the value of those years cutting his teeth in student politics. 'It was quite a revelation to me to see how politics was less about ideals and more about manoeuvres. For three years I sat among senior professors and high court judges who made up the governing body, but I don't think they liked me very much. Did I make a lot of noise? Well, I made a lot of enemies.' There were also achievements. 'We widened the narrow focus of the university court, and got more junior academic staff on. The whole thing changed.' Nevertheless, he did not think it was a very good use of three years of his life. 'And I am not forgiven by Edinburgh University.'[28] He still has doubts about the wisdom of that period. 'I feel in retrospect I could have done more if I had stood for the local council instead of being rector. It became a bit of a diversion.'[29]

However, Brown had also set up a commission to look into the university involving the community. On it sat Michael Ancram (appointed the Conservatives' constitutional spokesman in July 1997), George Foulkes (later International Development Minister) and numerous academic and community figures. It recommended far-reaching changes which have, over the ensuing twenty years, become gradually accepted: lifelong learning; more mature and part-time students; the opening up of the university to a wider admission; closer relationships between the university and the colleges around it, and a stronger link between university and local schools. All these recommendations came from the rector's commission. Some anticipated Brown's far-reaching ideas for lifelong education in the 1990s, such as individual learning accounts for all, and the University of Industry.

CHAPTER 4

THE MAN FOR MORNINGSIDE

UNIVERSITY POLITICS WERE STIMULATING, BUT THEY WERE hardly the real thing. By his own admission, Brown had been marking time during his drawn-out battles with the burghers of Edinburgh. The real action lay in the Labour Party, which increasingly began to claim his interest.

Brown cut his teeth in the two general elections of 1974, in February and October. The first was occasioned by the titanic struggle between the miners and the Conservative government of Edward Heath. The colliers' battle for higher wages had developed over the winter from a nationwide ban on overtime to an all-out strike on the model of their highly successful seven-week conflict of 1972, in which the Cabinet had been humiliated into conceding most of their demands.

In the early 1970s, there were still 30,000 coal miners in Scotland, many of them in the pits of Fife around Brown's home town, Kirkcaldy. They all belonged to the National Union of Mineworkers, and they all loyally joined the national strike on 9 February 1974, alongside 250,000 more around the country. There were fears that left-wing elements in the NUM would seek to destabilise the Conservative administration and precipitate its downfall by bringing the economy to a standstill.

Indeed, Michael ('Mick') McGahey, communist president of the Scots miners based in Edinburgh, caused a stir when he told Heath to his face in Downing Street that he wanted to change the government 'but by democratic means, through the ballot box'.[1]

This was the dramatic backdrop against which the February general election was called. Because so little coal was reaching the power stations, a state of emergency was already in place, and industry was working a three-day week. Across the UK, 750,000 workers were laid off, though Scottish industry proved more ingenious at maintaining production than most other parts of the nation. When Heath went to the country on 28 February, warning that it was time for moderate people to make their voices heard, Harold Wilson responded with the slogan 'Back to Work with Labour'.

In the chilly late-winter campaign, Brown went to work for the Labour Party in the constituency in which he was a member, Edinburgh Central, where the candidate was his near-contemporary at university, Robin Cook. The seat, a mixture of fine Georgian town houses and run-down inner-city tenements, had been held by Labour since 1945. The population was older than average and dwindling; only just enough remained to keep it a viable constituency. For the previous nineteen years, the voters had sent Tom Oswald, a former tram-driver in the city, to Westminster. He was reputed to be the most taciturn MP in the Commons, rarely troubling the Speaker, but diligent in his correspondence with constituents.

Oswald had retired, and Cook, aged 28, something of a D. H. Lawrence lookalike, was fighting to retain the seat. The future foreign secretary in a Cabinet with Brown was then a tutor–organiser with the Workers' Educational Association. Though only five years older than Brown, he had much more experience of politics in the real world. He was a member of Edinburgh City Council, and convenor (chairman) of its important Housing Committee. He had contested Edinburgh North, unsuccessfully, in 1970 when Heath came to power.

Brown had previously worked for Cook in 1970, delivering election literature. One leaflet depicted the Tory candidate, the Earl of Dalkeith, on horseback, with the legend 'Would You Vote For This Man?' This was designed to be satirical, though the earl could hardly have been a greater fan of the turf than Cook later became. Brown tramped the Tory northern suburbs of the city in that election, and in both elections in 1974 he acted as a sub-agent for Cook, working the terraces and tenements to get out the vote. Cook won, with a majority of 1,561, and across the country, Labour's fortunes revived just enough to nudge Heath out of office. Harold Wilson formed a minority government, and skilfully converted this into an administration with an overall majority – of only four – nine months later.

Brown was nearly chosen to fight Edinburgh South, home of middle-class Morningsiders but also to a growing public housing population, in the second poll of 1974. 'I was almost a candidate. I was invited by people to stand, but it just didn't work out. It would probably have been better had I done that.'[2] Very much so. It is possible his energetic brand of campaigning would have pulled it off. Labour's Charlotte Haddow, a local government officer in Edinburgh was a good candidate brought in at the last minute, and she lost to the Conservatives in October 1974 by only 3,226 votes. At 23, he would have been the youngest MP in the Wilson government. Haddow, now Mrs Stenhouse and chair of the Fife Health Board, is unconvinced: 'At that time, the seat was unwinnable.'[3] So close did he get to the nomination that some still believe he did fight the seat. The normally reliable *Scotland on Sunday* said in a profile that Gordon stood for Edinburgh South twice in 1974 'and was offered safe seats elsewhere in Scotland afterwards', but stuck with the constituency.[4] He did not stand then, but it was true he was offered a more secure berth a few years later – and turned it down.

Brown cast around for a parliamentary constituency to nurse, and began his tortuous climb up the ladder of the

Scottish Labour Party. He also began to stake out an intellectual reputation in the party, and in wider circles. While still
working on his PhD thesis on the relationship between the
trade unions and the Labour Party in Scotland, he was
appointed a temporary lecturer in the History Department at
Edinburgh University. It was the authorities' way, he thinks to
this day, of getting rid of him. 'They wouldn't have me full-
time. In a sense, they forced me out by offering me a part-time
job rather than full-time.'[5]

While still at Edinburgh in 1975, he galvanised the best
Scots thinkers into producing a ground-breaking set of essays
on the future of their country. Entitled *The Red Paper on
Scotland* (a deliberate pun on Swann's 'Black Papers' on education), it was published by the university Student Publications
Board. Officially, the 368-page book, edited by Brown, was his
swan-song as rector. In real terms, it was his attempt to put
together a broad church of thoughtful Labour activists who
could pull the party out of the intellectual doldrums in which
it was becalmed.

The first *Red Paper*, confined to education, had been pub-
lished in 1970. The second was a much more ambitious affair.
Brown described it as 'a forum for the left to express their views
on immediate issues'. The contributors ranged from academics
to community workers and trade-union officials. Hugh
MacDiarmid contributed, as did the playwright John
McGrath. Their subjects covered every aspect of politics from
North Sea oil to Highland landlordism, though with a strong
bias towards political economy. Jim Sillars, Labour MP for
South Ayrshire, whose disillusion with Labour later drove him
to quit and form his own Scottish Labour Party, contributed an
essay on land nationalisation. Overall, there was a definite
devolutionist tinge to *The Red Paper*, though party policy north
of the border at this stage was anti-devolution. Under pressure
from the Scottish National Party (SNP), which was running
strongly in the polls, this was set to change. Just weeks before
the October 1974 election, Harold Wilson rushed out a White

Paper on the future government of Scotland, full of vague promises about an elected assembly in Edinburgh. Once he was confirmed in Downing Street, he temporised, but by then the home rule genie was well and truly out of the bottle.

Brown's *Red Paper* was therefore timely and influential. The cover had a definite Old Labour feel to it: on the front, a forest of workers' hands raised in support for the work-in at UCS in 1971; on the back, a picture of the Leith dockers' strike during Lloyd George's premiership. Brown did not stint himself for space, giving twelve pages to his introduction: 'The Socialist Challenge'. It was his first political credo. He began confidently: 'The irresistible march of recent events places Scotland today at a turning point – not of our own choosing but where a choice must sooner or later be made.' The resurgent nationalism that was forcing the most significant constitutional decisions since the 1707 Act of Union was only one aspect of a revolt of rising expectations. 'The proliferation of industrial unrest and the less publicised mushrooming of community action also bears witness to the sheer enormity of the gap now growing between people's conditions of living and their legitimate aspirations.'

The 'great debate' on Scotland's future ushered in by the Kilbrandon Royal Commission Report of October 1973, which proposed a Scottish Convention of 100 members elected by proportional representation and with wide-ranging powers, had hardly been a debate at all, he argued. 'Dominated by electoral calculations, nationalist and anti-nationalist passions and crude bribery, it has engendered a barren, myopic, almost suffocating consensus which has tended to ignore Scotland's real problems – our unstable economy and unacceptable level of unemployment, chronic inequalities of wealth and power and inadequate social services.'[6]

Unemployment then was just over 4 per cent, substantially below present-day levels, but Brown was clearly intent on painting the big picture. Kilbrandon had identified a 'diffuse feeling of dissatisfaction . . . a feeling of powerlessness at the we/they relationship' in Scotland. But the basic questions which faced Scotland in the 1980s had not been asked, much less answered: who would exercise power and control the lives of people? How would material resources and social energies be harnessed to meet the needs of 5 million people? What social structure would guarantee 'the planned co-ordination of the use and distribution of resources in a co-operative community of equals?'[7]

Brown insisted that Scotland's social condition and political predicament cried out for 'a new commitment to socialist ideals, policies and action' emerging from far-reaching analysis and a bringing together of many positive insights, responses and analyses. An exercise, in fact, like *The Red Paper*. The 24-year-old prophet demanded 'a new social vision for Scotland which begins from people's potentials, is sensitive to cultural needs, and is humane, democratic and revolutionary'. He was ready to offer that vision. He thought it was 'increasingly impossible to manage the economy both for private profit and the needs of society as a whole'. Paradoxically, working-class industrial and political pressure in Scotland had been contained 'by the accumulative [sic] failures of successive Labour governments'. Socialism had, fifty years previously (in the period that he had been studying for his PhD) been an urgently felt moral imperative. 'Today, for many it means little more than a scheme for compensating the least fortunate in an unequal society.'[8]

Labour had two choices: resist the pressure for change, and see the SNP take over, or harness the current dissatisfaction in a socialist strategy that not only forced the pace of advance towards socialism in Britain as a whole but revitalised the grass roots of Scottish society. Scots socialists could not support a strategy for independence that put off meeting urgent social and economic needs, 'but nor can they give unconditional support to maintaining the integrity of the United Kingdom – and all that that entails – without any guarantee of radical social change'.[9] This open questioning of the UK union set Brown apart from the majority in the Scottish Labour Party, including Robin Cook for whom he had been campaigning only months previously. But it brought him to the forefront of a more challenging style of campaigning, and closer to some of the younger, sharper minds on the left. 'All the older people hated him. Those over 50, old Labour, just couldn't stand him,' recalls Henry Drucker, at the time a young academic activist in the party. 'He was too fast for them, too clever, too popular, too good with the press. But he was the future.'[10]

However, Brown did not offer his own detailed prospectus. On social needs, he reviewed the evidence put forward by various contributors. On community democracy, he was at his most fundamental; yet it was still a broad-brush, almost wishful-thinking, approach: 'If the prospects for the least fortunate are to be as great as they can be, then they must have the final say – and that requires a massive and irreversible shift of power to working people, a framework of free universal welfare services controlled by the people who use them.' Socialism would also have to be won 'at the point of production', – and that demanded ending the power of a minority 'through ownership and control to direct the energies of all other members of our society.'[11]

Turning to economic prospects, Brown criticised the failure of existing economic strategies, accused the oil companies of 'a strike of capital' aimed at halting socialism and poo-poohed the £200 million resources of Labour's new Scottish Development Agency as 'insufficient'. The market, he wrote, could no longer be seen as the efficient allocator of resources. The logic of current economic development pointed to a planned economy. The private control of industry had become a hindrance to 'the further unfolding of the social forces of production'. The erosion of the power of the market was now 'the forging ground for socialist progress'.[12]

In order to determine the political distance that Gordon Brown has travelled since those intoxicatingly ideological days, it is useful to record what he actually proposed. 'The public control of industries essential to the provision of social needs and services, the priorities being building and construction, food and food processing, insurance and pensions; the industries essential to the planning of services vital to the economy – the priorities being energy as a whole, land, banking and foreign trade; industries whose monopolistic position threatens the ability of society to plan its own future – the priorities being the taking over of the assets of the major British and American multinationals in Scotland; and industries essential to regional development – in Scotland's case shipbuilding and textiles being obvious cases.' Fortunately for the chancellor and the tax-payer, this 'major erosion of the power of the British upper class' could be enacted without compensation, though a new world economics framework, possibly under United Nations auspices, would be required.[13]

On workers' power, Brown praised the proposals of the Nottingham-based Institute for Workers' Control (whose presses printed *The Red Paper*) which called, naturally enough, for more workers' control of industry. 'Workers' control on an international scale is clearly an alternative to nationalism,' he wrote. The industrial workers of Scotland had 'implicitly if not explicitly' rejected the values of capitalist society. Spurning the SNP's 'new politics' that 'reject class warfare' as 'the familiar priorities of wealth and power over people', Brown urged an almost mystical creation of a socialist society 'within the womb of existing society'. Socialists should not put their faith in an Armageddon of capitalist collapse, 'nor in nationalisation alone'. No, there must be a far-reaching movement of people and ideas, stimulating people to see beyond their existing condition. In turn, the labour movement in Scotland should give a positive commitment to creating a socialist society, 'a coherent strategy with rhythm and modality to each reform to cancel the logic of capitalism and a programme of immediate aims which leads out of one social order into another'.[14]

The language is interesting. When he talks of Armageddon and socialism 'not by nationalisation alone', there are echoes of the sermons ('not by bread alone') given by his father that the young Gordon heard by the hundred. They made a deep impression on him. He has a bound copy of them. There are also obligatory references to Gramsci's *Prison Notebooks*, the works of E. P. Thompson, Michael Barratt Brown and Ken Coates, the New Left of the day. He imitates their earnestness, and sometimes, it must be said, their verbal flatulence. Brown was in a soaring frame of mind, and it would be easy to dismiss his first lengthy published political testament as the flight of fancy of a twenty-something just getting his first job as a temporary lecturer. There would be some justice in the charge. His vision for industry reads like a shopping list scribbled on the back of an envelope. In contrast to his later intellectual rigour, this statement of beliefs and principles has not been thought through. It is a vision of the promised land, rather than a down-to-earth programme, but there is an underlying sense of goodness and altruism that has stayed with him down the years. The emphasis on socialism as making the most of every person's potential was at the heart of *The Red Paper*. That, too, has remained a constant theme. In 1975, he spoke of 'the gap between what people are and what they may have it in themselves to become',[15] a feature of his philosophy in the 1990s.

He could be practical, too. A few lines after rhapsodising over 'rhythm and modality', Brown called for a concerted programme of political education. He pointed out that Scotland had no political newspapers, no socialist book club, no social labour college or workers' university and only a handful of socialist magazines and pamphlets. 'We need all of these now.' And, indeed, still do. He ended with a roll-call of Scotland's socialist pioneers, his heroes: Hardie, Smillie, Maxton, Maclean, Gallacher and Wheatley. Keir Hardie, founder of the Independent Labour Party (ILP) and the first socialist MP, whose socialism 'in practice owed more to religion than economics';[16] Robert Smillie, a miners' leader from Lanarkshire; James Maxton, an ILP Glasgow schoolteacher who fought for the poor, the homeless and the unemployed in the Commons during the Depression and the war; John Maclean, a Marxist and 'great folk hero of Scottish socialism' jailed for three years in World War I for sedition (urging strikes); Willie Gallacher, a communist leader from the 1920s; and John Wheatley, who served as health secretary in Ramsay Macdonald's 1924 Labour government. In all, a sextet of dedicated men, who had suffered for socialism. These men, Brown maintained, knew that social-ism would not be won until people were convinced of the need for social control. He ended with a statesmanlike plea: 'The Scottish Labour movement is uniquely placed today to convert the present discontent into a demand for socialism: we will fail only if we ignore the challenge.'[17]

Publication of *The Red Paper* fed naturally into the discon-tent over 'whither Scotland?' among Labour activists and key media figures. But, despite its radical tone, it did not create waves through the population at large. There were several reasons for this. Scotland, like the rest of the UK, now had a Labour government: one, moreover, that was on the closest of terms with the trade unions through the 'social contract' with the TUC. This cosy arrangement had just delivered a flat-rate pay rise of £6 a week to all employees, the largest percentage wage increase the low-paid had ever received. There was a lull in the industrial unrest that had so fired Brown's vaguely syndi-calist talk of pressure from the workers. The hated 1971 Industrial Relations Act aimed at curbing the power of the unions had been repealed, and replaced by legislation enacted by Employment Secretary Michael Foot that restored their rights. Harold Wilson gave the Scots the prospect of limited self-government and tax-raising powers in a White Paper, *Our Changing Democracy*, published in November 1975.

Some of Labour's home-rule hard-liners decided they had had enough, and quit to form the breakaway Scottish Labour Party. Its leader was Jim Sillars, MP for South Ayrshire, who had written for *The Red Paper*. According to some, he would have liked nothing more than for Gordon Brown to follow him. 'Gordon was the key figure when Sillars set up the SLP,' said Henry Drucker, author of a book on the breakaway party. 'The person he most wanted to join was Brown. He knew if he could get Brown he would get the entire younger generation in Scotland.'[18] Sillars was well aware that Brown was a coming man in the Labour Party. 'I had never any doubt in my mind that Gordon would become an MP.' But he disputes Drucker's claim that he was tempted to recruit him. 'That is one of the mistakes we made. They argued that we had carefully prepared the SLP. Really, it was a rush of blood to the head, an enormous Scottish rush down the hill. There was never any idea of recruiting significant individuals. If they wanted to join, they did. No approach was made to Brown by me. I don't think that it is in his nature in any event to take that kind of gamble. He had a fairly set course for the top.'[19] The SLP was formally launched in January 1976, at a meeting in Glasgow attended by nearly a thousand potential recruits. But it was soon riven by factionalism – the old enemy of the left – and folded after the 1979 general election. 'It was one of the balls-ups of history,' reflects Sillars.

Brown was moving further into the mainstream, rather than to the left. He was also chafing at the indifference of his alma mater. 'They wouldn't give me a full-time job because of my politics, because I was controversial. I had to move.'[20] In 1976, he moved to Glasgow to take up a lectureship in politics at the city's College of Technology. He was to stay there for four years, mixing academe with politics. Like Robin Cook, he went into trade-union education. He was a tutor for the Workers' Educational Association, doing courses in politics and labour history – while writing his PhD thesis on the relationship between organised labour and the party in Scotland. He always joked that his courses were not the most popular. To his chagrin, he noticed more students signing for the gardening courses.

Brown was still living in Marchmont Road, in Edinburgh South constituency. He had always been active in the university Labour Club, building up membership to record levels in the early 1970s when he was chairman, organising for the Chile Solidarity Campaign after the bloody overthrow of the Marxist president, Salvador Allende and supporting the miners' strikes. At the end of the big strike in 1974 that led to the downfall of the Heath government, he and fellow students were feted by the Scottish miners' leader, Mick McGahey in the Liberton miners' welfare club in south Edinburgh. Now, he threw himself into the work of his local party: becoming first chairman of a branch, then secretary of the constituency party. His devotion to duty was rewarded in 1976 with the prize of prospective candidacy for the Edinburgh South seat. Brown readily admits that 'these were difficult times for Labour. You knew things were going wrong.'

For the party, perhaps, but not necessarily for Gordon Brown. He had made his mark as a man of the future. The leading journalist Neal Ascherson described him as 'the outstanding Scot of his generation.' Friends at the time concur in their description: a prodigious worker, attending meetings three nights a week and devoting all his weekends to political activity. They also recall that he carried around plastic bags stuffed with newspaper cuttings and statistical papers on issues close to his heart. Faced with an awkward question, he would fish about in the pile of documents and triumphantly pull out facts and figures to prove his point. He was praised for his 'intense focus', but fellow-workers in the party shook their heads in disbelief at the general air of disorganisation that surrounded him. He hated the tag of 'intellectual', insisting, 'Call me a propagandist, a polemicist – anything but that.'[21]

Yet that is how he was seen. As an unnamed senior Scottish trade unionist put it: 'Some people have degrees and you'd never know it, but this guy certainly gives off an aura of intellectualism. He is really too clever by half for a party – and a country – suspicious of intellectuals. And with the best will in the world, there are insufficient ways for someone like him to project himself in Scotland. To make it big, he'd have to go to London.'[22] In truth, that was his destination. Edinburgh South looked the perfect launch-pad. The constituency was gradually changing. More students were moving into halls of residence built by the university: enough, Brown hoped, to tip the scales his way. He was also climbing the ladder of the Scottish party. A brilliant speech at the party conference in Troon in March 1976 brought him to the attention of the right people. He stood for the party executive that year, and got on first time.

Brown interpreted his role as a prospective parliamentary candidate in the broadest possible manner. In September 1976, on the eve of the Labour Party conference in Blackpool, he took the battle for devolution into the enemy camp, inviting five English Labour MPs who had joined with Tam Dalyell, the MP for Linlithgow, in an anti-home rule campaign to visit Scotland to examine at first hand the arguments for devolution. 'Your opposition to devolution is born out of a complete misunderstanding of the mood in Scotland,' he argued. Nothing came of the initiative, but Brown's passionate advocacy of the devolution case aroused the notice of older hands on the Scottish party executive, who marked him out for higher things.

Brown had not long immersed himself in the task of turning Edinburgh South into a winnable seat when a prize opportunity arose to get into Parliament in a by-election in Hamilton, the county town of Lanarkshire, just south of Glasgow where he now worked. The sitting MP, NUM-sponsored Alec Wilson, had died. Though the local coalmines were closing rapidly, Hamilton was still a working-class town. It looked ideal for his purposes. The seat had once been lost to the SNP, in 1967, when Winnie Ewing became the first Nationalist to enter Parliament – also at a by-election, when the Labour government's fortunes were ebbing. But it was now regarded as reasonably safe, certainly in a safe pair of hands. Gordon's parents were now living in the town, since John Ebenezer Brown had moved to St. John's Church there, that year. The SNP was fielding another woman candidate, Margo Macdonald, who married Jim Sillars. Scottish politics may be a broad church, but it is often a small one. Influential figures in Hamilton Labour

Party, including the secretary, Alec Reid, urged Brown to go for it. He consulted Jimmy Allison, the party's Scottish organiser, who noted that Gordon had already been selected for Edinburgh South, the constituency he failed to land in 1974. 'He came to see me in my office. He was being pressured by certain people in Hamilton to go for it. But he didn't want to desert the people in Edinburgh South. I could tell he was uneasy about leaving them in the lurch. We discussed it, and he decided to stay.'[23] Brown remembers: 'I was invited to stand. I was offered nominations. Seven branches sent letters to me inviting me to go for nomination. They wanted someone with a local connection, and my father was a minister in the town. But he was in hospital, and I was already a candidate elsewhere. I didn't think it was the right thing to do. I pulled out.'[24]

Others have less charitable recollections. Alf Young, then a young research officer for the Scottish party and now deputy editor of the Glasgow *Herald*, insists: 'I got a nomination and said I would stand. Gordon telephoned me, and asked me if I would step aside. We had a very good and reasonable relationship, but I said, "I'm not. If people want you to stand there should be an open election. The membership should make their choice." He got really agitated about it. It was only then I realised how desperate he was to get into Parliament, how intensely important it was to Gordon's life plan and game plan to be an MP.'[25]

Young told Brown he stood no chance against the General and Municipal Workers' Union machine gearing up to take the seat. Sure enough, George Robertson, the defence secretary in Tony Blair's 1997 Cabinet, who was then a little-known official of the GMW (now the GMB), won the nomination and easily retained the seat for the government. Ms Macdonald was to have her revenge on Labour later.

Soon afterwards, most trade unionists attending the September 1978 Trades Union Congress in Brighton thought they heard James Callaghan, the prime minister, signalling his intention to call a general election in October. Then he sang,

'Can't get away to marry you today/My wife won't let me', and most political observers assumed he had ruled out an autumn poll. They were right. His government was now in a minority, dependent on support from nationalists of every stripe, and vulnerable to ambush by an increasingly confident Conservative Opposition under Margaret Thatcher. Chancellor Denis Healey's policy of holding down wage rises to 5 per cent – without any agreement with the TUC, the much-vaunted social contract now being in tatters – proved futile and self-damaging. The 'winter of discontent' of 1978–79 set in, and nowhere more so than in Scotland.

The political situation in Scotland was doubly difficult, because Scots voters were already preparing for a referendum on the Callaghan government's devolution proposals. These, in turn, had divided the Labour Party in Parliament. Robin Cook MP, for whom Brown had worked so hard, was now the most high-profile Scots politician opposed to devolution, going so far as to say he wanted to 'kill the issue'.[26] John Smith, later party leader and Brown's mentor, was eloquently in favour, but there was a serious risk that the referendum could fail: not because the majority would be against, but because, in Cook's words, 'we shall have such an unimpressive proportion voting that no government in their senses would be able to claim that they have a mandate for such major constitutional change'.[27] To achieve this end, anti-devolution MPs led by George Cunningham, MP for Islington in London but a Scot, had inserted into the Scotland Bill a requirement that 40 per cent of the Scottish electorate – not merely of those voting – must support the devolution package for it to be implemented. The Scotland Bill went on to the statute book in this form in July 1978. Gordon Brown, a powerful advocate of Labour's version of home rule, had been chosen to chair the Scottish party's Devolution Committee. It was an extraordinary choice. He was only 27, yet here he was in charge of delivering a central plank of Labour government policy for Scotland. In some senses he was the obvious choice: untainted by the old right-wing hostility to limited home rule, and capable of seeing a compromise that would suit a majority of Scots. His former political ally Robin Cook argued that Labour could not oppose nationalism by creating some kind of middle way. Brown was convinced it could be done. From being an early supporter of devolution, Cook had swung over to the other side. Alf Young, the party research officer, watched the contest. 'There is a very, very powerful thread of pragmatism in Gordon Brown's character,' he observes. 'If you bring that up to the present day – what he did then and what he does now in terms of the fiscal constraints he has adopted willingly to abolish Labour's tax and spend image and ensure victory – there is some kind of willingness to compromise in pursuit of a bigger objective that was already present in the 1970s. Cook has now joined him in that process.'[28] From that period dates the chasm between Brown and Cook. In the words of a veteran Scots Labour MP to the author: 'Cook hates Brown for "selling out". The difference is, Cook did it later'.

Referendum year opened inauspiciously. More than five thousand Scots lorry drivers were doing their bit for the trade unions' winter of discontent by striking, and many more roads than usual were blocked by snow because there were not enough gritters. There were calls for troops to be used. Thirty thousand workers were laid off. Edinburgh airport was closed for a day by striking ground staff, and there was even a walk-out by hospital workers. There were food shortages in the city, and some shops reported panic buying by housewives. 1 March 1979 was set for devolution day, when 4 million Scots would decide on their future.

Labour insiders now say the party's campaign was pretty hopeless from the start. The party of government, divided over the issue, refused to co-operate with the SNP's 'Scotland Says Yes' campaign, and ran its own. But enthusiasm was limited. Brown was tireless, speaking to many meetings, yet audiences were often sparse. The only gatherings that really caught the public imagination were mounted by the Sillars–Dalyell road show, barnstorming round Scotland urging 'No'. Party officials like Alf Young 'kind of knew' what was in store. 'The campaign was left to the enthusiasts like Gordon Brown. It meant a hell of a lot of work devolving on a few shoulders,' he recalls. 'It was pitiful how much real effort was put into delivering the goods. Remember, in 1974 the party had voted against devolution. It had to be dragged kicking and screaming into a commitment by growing support for the SNP.'[29]

On 7 January, Brown treated a local devolution meeting to a few statistics. The Scottish Office, he pointed out, was currently responsible for spending more than £70 million a week, yet only five ministers were responsible for expenditure decisions. The secretary of state answered questions at Westminster only once every three weeks. 'An extra 5p per person per week is not a high price to pay for democratic control over an assembly that will spend more than £8 million a day,' he declared.[30] Perhaps not, but the opinion polls on home rule were discouraging. National opinion polls painted an even bleaker picture: as James Callaghan pleaded with TUC leaders to do something about the tidal wave of strikes that was drowning his government, a MORI poll on 6 February put Margaret Thatcher nineteen points ahead of Labour. Callaghan promised to travel to Scotland to campaign for 'a big Yes', but it was rapidly becoming evident that his minority administration would not hold on to power long enough to carry through even its limited devolution package. As the bank rate of interest surged up to 14 per cent, Robin Cook dismissed devolution as 'irrelevant to the real problems we face. Given the present economic situation, to go ahead with devolution seems to be like fiddling while Rome burns.'

The package on offer to the Scots people was for an elected Assembly of 150 members sitting in Edinburgh – the first such legislative body in Scotland since 1707. It would begin sitting in 1980, and would have a budget of £3,300 million. An extra 750 civil servants would be recruited, and a further 240 support staff. An Assembly chamber was practically ready: the premises of the old Royal High School, on Calton Hill, refurbished at a cost of £3 million. The Assembly, elected every four years, would have devolved power over health and social work; schools and education (including universities); housing; local government; transport; the law; the arts; fishing (inland); tourism; the fire services, and, dear to Scottish hearts, alcohol licensing laws. Westminster would retain control over defence; foreign affairs; European Community links; energy and North Sea oil; economic policy; taxation; industrial relations and industrial policy; forestry; abortion; betting; the police; food and drug control; and weights and measures.

Gordon Brown stumped his patch pushing the case for a 'Yes' vote. Speaking at Edinburgh University on 19 February, he excoriated 'Tory turncoats' who had twisted and turned on devolution six times in only ten years without producing a real alternative to the Scotland Act. 'They are putting party politics before the constitutional future of this country,' he declared. 'Mrs Thatcher, who said after her election as leader that the Tories are pledged to a Scottish assembly has now thrown any claim to honesty to the winds.' By turning their backs on devolution – of which they had been half-hearted advocates – the Conservatives were 'playing into the hands of the extremists and wreckers who want to break up Britain'. This scathing reference to the SNP showed how far Brown had travelled since the days of *The Red Paper* barely four years previously, when he was not willing to guarantee the integrity of the UK. Unfortunately, the biggest threat to the right outcome of the referendum lay less in the Tory party and the Nationalists than among his own ranks. Andrew Marr noted: 'Local parties were sometimes split. About a third of constituency Labour parties declined to campaign at all, and many others had members working in the "no" camp as well as the "yes" one. Indeed, neither camp existed as a single entity, since both the pro- and anti-devolutionists were split into rival campaigns.'[31]

Brown ploughed on, predicting in a speech on 22 February that 'The next twenty years will see Scottish society change more quickly than ever before.' The Assembly would be one of the biggest challenges in Scotland's long history, responding to the breathtaking social changes in the 1980s and 1990s. He linked home rule to a forthcoming 'leisure revolution', with people retiring earlier, living longer and enjoying a shorter working week. The Assembly's task would be to co-ordinate public support for sports, arts, education, youth and community services and 'tap the potential of the Scottish people, many of whom have felt themselves to be at a dead end.' The Scottish TUC came out in favour, the Confederation of British Industry against. Meanwhile, the winter of discontent ground on, dragging down the government's credibility, and with it hopes of a 'Yes' vote. A week before polling day, forty thousand Scots civil servants stopped work for a day.

The chairman of the Devolution Committee could not let up, however. Brown announced that he would address thirty meetings in the final seven days of the campaign. At a meeting in Lothian, he reminded voters, 'It is ten years since the Kilbrandon Commission was set up to examine the case for devolution, and four years since the first White Paper committing the government to a Scottish assembly. To be swayed now by the scaremongering and false fears peddled by the money men of the "No" campaign would be like scoring an own goal in the last seconds of a big match.' To continue the footballing metaphor, the real problem was that the spectators were drifting off the terraces. Many could not work out the direction in which Labour was playing. Michael Ancram, prospective Conservative candidate for Edinburgh South – the constituency for which Brown had been selected – came out virtually on the eve of polling day to denounce 'the cruel deception' of devolution. 'The only thing that will change is that Scotland will have more government, more civil servants and more politics – all of which it has too much already.'[32] The 'Yes' campaign was not helped by a BBC Wales opinion poll showing that the Welsh, in a parallel referendum, were poised to reject devolution by a margin of two to one.

Polling day dawned with a heavy frost and snow showers. A low to just-reasonable turnout was reported from the 5,700 polling stations scattered around Scotland. In order to win, Brown and the government would have had to secure 1,498,844 'Yes' votes from 3,747,112 electors – the magical 40 per cent threshold laid down in the Scotland Act. The early returns were bad. Dumfries and the Western Isles said 'No'. News also came in that Labour had lost two key English by-elections, at Clitheroe in Lancashire and Knutsford in Cheshire, both recording a swing in excess of 10 per cent against Labour. The Tory party chairman, Lord Thorneycroft, urged Callaghan: 'In the name of God, go!' When the referendum votes were counted, those in favour of devolution had a majority of 77,435. It was not enough. In a 63.7 per cent poll, the Scots voted 32.8 per cent 'Yes' and 30.8 per cent 'No'. Robin Cook was vindicated. Gordon Brown was devastated, though he had seen it coming.

Explanations and recriminations followed thick and fast. It was a bad time for Labour. The referendum had been used to record a vote against an ailing government seemingly incapable of ending the industrial unrest that had hit sector after sector for five months. There had been no 'plain man's guide' to devolution, as there had been on the EEC in the 1975 referendum on the UK's entry into Europe. After the failure of the referendum, Scottish Secretary Bruce Millan was obliged to put forward a parliamentary order repealing the Scotland Act, thereby losing the support of the eleven SNP MPs and the two breakaway Scottish Labour MPs – and sealing the fate of the Callaghan administration.

Labour's Scottish party executive held an inquest on 3 March, and reaffirmed its commitment to devolution, and urged the government to do likewise. The SNP warned that it would withdraw its parliamentary support and force an early general election if Callaghan did not try to drive through an assembly. Bad luck would have it that Labour's Scottish party conference was scheduled that week in Perth. The executive reaffirmed that its 'historic commitment' to devolution was 'as old as the Labour Party itself', which was an interesting variation of the truth.

Unrest continued. In Scotland, teachers struck, and civil servants came out again. At Westminster, in the absence of any move to sustain the devolutionary momentum (a process that became known as 'the Frankenstein solution'), the SNP carried out its ultimatum, and put down a motion of censure against the government. Thatcher jumped on to the bandwagon: here was her chance to bring down Callaghan. Election fever broke out, and the stock market put on a billion pounds in one day. Gordon Brown tore into the Nationalists and the Tories: 'What will Scotland gain from a No-confidence vote?' he demanded. It would do nothing but harm to the fight against unemployment and inflation. 'The people will judge harshly the Nationalists who said last month there would be no devolution for Scotland for twenty years if the Scotland Act failed, and are now not even prepared to allow another twenty days' discussion. It is also dishonest of them to vote with the Tories who offer Scotland nothing but fewer jobs and higher prices and public spending cuts.'[33] In his heart of hearts, he knew the game was up and he was already fighting the general election. It came quickly enough. Without the Nationalists, Callaghan lost the censure motion by one vote. On 29 March, he asked the Queen to dissolve Parliament.

Labour went into the election on the back foot, trailing heavily in the polls and mauled by the referendum defeats in Scotland and Wales. The party's 9,000-word manifesto, *The Labour Way is the Better Way*, tried manfully to instil fear of what a Conservative government would do: scrap the Prices Commission, which had a poor record for holding down inflation, and introduce curbs on the trade unions, which many voters, influenced by screaming headlines like the *Daily Mail's* 'Now We Can't Bury Our Dead', thought were long overdue. Civil servants marked the opening of the election campaign by staging a one-day strike which brought out half a million people and brought the business of government to a standstill. Labour promised pension increases, the abolition of TV licences for pensioners, tax cuts for some and help with home-buying for young people.

Polling day was set for 3 May. In Scotland, Scottish Secretary, Bruce Millan promised that Labour would continue with measures that had saved a hundred thousand jobs in the motor industry, shipbuilding and other sectors north of the border. He pledged that the budget of the Scottish Development Agency would more than double to £800 million a year – as Brown had recommended in *The Red Paper*. And he reaffirmed the party's commitment to devolution, without spelling out how it would be implemented.

It was a tough time to try for Westminster, but Brown threw himself into the fray with characteristic enthusiasm. 'We really did canvass it very hard. I was the candidate for three years. This is a long time in what is not a winnable seat.'[34]

On 11 April, Brown contributed a long feature article to the *Edinburgh Evening News* on the issue of housing in the city. The Scottish capital, he argued, needed a five-year housing plan, one that was 'grounded in what people need and can afford'. More homes were needed in the city centre, particularly for young people and those who needed sheltered accommodation. He called for radical initiatives in tenant management of public housing schemes, and more resources to upgrade housing stock. Back on a familiar hobby-horse, he demanded more resources for community facilities. It was a workmanlike piece, but dense and packed with statistics: nothing like the soaring vision of *The Red Paper*, and unlikely to pick up many unconverted voters.

In Morningside, it was a five-man contest. Brown's main rival was the Tory, Michael Ancram, 33, an advocate, vice-chairman of the Scottish Conservative Party and fighting his first seat, too – but inheriting a 3,226 majority from Michael Clark-Hutchinson, the retiring MP. The SNP fielded Robert Shirley, a 51-year-old economics lecturer, fighting this seat for the third time. The Liberals were represented by Bryan Lovell, 39, his party's Scottish energy spokesman and yet another lecturer, and there was a candidate from the Ecology Party, political novice Stewart Biggar, a 28-year-old researcher. Brown had smartened up his appearance for the campaign. Press pictures show his hair was cut respectably, just on the collar, barely an inch longer than the Tory candidate's.

The Conservatives banged away on the devolution drum, turning Labour's referendum defeat to their advantage. They argued that the 1 March poll result was not a sufficient basis on which to proceed with major constitutional change (a view shared by leading Labour figures), but made vague promises about an 'all-party conference or committee' to see if agreement could be reached about the system of government in Scotland. An unrepentant Gordon Brown told the *Edinburgh Evening News* that he still wanted to see a Scottish Assembly set up as quickly as possible. If Labour were returned to power with a working majority, they should implement the Scotland Act without further delay. Failing that, he was willing to look at the Tory option. 'I still think, however, that given the referendum result, inter-party talks should be held to discuss the way forward.'[35]

Given the unpopularity of the unions at the time, Brown was courageous in his defence of the labour movement. He firmly rejected suggestions of legislation on picketing, unofficial strikes or wage settlements. 'What we require is agreement and consultation, not legislative confrontation,' he urged. 'There is a new accord between the government and the trade unions to reduce inflation to five per cent over the next three years, to stage annual talks on an acceptable norm for wage settlements and find ways round the difficulties posed by picketing and unofficial strikes.'[36] The TUC and the government had indeed signed a new 'concordat' on 14 February, St Valentine's Day, agreeing inflation targets and an annual wage assessment. The TUC would also issue guidance on picketing, on 'flexible use' of the closed shop and on the way industrial disputes should be run. However, this revived form of the original social contract came too late to rescue the government's fortunes. Brown's Conservative rival offered 'an immediate curb on secondary picketing – an unnatural and unjustified extension of the strike weapon'.[37]

In Edinburgh South, what concerned the voters was vandalism. Ancram cited his own experience in court as a lawyer. 'Too often sentences have little or no effect on the criminal. We should introduce a new crime of vandalism.' Brown agreed that vandalism had become a problem, but said harsher penalties were not the answer: 'There is no evidence that stiffer penalties cut crime. I do not believe in being soft, but the idea that you can solve the problem by beating, flogging and hanging is complete nonsense. We should try instead to give young people a greater sense of responsibility and community involvement.'[38] He pressed for more public investment to create jobs, and more cash for the local neighbourhoods of Inch and Gilmerton which had been 'starved of resources' by the city's Tory-controlled council. Brown sounded more like a traditional Labour candidate than the *Red Paper* visionary: anxious about dampness in council houses, and concerned about vandalism, the stock-in-trade of pavement politics. He knew well enough that the election had to be fought at that level. 'We worked that constituency really hard,' he recollected years later.

His hard work paid off, but not enough. On a bright, crisp 3 May, the electors of Edinburgh South returned Michael Ancram to Parliament. His majority over Labour was cut by almost a thousand votes, to only 2,460, but the Tory vote went up by three thousand to 17,986. Brown put on nearly four thousand to poll 15,526. Both benefited from a collapse in the SNP vote, which fell by more than half, letting the Liberal into a poor third place. The Ecologist got only five hundred votes. The trend to Labour was established by Gordon Brown, but it was to be eight years before his protégé Nigel Griffiths brought it firmly into the fold. Ancram was generous in victory, though with a snide attack on Brown's party: 'He was an excellent opponent, very courteous and thoughtful. He is clearly a rational man, but his problem is that his qualities are not necessarily those that will serve him well in today's Labour Party.'[39]

In Scotland, the election went surprisingly well. Labour polled 42 per cent of the popular vote, and won 44 of the 71 seats. The Conservatives took 31 per cent, and secured 22 seats. The SNP, on 17 per cent, were cut from eleven seats to two, and the Liberals on 9 per cent got three seats. Nationally, it was a completely different picture. The Conservatives won handsomely, garnering 339 seats and an overall majority of 144. Thatcherism was born.

CHAPTER 5

VICTORY AND DISASTER

THATCHER'S OVERWHELMING VICTORY BROUGHT FORTH A wave of recriminations. At a meeting of the Shadow Cabinet six days after the election, Jim Callaghan, just unanimously re-elected as party leader, exploded: 'I'll tell you what happened. We lost the election because people didn't get their dustbins emptied, because commuters were angry about train disruption and because of too much trade union power. That's all there is to it.'[1] It was rather more complicated in Scotland, where devolution had created a sharper campaigning edge for Labour, but also exposed the party's internal divisions on home rule. On balance, Labour's principled stand, contrasting with the SNP's opportunism, stood the party in good stead. In the European parliamentary election that came a month after the general election, Labour took 33 per cent of the votes cast in Scotland (less than 1 per cent fewer than the government) and won two seats, against five for the Tories and one for the SNP. The party was down, but decidedly not out.

Gordon Brown was at a crossroads. Defeated in a seat he had imagined he could win, he was now just another ex-candidate among many, albeit one with a place on the party executive in Scotland. He was still writing his thesis, and lecturing at

Glasgow College of Technology. But he was ready for a change, a move to a new discipline. 'It seemed right to get some experience in another area,' he said later. 'I knew people at Scottish Television. They invited me to make a film about the state of the Scottish economy, while I was still lecturing. I did so, and that seemed to go quite well. They gave me a job – a contract – to do work with them for a time. The pay was £200 a week – more than I was getting as a lecturer.'[2]

So in 1980 he joined STV as a programme producer. He worked first on *Ways and Means*, a political programme for Scotland, covering the big issues of the day. But in the run-up to the next general election, he felt his active role in politics might compromise his journalistic impartiality. Another explanation circulating in later years suggested that he was taken off-screen as a result of a complaint – not from a political opponent but from a Labour MP. Whatever the reason, Brown moved into consumer programmes. He became editor of *What's Your Problem?*, a weekly vox-pop show that took up the complaints of the Scottish people, and gave the programme a social conscience: advising viewers how to claim benefits. 'We were trying to get justice, social justice for consumers,' he recollects. Gordon was joined on the programme by his elder brother, John. He also turned his hand to literary matters, producing *Between the Lines*, a books programme, and finally to sport. In 1982, he went out to Spain to do the pre-work for Scotland's bid for the World Cup, meeting his hero Jock Stein. This excursion also yielded an STV book, *Scotland and Spain: The World Cup*.

Brown enjoyed television. STV was a good company to work for. The work was stimulating, and it made him more succinct in his style. Here, plainly, are the origins of the sound-bite style that made him so effective at policy presentation and attack years later. He is reticent on that score, admitting only that 'TV is a very tough medium. You have to say what you want in a very short period of time. You have to say things succinctly to get your message across.'[3] He also did a number of controversial investigative programmes, including one on the North Sea oil companies, *Rigs to Riches*, which showed that most of the oil companies had not paid Petroleum Revenue Tax. Another programme dealt with corrupt property deals in Glasgow.

It was as well that he was enjoying his new professional life, for politics grew steadily more bleak. The strongly ascendant left seized the opportunity of a weakened leadership to begin a concerted drive for constitutional – i.e., political – change in the party. Labour's annual conference in 1979 voted that it be made mandatory for sitting MPs to stand for re-selection, a move that would encourage constituency hard-liners to dump 'moderate' members of parliament. James Callaghan quit as leader, plunging the party into fresh uncertainty. In the poll of MPs that followed, Michael Foot beat the former chancellor Denis Healey on the second ballot by 139:129, prompting another Labour ex-chancellor, Roy Jenkins, to announce that the time had come for a political realignment of the centre. Moves to set up a Social Democratic Party were already under way, in a breakaway from the right comprehensively more damaging than the previous haemorrhage of talent in Scotland to Jim Sillars's SLP.

North of the border, the committee set up to push through the internal Labour Party reforms was led by Brown's hard-line rival on the Scottish executive, George Galloway (later MP for Glasgow Hillhead). Within days of the party conference, he organised a conference in Glasgow on 13 October 1979 to popularise the changes that transferred much power to left-wing activists in the constituency. Among the handful of Tribunite MPs attending the City Hall gathering was Robin Cook, who was emerging as a left-wing opponent of Brown. The leftward surge of the party put Brown in a somewhat awkward position. He was not by nature a left-wing cohort of the Bennite variety. He never, for instance, joined the Campaign for Nuclear Disarmament, not even at university when it was fashionable to do so, and not when he became involved with the Transport and General Workers' Union, which was strongly

associated with CND. As he matured from the fundamental-
ism of *The Red Paper*, Brown's political outlook became
grounded more in ethical socialism, based more on the values
of the Kirk than those of Marxist ideology. Jimmy Allison, the
party's Scottish organiser, who built up a friendly relationship
with Brown during this period said of him, 'He was a person
who had a great deal of talent and believed in Christian
Socialism. Many people claim that their politics are based on
such principles and there is no shortage of Christians in the
Tory Party who think that they have a direct link with their
God. But Gordon Brown, I found genuine.'[4] Jim Sillars concurs that Brown was 'mainstream, never lined up with any
faction. You could not have said he identified himself with the
right-of-centre. He wasn't malicious in discussion or debate.
He participated at a very good intellectual level, not on the
basis of personality clash or ideological labels.' Naturally, this
style had a practical side. Brown 'knew the right buttons to
press. He knew the right people to contact and how to establish a network of contacts who were broadly influential in different sections of the party,' reflected Sillars.[5] However, another
trade union official later put it: 'He used to vote all over the
place on the executive as his conscience dictated. Now he votes
according to block considerations. He realises you can't operate
as an individual, however bright, in the Labour Party.'[6] The
newly ascendant hard left found Brown's style antipathetic, but
difficult to condemn. On the Scottish executive, a group round
Galloway and Bill Speirs, assistant general secretary of the
Scottish TUC, sought to put the brakes on his gradual rise up
the political ladder, but without success.

The threatened breakaway by Labour's Gang of Four –
David Owen, Shirley Williams, Bill Rodgers and Roy Jenkins
– was accelerated by the party conference decisions in 1980 to
withdraw from the Common Market and to establish an electoral college for choosing the party leader and deputy leader.
The final break came in January 1981, after Labour's special
conference at Wembley gave the trade unions the largest share

of votes in the electoral college (40 per cent), with MPs and local parties sharing the rest. The party in Scotland was in favour of the policies that triggered the breakaway. Indeed, the Scottish conference in 1980 voted not just for unilateral nuclear disarmament but for complete UK withdrawal from NATO. Only one of Scotland's Labour MPs, Robert McLennan, MP for far-flung Caithness and Sutherland, joined the SDP. The party in Scotland has always been more to the left than elsewhere and suffered fewer defections.

Nevertheless, the tensions set up within Labour by the lurch to the left and the rise of the SDP did reverberate in Scotland. Unemployment was rising sharply under Margaret Thatcher, and a protest demonstration was organised in Glasgow for 21 February 1981. There was nothing unusual in this. Demonstrations were everyday fare for Scottish socialists. This one, however, was to be addressed by Michael Foot, the party leader. The hard-left Labour Co-ordinating Committee insisted that Mick McGahey, the much-respected communist miners' leader should also speak. Officials in Keir Hardie House, Labour's Scottish HQ in Glasgow, refused permission. On the day, 100,000 workers marched through the city to hear Foot. McGahey did not address them.

This superficially trivial incident provoked an almighty row within the Scottish executive months later, when the hapless Michael Foot was present. The 'strictly private and confidential' minutes of the meeting in Keir Hardie House on 14 November 1981 are deeply revealing about Gordon Brown's developing political outlook. George Galloway, the left's chief spokesman, was in the chair. He excoriated Foot for denying Tony Benn – who had recently been narrowly beaten by Denis Healey for the deputy leadership – his support for the Shadow Cabinet, on the grounds that Benn would not accept collective Cabinet responsibility. This decision, he argued was 'little short of disastrous'. Galloway also criticised Healey for not toeing the party line on unilateral nuclear disarmament. Two of his comrades swiftly piped up in support.

Gordon Brown sprang to the aid of his leader and deputy leader, disagreeing 'completely' with Galloway's comment. The matter had to be put in perspective. 'We need to win the support of the voters. Anything which prevents this and which puts the relationship between the party and the trade unions in jeopardy is not only needless but harmful. What is needed is a tri-partite agreement, the drawing-up of a Draft Manifesto and the issuing of it as a public statement of the party's position. If some on the right or the left of the party could not accept this, so be it. But I believe it would be possible to draft such a manifesto and receive the overwhelming support of party members. Having done this, we have to go and sell it to the country and start a moral crusade backed by the vast majority of party members.'[7]

His comments are revealing in a number of ways. First, Brown was the only speaker to state the obvious fact that winning the support of voters must be the overriding priority. It sounds trite today, but such a view was practically a heresy in the early 1980s, when the dominant left was more interested in ideological purity than in electoral popularity. Second, Brown's deferential nod towards the unions and their special relationship with the party should be noticed. He was deeply involved in trade-union education work and promoting the labour movement's grandly titled Alternative Economic Strategy, a statement of anti-Thatcherite economic policy. Third, his proposal of a tripartite agreement (presumably between the unions, the national executive and the parliamentary party) was not new. There had been similar initiatives before by the TUC–Labour Party Liaison Committee, which brought together politicians and union barons. What was new – utterly new – was his idea that the policy statement should be published as a draft election manifesto: an idea that pre-dates Tony Blair's similar exercise in the run-up to the 1997 general election by fifteen years, and clearly signposts the origins of Labour's hugely successful *Road to the Manifesto* of 1996. His rejection of a right or left veto on such a step is interesting confirmation of contemporary judgments that Brown (still aged only 30) was by now very much a mainstream figure in the party. And furthermore, his suggestion of a 'moral crusade' not only underlines the perceived basis of his politics, but pre-dates Blair's 'Big Idea' commitment to similar principles many years later. In such brief form, Brown laid out a vision that eventually came to pass. In keeping with the internecine warfare politics of the time, it was ignored. The meeting ended acrimoniously, and the bad feeling endured during an informal 'mingling' held afterwards in the boardroom of Keir Hardie House. The following day, Scottish papers carried stories that an MP had been jostled by left-wing members of the executive. Scots politics could sometimes be a painfully physical affair.

The PhD thesis on which Brown had been toiling intermittently for the best part of a decade was now brought to a swift conclusion. He only just made it. The 532-page tome, lodged today in the Special Collection of Edinburgh University Library, was delivered at the last possible moment after Brown telephoned his flatmate in Marchmont Road from Edinburgh airport, where he was on his way to Spain to prepare STV coverage of the 1982 World Cup football tournament. Could someone get his thesis down to the binders? It was delivered with five minutes to spare.

The contents are rather less racy than the anecdote. Entitled 'The Labour Party and Political Change in Scotland, 1918–29', the thesis examined the politics of five general elections and in particular the rise of socialism. In the first half of this period, to 1924, he concluded, Labour established itself as the alternative party of government, but socialism failed to establish itself as a dominant ideology. In the second half, he found that by 1929 'the differences between the Labour and Conservative Parties appeared to the elector to be less matters of fundamental dispute than qualitative differences over how far economic and social reform should go'. Labour won thirty-six seats in the election of 1929, but only 6 per cent of Labour election addresses north of the border mentioned socialism.

The campaign that year reflected how far Labour had become a party which grounded its electoral appeal in social and economic reforms 'rather than full-blooded socialism'. Shades of *The Red Paper*! Brown had clearly read deeply among Scottish Office reports for the period (some of them, naturally, 'confidential') and he uncovered much new material from the minutes of the Independent Labour Party, whose leader, James Maxton, was becoming something of a political idol. He also traced Labour's varying enthusiasm for devolution in Scotland, noting that the sense of Scottish separateness was never sufficiently strong to force Labour into a really decisive stance: the popular demand for home rule took second place to the demand for action on unemployment, the Poor Law and other social and economic questions. 'The real problem for Scottish Labour was that it wanted to be Scottish and British at the same time,' he concluded presciently. Amid the thickets of statistics in his thesis can be discerned Brown's emerging political philosophy: pragmatic, non-ideological and fired by social concern.

Brown's educational missionary work for the unions brought him closer to the heart of the complex web of relationships within Scottish politics that could deliver his heart's desire: a safe seat. These were promising times for Labour, despite the party's bitter internal divisions. The SDP was gaining ground – Roy Jenkins won a by-election in Glasgow Hillhead on 25 March 1982 – but nationally Labour was benefiting from the huge unpopularity of the Thatcher government, brought about largely by recession and unemployment. As vice-chairman of the Scottish party that year, Brown's profile in Scotland was high, and he was discreetly engaged in the search for the right constituency.

Then came disaster, in a form so unpredictable that political certitudes were swept aside. General Galtieri mounted the Argentine invasion of the Falklands Islands on 2 April 1982, and with one patriotic bound Margaret Thatcher was free of her electoral unpopularity. Britain's brilliantly successful campaign to retake the South Atlantic territories with a combined-service task force revived the Conservative government's fortunes and allowed the prime minister to proclaim that she had restored Britain to its rightful place in the world. Some Scottish Labour MPs voiced their opposition to the war, and many Scots were less enthusiastic about the war than the flag-waving jingoists south of the border. But as a political fact, Thatcher's adroit exploitation of the Falklands issue made it infinitely less likely that a divided, left-leaning Labour Party could win enough seats across the country in a general election to unseat the Tories. In Scotland, the picture was less gloomy. After the loss of Glasgow Hillhead, Labour easily retained Coatbridge and Airdrie and Glasgow Queens Park, where the death of the sitting MPs forced two further by-elections in 1982. The Tories performed badly in these Labour heartlands, and the SDP lost a deposit.

Organisational shortcomings remained a problem. Michael Foot had mistakenly believed that Labour could win a legal action against the Boundary Commission, whose report redrew the constituency map of Britain. Consequently, Scottish Labour was late in fielding a full list of candidates. At the eleventh hour, an opportunity arose for Brown to go for a seat on his home ground of Fife. Boundary-redrawing had given the old Kingdom an extra seat, making the total five.

The new constituency of Dunfermline East was carved out of the centre of the region, taking in the dockyard and naval base community of Rosyth, and the pleasant seaside towns of Inverkeithing and Aberdour on the Firth of Forth. It was based, however, on the mining town of Cowdenbeath in the heart of the Fife coalfield, and took in the surrounding pit villages of Lochgelly, Ballingry, Lumphinans, Kelty, Lochore and Kinglassie. These communities used to be known as 'Little Moscows', on account of the strong local adherence to communism – there is a Gagarin Way, named after the Soviet cosmonaut, in Lumphinans to this day. Willie Gallacher was Communist MP for much of the area from 1935 to 1950, when it was part of West Fife constituency, and the tradition endured right into the mid-1980s.

It was certainly a communist stronghold in 1945 when Willie Hamilton, a Geordie, came to contest the seat for Labour. He insisted that the miners 'were not Communist in the political sense', but were disillusioned with 'the apparent lack of militant leadership from both their trade union and the Labour Party'. Hamilton found Lumphinans, birthplace of the Moffat brothers – the notorious communist leaders of the Scottish Miners' Union – was 'full of miners' rows, depressing slums owned by the Fife Coal Company – a real hotbed for the breeding of extremist politicians and agitators'. He had to campaign there from the top of an air-raid shelter, with 'Bevin Boys' (men who went to work in the mines rather than do military service in the war) acting as his bodyguard. Hamilton also had a meeting in North Queensferry (where Brown now lives). It was 'a wee community' of a thousand souls. Hamilton thought it 'looked like a God-forsaken village'.[8] He announced his arrival there with a borrowed school handbell. Labour won the general election that year, but West Fife stayed communist. Gallacher's majority was down sharply, however, and five years later the miners who had seen their pits taken into public ownership by the Attlee government opted emphatically for Labour. In parliamentary terms, it has been safe Labour territory ever since.

The boundary changes that produced Dunfermline East welded this staunchly socialist coalfield to a coastal strip that runs along the north shore of the Firth of Forth, by the magnificent railway bridge and its modern road neighbour, through residential North Queensferry and Inverkeithing to Aberdour. It was an inviting prospect for a would-be MP, being much safer than the other new constituency of Dunfermline West. Willie Hamilton decided to stay with Central Fife, another freshly created constituency based on the new town of Glenrothes. It was expected that Dick Douglas, the outgoing MP for Dunfermline Boroughs, would exercise his prerogative to choose the safer of the two new seats created from the coast and the coalfield. That was the Labour Party rule. It favoured sitting MPs. Douglas signalled his wish to represent Dunfermline East.

But there was also another rule, which laid down that a new constituency could decide whether to have a 'one-person short-list' (i.e., Hobson's choice) or to throw open the candidacy to a selection conference. There was hostility to Douglas in the fledging constituency party. The party chairman, David Stoddart, a colliery mechanic on the left of the party, recalls: 'Dick Douglas said he wanted it. A number of us said he wasn't having it. He lobbied us and telephoned us and took us to tea and every damn thing. My reply was, "Look, we will be holding a selection. If you want to throw your hat in the ring, you can. But you're not going to walk in and claim it as yours – because it isn't yours."'[9] At the inaugural meeting of the Dunfermline East CLP, a motion to have a reselection conference was put by Alex Falconer, senior Transport and General Workers' Union shop steward at Rosyth dockyard, and seconded by a dockyard electrician, Jock Penman. It was carried overwhelmingly. Dick Douglas, accordingly, was out of the picture. He subsequently claimed his place in Dunfermline West and won the seat.

The election was only a matter of weeks away, and the constituency was still without a candidate. But ambition abhors a political vacuum, and interest was already aroused. Bob Eadie, a full-time organiser for the electricians' union, the EETPU, aged 40, began collecting nominations. His father, Alex, was an NUM-sponsored MP for Midlothian, and had served in a Labour government as junior energy minister to Tony Benn. The miners still felt a proprietary interest in the seat, and Eadie – a product of the right-wing electricians' union machine – was regarded as too moderate. David Stoddart approached Tom Dair, a 48-year-old mechanical engineer at Comrie colliery who was also a member of Fife Regional Council. Dair, a popular chairman of the council's Education Committee, had previous parliamentary ambitions. He reached the short-list in Dunfermline in 1976, only to be beaten by Dick Douglas. 'Bob Eadie was even further to the right than Dick Douglas,' says Stoddart. 'I telephoned Tom Dair, and urged him to stand. He wasn't too keen, but he agreed.'[10]

Unbeknown to either of these hopefuls, Gordon Brown was beavering away on his own candidature. His political ambitions had been nurtured by some of Scotland's most astute power-brokers for several years. Brown's political power base was the Rosyth dockyard, then the biggest industrial employer in Scotland, employing nine thousand men, and the Transport and General Workers' Union was the dominant union in the yard. At this time, the TGWU, Britain's biggest union, with two million members and enormous political clout, was pushing the labour movement's Alternative Economic Strategy (AES), a socialist programme for industry – which had many points of contact with Brown's *Red Paper*. The union was on the lookout for articulate voices to popularise its policies, and Brown fitted the bill admirably. His first contact with the formidable TGWU local machine was Alex Falconer, the union's chief shop steward at Rosyth (and now MEP for Mid-Scotland and Fife). Brown met Falconer at the Scottish party conference in 1976. He was recruited into the TGWU, and became involved in the union's political education work.

He had also been talent-spotted by Jimmy McIntyre, who ran the TGWU's Dunfermline office. McIntyre is one of the labour movement's unsung heroes. He died of mesolothemia in 1985, but before that had been Fife district organiser. He had built up the union's membership, recruiting widely in unskilled areas, and had put his faith in union education, politicising a generation of young shop stewards, of whom Alex Falconer was one. McIntyre introduced Brown to the Fife TGWU scene, encouraging him to go for a seat. The two sat together on the Scottish party executive, and from 1979 onwards their friendship was cemented by a mutual friend, Tom Donald, a local Fife journalist.

Defeats for Labour in 1979 in the Scottish referendum, the general election, local government elections and the European elections prompted the union to look for new blood. 'Jimmy McIntyre, recognising Gordon Brown's obvious talent, recruited him into our union,' recalls Falconer. When the prospect of Dunfermline East opened up, the TGWU had 'another comrade' in mind, but he left to seek out a different parliamentary seat. 'Meanwhile, Gordon had been active at meetings of the TGWU Political Committee and had participated in a number of weekend schools run by the union, along with the likes of Adam Ingram, John Reid, Lewis Moonie and Norman Godman.' These men are now MPs for East Kilbride, Motherwell North, Kirkcaldy and Greenock/Port Glasgow respectively – a tribute to the efficacy of the system. 'A large part of these schools was devoted to the union's policy of the Alternative Economic Strategy and the role that shop stewards and the wider membership could play in the development of the AES when Labour were in government. After all, we were all Bennites then,' says Falconer.[11] Not quite. Brown – then invariably referred to in the media as 'Dr Brown' – was portrayed in the *Dunfermline Press* as 'politically Left of the centre of the Labour Party' but described himself as 'an old-fashioned Tribunite'.[12]

The TGWU decided to 'sponsor' Dunfermline East, which would benefit the local party by several thousand pounds at election time and an annual stipend of around £600 for organisational expenses. Jonathan Wills, Brown's university friend, who was now working for him politically, recollects, 'Thanks to the introduction from Jimmy McIntyre, Gordon quickly won friends and influence among shop stewards and branch secretaries with his charm, quick wit, oratory and willingness to speak anywhere, at any time, however personally inconvenient.'[13] Falconer, by now the lay political education officer for the TGWU locally, set about introducing Brown to the area. A workplace branch of the Labour Party was set up in Rosyth dockyard and the neighbouring naval base, which brought him

into contact with activists of other unions. He was also invited
to visit those Labour Party branches that would be within the
boundaries of the new constituency. Nothing was left to
chance. 'Overall, Gordon was well received,' says Falconer. He
picked up two nominations from the TGWU, and two from
party branches, Kelty and Rosyth East.

There was one very special friend aspiring candidates for
TGWU sponsorship had to make, and that was Hugh Wyper,
the boss of the TGWU in Scotland. 'Again, Jimmy McIntyre
made the introduction,' recalls Wills. 'Hugh was a canny, not
to say calculating, man who ran a tight ship. He was also
extremely stimulating company. There was just one small problem. The man who ultimately decided who secured the nomination for all these TGWU-sponsored fiefdoms was not a
member of the Labour Party. He was a member of the
Communist Party, and always had been. Jimmy McIntyre
didn't like this anomaly, and neither did Gordon. But you had
to have Hugh on board to clinch it, and Gordon, like so many
others now prominent in the Labour Party, must have gone
through the traditional initiation rite of taking tea with Hugh
in his Glasgow office.'[14] Brown also won the backing of Alex
Kitson, deputy general secretary of the TGWU in London.
Kitson, a calculating Left-winger who came up through the
union ranks in Edinburgh and formed part of a double-act
with Wyper, was hugely influential in reorientating the Scottish
labour movement to the left in the late 1960s and early 1970s.
He was also in charge of picking winners for the TGWU parliamentary panel (he singled out Harriet Harman as promising
material), and fully approved of the choice of Brown. 'He made
a good impression on me,' recollected Kitson. 'I knew a lot of
his contacts at STV. He always had a high profile – not up
front, shouting, but his name cropped up, his philosophies, his
ideas, in the *Scotsman* and the *Herald*. That built him up.'[15]

An unexpected late intervention almost scuppered Brown's
political career before it took off. The mystery 'comrade' who
had shown an interest in Dunfermline East revived his claim

just as the carefully organised plan was about to come to fruition. Soon after the March 1983 Scottish party conference – at which Brown was elected chairman of the Scottish party unopposed – Falconer attended a weekend school run by the TGWU and Oxfam. Hugh Wyper and the 'comrade' approached Falconer, with a view to reintroducing his candidature. 'I advised that if the union wanted to do this, then it could be done, but pointed out that we had already introduced Gordon into the area, and any change now would likely upset the Labour Party branches. This could hit us badly in a number of ways. It would affect our chances of securing a re-selection conference, and the union would lose the nomination for the seat. It could, in fact, be construed as a form of gerrymandering, losing us the goodwill we had built up over the years. The comrade agreed, and we resolved to continue supporting Gordon Brown.'[16] Once the re-selection conference had been secured, Falconer then got himself elected minute secretary. This role may sound tedious, but it was critical. As minute secretary, he had unparalleled access to the addresses and telephone numbers of the branch delegates who would choose Labour's candidate. Brown's backers were at an advantage: they could discreetly lobby the 'selectorate' in advance of the day of decision.

More than sixty delegates turned out for the selection conference in Broad Street Centre, Cowdenbeath, on 16 May 1983. Brown travelled by train from Edinburgh, accompanied by Wills for much of the way. 'I expected Gordon to be confident and cheery but I could hardly get a word out of him. He sat, the picture of grumpy, agonised misery, scrawling the umpteenth redraft of his speech.'[17] McIntyre and Falconer picked up Gordon from Cowdenbeath station. They, too, found him nervous. Falconer assured him that he was one delegate short of an overall majority on the first ballot. If he made a good speech, he would win it on the first ballot.

There were three candidates: Brown, Tom Dair and Bob Eadie. Stoddart was in the chair. He describes the meeting as 'a humdinger, like a big rally'. He did not know Brown, but he had heard him speak once before and had been 'quite impressed'. Officially, the local branch members and trade-union affiliates were not mandated but had a free vote. Unofficially, of course, many delegates arrived with clear instructions in their pockets. This was particularly true of the union delegates. 'It was a foregone conclusion,' insists Wills. 'Not just because it had been stitched up in advance (which of course it had been by Jimmy McIntyre and the TGWU boys in the dockyard) but because Gordon really did win over the delegates' hearts and minds.' He promised delegates he would 'knock on every door in the corridors of power' to promote the interests of his constituents. He would champion the claims of ten thousand pensioners and demand a better deal for ten thousand children 'whose future is being threatened by Tory government cuts in educational spending and the real value of child benefit'.[18] As his TGWU minders had predicted, Brown won on the first ballot. 'Gordon swept the board,' recalls Stoddart.[19] Brown took thirty-four votes, Dair eighteen and Eadie trailed behind with ten.

The crafty – ruthless, even – campaign to secure the safe seat of Dunfermline East for Gordon Brown may appear unsavoury at this distance. It is certainly at odds with the image of Brown the moderniser, the champion of one member, one vote and of internal party democracy. But machine politics were the order of the day in the Scotland of the late 1970s and early 1980s. The unions were masters of the levers of that machine. Their support was critical. It often meant the difference between winning and losing the nomination in a key seat, as Brown's rivals for his constituency swiftly discovered. That the Communist Party was closely involved in this process, ostensibly at arm's length, but in reality at the heart of the wheeler-dealing, was also accepted, if reluctantly as in Brown's case. Communists in Scotland were, in any event, much more respected for their educational work and industrial realpolitik than they were south of the border. In sum, what the carefully planned operation to ease Brown into a safe seat tells us about him is that he is – quite unlike Tony Blair – very much a 'party man'. He knows Labour's highways and byways, and he is at home there. He was a Labour activist from his teens. He was on the Scottish party executive in his mid-twenties, a sure sign of a man determined to climb the party's greasy pole. And he was chairman of the Scottish party in the year he stood for Parliament.

With the general election pending, Brown had to find an agent quickly and suggested David Stoddart, chairman of the local party. Stoddart spluttered that he hadn't even voted for Brown, but Gordon said it didn't matter to him. This play-within-a-play had also been rehearsed in advance. Jimmy McIntyre, Falconer and Brown had previously agreed that if they pulled off the nomination Gordon would propose Stoddart as his agent in order to maintain unity and maximise support. Stoddart accepted. The final part of the plot was now in place.

The problem now was to raise his profile in the constituency. He may have been well-known in the Glasgow machine of the Labour Party, but nobody knew him in Fife, which he had left sixteen years previously to go to university. Officials hastily arranged a score of public meetings, often two or three in an evening. He addressed a dozen people in sheltered accommodation and moved on to a dockyard-gate meeting where more than a hundred might gather. Brown organised his own supporting speakers, some of who – like Lawrence Daly, general secretary of the National Union of Mineworkers – were Fifers 'coming home'. Others, like Jimmy Reid, the hero of the UCS work-in, were household names in Scotland. Douglas Henderson, the minister for Europe in Tony Blair's 1997 Cabinet, who was then a humble official of the GMB general union, also appeared on platforms with him.

The *Scotsman* assessed the seat as 'safe Labour', suggesting that a notional majority based on 1979 voting patterns could be as high as 14,800. However, it also noted that unemployment was rife, rising to 33 per cent in some pockets of the old mining areas. 'Unemployment is not just an issue, it is a way of life,' the paper observed. It also detected a strong left-wing tradition, albeit softened from the days of Willie Gallacher. Ballingry still had a Communist councillor, and elsewhere seven Labour councillors had been returned unopposed in the local elections of May that year. Brown had four opponents. The Liberal/Alliance candidate, David Harcus, a solicitor, and another graduate of Edinburgh University fighting his first election, was thought likely to present the greatest danger. Clive Shenton, the Tories' choice, a 36-year-old Durban-born advocate who had served in the Black Watch before graduating in law from Brown's alma mater, tried to frighten the voters with scare stories of a threat to jobs at Rosyth. The Scottish Nationalists fielded George Hunter, aged 53, a telecommunications engineer. And the Communist Party refused to support Brown, standing their own candidate, Alex Maxwell, a production controller for the National Coal Board, against him. The CP fought ten seats in Scotland that year, on 'Left and progressive policies'.

Gordon Brown was fighting a seat that could only fall victim to a political landslide. He could not lose. Equally, his party could not win, nationally. In Glasgow, the party's Scottish organiser put in his safe an internal report predicting that the Tories would have an overall majority over Labour of 120 seats, principally because of the unattractiveness of Michael Foot as leader and the party's disunity. Additionally, Labour had adopted a 15,000-word manifesto, *New Hope for Britain*, which was easily the most radical set of policies it had put before the electorate since 1945. The manifesto favoured withdrawal from the European Economic Community, unilateral nuclear disarmament and strong intervention in industry. It was memorably described by Labour's Gerald Kaufman as 'the longest suicide note in history'. Margaret Thatcher called it 'the most extreme manifesto ever put before the electorate'. Even Tony Benn admitted to his diary that 'the Shadow Cabinet wouldn't implement it if they were elected'. The Tories said it would cost £70 billion to put into action; Labour said it would be only £11 billion. Either way, it cut little ice with the mass of ordinary voters, who were more impressed by Margaret Thatcher's recapture of the Falkland Islands.

British patriotism was not Fife's stock-in-trade, however, and Brown wisely campaigned on jobs, jobs, jobs. Labour's central aim, he argued, was to cut unemployment to a million within five years. To achieve that, Labour would need five years of economic growth. The economy would be expanded by 'a strong and measured increase in spending'. The SNP also concentrated on employment, promising to create 220,000 jobs in Scotland within three years, financed by North Sea oil revenues. In contrast to Labour's poor showing south of the border, opinion polls in Scotland put Labour ahead, though by a dwindling margin. On 20 May, System Three in the Glasgow *Herald* had Labour on 44 per cent (down 5 points on the previous week), the Tories on 32 per cent (up 8), the Liberal/ Alliance on 12 (up 3) and the SNP on 12 (down 1). That same day, after a marathon battle, Tony Blair, an Edinburgh-born lawyer, was adopted as Labour candidate for the safe seat of Sedgefield. A few days later, MORI in the *Scotsman* had Labour down to 39 and the Tories up to 34. Nationally, Labour's share of the poll slid alarmingly to between 28 and 30 per cent, as Labour's general secretary, Jim Mortimer, committed the gaffe of saying that the national executive had reached the unanimous view that Michael Foot was still leader of the party. Labour also suffered from internal divisions over the Polaris nuclear deterrent, a sensitive issue in Rosyth, where the Polaris submarines went for refit.

John Smith, Labour's energy spokesman, tried to keep the election on track, pointing out in a speech on 30 May that 125 men and women had lost their jobs in Scotland every day since Thatcher took office in 1979. Moreover, 128,000 Scots had been out of work for more than a year, and there were seventy school-leavers chasing every job vacancy north of the border. Yet on 3 June, a few days before polling day, the Department of

Employment announced good news for the Conservatives on the jobs front. The 'headline' count of unemployment fell by 121,000 to 3,049,351. The government was obliged to admit that the underlying trend (which economists watch) was up, but most voters only read the headlines. That day, Brown appeared at a press conference in Glasgow to accuse the government of a 'Watergate-style cover-up'. He told reporters that 'concerned civil servants' had informed him that Prime Minister Thatcher had personally ordered the destruction of internal Government social security documents to prevent them being leaked during the campaign – presumably to stop them getting into Gordon's hands.

Nevertheless, he was confident he knew what was in these documents. 'The cover-up in Whitehall is to hide the fact that under the Tory microscope are detailed plans for abolishing mortgage tax relief, abandoning the Wages Councils, ending the present system of child benefit and forcing everyone to take up private medical insurance – with charges for visits to the doctor under consideration.'[20] That these ideas were not in the Conservative manifesto did not divert his wrath. 'They didn't tell us [in the last manifesto] they would break the link between pensions and rising earnings, and abolish earnings-related supplements for the unemployed, cut maternity and invalidity benefit, issue a White Paper on means-tested death grant and push up the numbers of people who depend on the means test to more than seven million.' This was not the old Tory party of Butler and Macmillan, he declared (though it is difficult to believe he would have been any less withering about them). 'What we have is a new Tory Party that genuinely believes that state support should only be provided for the wholly desti-tute.'[21] It was a powerful shot, and he followed it up with another leaked document, this time an internal Coal Board paper showing that the mining industry would shed ten thou-sand jobs in Scotland over the next few years – one in three. John Smith said, 'It is real. It is planned. It is lethal.'[22] It proved to be all three.

On the eve of polling day, Labour fortunes in Scotland staged a last-gasp recovery in the opinion polls, bounding back up to 41 per cent, with the Tories down to 27 per cent, the Alliance on 20 per cent and the SNP on only 11 per cent. Nationally, the roles were reversed. Thatcher was ahead on 47 per cent, and Labour was level-pegging with the Alliance on 26 per cent, the party's worst performance in living memory. In Dunfermline East, Gordon Brown romped home, taking 18,515 votes (51.5 per cent of the votes), a majority of 11,301 over the Liberal/Alliance on 7,214 (20 per cent). The Conservative came third with 6,764 (18.9 per cent), the SNP fourth with 2,573 (7 per cent), while the once-conquering Communist Party trailed in last with a risible 864 votes (2 per cent). The turnout was 71.2 per cent. In neighbouring Dunfermline West, Dick Douglas held on, but by fewer than 2,500 votes.

After the count in Lochgelly Town Hall, Brown and his party workers gathered in David Stoddart's council house nearby for a celebration-cum-wake. At one o'clock in the morning, expecting a Fifers' party, Jon Wills found him close to despair instead. 'In the front room, the new MP for Dunfermline East squatted on the floor in front of the telly, utterly dejected. He had just achieved something he'd worked on for a decade, but victory had turned to ashes as he watched Thatcher's rout of Michael Foot's Labour Party.' Wills made vapid, encouraging remarks about celebrating his own victory and rebuilding for the next election, but Brown was not to be cheered. 'It's a bloody disaster, Wills,' he said. 'There's some beer in the kitchen.'[23]

Brown had finally made it to the green leather benches of Westminster, but his personal victory was soured by the terrible drubbing meted out to his party, which was back in Opposition against a Thatcher government that had an impregnable majority, and which had a failed leader and a quiverful of discredited policies. At the Scottish miners' gala in Edinburgh two days after polling day, John Smith told the working-class throng that young people were apathetic and uninterested in what Labour had offered. There existed, he warned, 'a whole generation of young people to whom the message of socialism has not reached'. In the absence of power, this would become Brown's theme for the future.

CHAPTER 6

AMBITIOUS BACKBENCHER

ARRIVING AT WESTMINSTER IN LATE JUNE 1983 WAS simultaneously an exhilarating and a dispiriting experience. Brown was at last where he wanted to be, but Labour had been crushed on its most radical platform since 1945, a manifesto that could have been culled from the pages of his own *Red Paper* of the previous decade. Margaret Thatcher had a majority of 144 over the combined Opposition, and Labour had a leadership crisis on its hands. Michael Foot indicated that he would not accept nomination to continue as leader, and there was an immediate scramble for the post. Neil Kinnock swiftly emerged as soft-left front-runner against right-wing Roy Hattersley and the anti-Common Market Peter Shore, easily the most experienced Cabinet veteran. Gordon Brown was a natural Kinnockite. More and more, he was becoming associated with what was known as the 'soft-left' of the Labour Party, its reformist and modernising wing. He joined the moderate-left Tribune Group, in which Kinnock was a leading figure, and moved easily into the inside track as a member of Kinnock's leadership campaign committee, the only member of the new intake to do so.

His first priorities, though, were to obtain an office in the

gloomy chaos of Westminster, and to find his political feet in
the Commons. He also had to find somewhere to live. Initially,
he took a room in Dolphin Square, before renting a flat in the
Barbican, the GLC's 'jewel in the crown' estate in the City –
where, incidentally, he was a neighbour of Arthur Scargill. At
Westminster, he was given a room off the main committee cor-
ridor, to be shared with another new Labour member who had
also secured a safe seat at the eleventh hour – Tony Blair. The
two shared a tiny, windowless office, facing each other across
desks jammed tightly together by the wall. There was little
space left for filing cabinets or shelves, and Brown's moving
paper mountain often encroached on Blair's desk, to the tidy
lawyer's intense irritation. The new MP for Sedgefield was not
used to living amid such chaos, yet he swiftly realised that it was
a most fortuitous turn of events. Here was a political heavyweight who could teach him much. In the words of his first
biographer, 'Blair was immediately captivated by Brown's
breadth of knowledge and his insight into the workings of the
party.'[1] Brown was so obviously the senior of the two, remarked
his younger brother, Andrew (his Commons assistant at the
time), that 'No one who looked into that office would have
believed that it would be Tony Blair who was prime minister.'[2]

There was a constant flow of chat and ideas across Brown's
crowded desk. Blair learned from him how to master the black
arts of media manipulation: how to handle radio and television, and how to write a press release so that it would actually
appear in the newspapers rather than end up in the bin. Blair
himself confessed, 'My press releases used to read like essays
before Gordon showed me how to write them.'[3] Brown also
taught the young barrister how to structure his speeches, how
to appeal to a mass audience and how to encapsulate a complicated idea in a simple phrase. This skill, the outcome of his
years in television, brought the sound-bite into British politics.

Brown took his time settling in at Westminster. He did not
even hurry to be sworn in by the Speaker. He did not take the
loyal oath until the third day of swearing-in, on the afternoon

of 21 June. He waited in line by the despatch box just behind Neil Kinnock and a clutch of other Labour members, including the *ancien terrible* Ian Mikardo. Brown's was the last name on the list of those who took the oath or made an affirmation that day, before the House was adjourned at five minutes to eight.

Some new members cannot wait to make their maiden speech, fearing that the longer they wait, the bigger the mess they will make of it. Others put it off as long as possible, for much the same reason. Gordon Brown waited just over a month before speaking for the first time in a debate on social security on the evening of 27 July. Social Security Minister Rhodes Boyson defended an inflation-linked 3.7 per cent rise in pensions on the grounds that low inflation rates were good news for the economy, for pensioners and everyone in Britain. Supplementary benefits for the needy went up by 4.3 per cent. Unemployment benefit had been fully protected against inflation since 1978, claimed the strangely Edwardian figure of Dr Boyson, whose mutton-chop whiskers were a political trademark.

Brown would have none of this complacency. He listened patiently to speeches from the government and his own front bench before rising at 6.45 p.m., to point out that, as a member representing a constituency where one in seven voters was dependent on means-tested benefit, it was appropriate for him to make his maiden speech in a debate on social security. First, he paid tribute to the two MPs who had represented parts of his seat before the boundary changes, Willie Hamilton and Dick Douglas, both of whom had been returned to the Commons. Relatively few MPs could enjoy the company and support of their predecessor, 'especially on the Labour side', he added wryly. They shared his view that the greatest threat to the ideals of personal responsibility the Thatcher government so stridently espoused, indeed 'the grossest affront to human dignity and the gravest assault, on any view of social justice, is mass unemployment and its inevitable consequence, mass poverty.

'The people of Dunfermline East know about unemployment and poverty,' he thundered. 'They live in a community
that was once at the heart of the mining industry: 30,000
miners were employed in 66 pits in the county of Fife in 1913.'
At nationalisation in 1947 there were still 20,000 miners at
work in 33 pits. 'Yet today there is not one pit in my constituency, and only six in the county of Fife.' The newer industries – petrochemicals, electronics and computers – had not
yielded the jobs that had been promised. The result: four thousand officially on the dole, a figure that obscured 'a larger truth'
that six thousand men, women and teenagers were without a
lasting job.[4]

Brown sought to bring the statistics into an understandable
human scale. Dunfermline East, he told MPs, was a constituency of small communities, villages and towns, the largest
with a population of only twelve thousand. 'Community by
community, village by village, town by town, we can see how
the mass casualties of the Conservatives' economic war of attri-
tion translate into human disappointment and suffering: nearly
400 out of work in the one small village of Kelty; 530 out of
work in Cardenden, Kinglassie, Bowhill and Dundonald, 800
out of work in Cowdenbeath and Lumphinans, and 1,000 out
of work in Lochgelly, Ballingry and Lochore.' Even in the more
prosperous coastal communities of Aberdour, Dalgety Bay,
Rosyth and Inverkeithing, there were more than a thousand
people on the dole.

These local figures, 'a new arithmetic of depression and
despair', had come to Brown almost by accident. They were not
routinely published, but were available only on request from
the Manpower Services Commission. Brown served notice that
until the government recognised that 'unemployment is the
disease, and not the cure for the disease', and accepted the
blame for continuously rising unemployment as freely as they
took the credit for falling inflation, he would ask the secretary
of state for Scotland month by month, community by community, to publish 'these tragic tolls' so the real nature of unem-

ployment was visible for all to see.

Brown then pulled another rabbit out of the hat: the 'true but unpublished' figures for those claiming supplementary benefit in Dunfermline East. They totalled eight thousand, meaning that no fewer than fifteen thousand men, women and children were dependent on means-tested benefit. The numbers had doubled in five years as a result of unemployment. In Scotland as a whole, he reckoned, the number of people living at or below the government's poverty line was more than a million – one in five of the population. Yet a family of four with no breadwinner would have to live on £59.20 a week, while pensioners had less than £5 a day to meet their needs.

'This is all because the government's philosophy is that the rich must get rich by way of tax cuts and that the poor must become poorer to ensure true prosperity,' he added witheringly. Perhaps the Conservative members did not realise that supplementary benefit for the jobless, when compared with average earnings, was now at a lower level than the National Assistance Board rates of 1948, and benefit levels were dwindling to those of the Poor Law in the 1930s. He asked detailed questions about the prospect of cuts in unemployment benefit, warning, 'I expect detailed answers.'

He went on to examine the case for the so-called 'incentive approach' to unemployment. 'It seems that the government are saying that the problem, as they see it, is no longer unemployment but the unemployed. They seem to be suggesting that benefits as low as £26 a week are deterring the unemployed from seeking jobs. They are implying that in future benefits should be set at a level that will not even permit a minimum of dignity and comfort. They are apparently suggesting that they should be lowered to a level that will be only a fraction or proportion of the lowest wages in the market place, irrespective of whether such wages can offer or guarantee subsistence.' Expert evidence rejected this analysis. The Institute for Fiscal Studies found that only one person in forty received more in benefits than they would have got in work. The economist Samuel

Brittan said there was 'a logical as well as a technical flaw' in the case for cutting benefits, and even a previous social services secretary had admitted there was no evidence that benefit levels deterred the unemployed from seeking work. The whole argument was 'designed to obscure what everyone knows: if there are no jobs, no amount of poverty and no amount of destitution will create jobs where none exist'.

The chance of a labourer getting a job in his constituency were 150:1 against. For nearly five hundred teenagers who had just left school, there was only one vacancy in the local careers office. Where would the jobs come from? Brown asked. Then, in a passage that caught the attention of the House, he asked Dr Rhodes Boyson if he still believed, as he had said in *Centre Forward* in 1978, that there were plenty of jobs around for the unemployed as window-cleaners: 'I shall believe that there is a shortage of jobs when two window cleaners call for my custom in one week, one month or one year.' Boyson had also said that to become a window cleaner, little equipment was needed – a bucket, a leather or two, and a ladder.

Perhaps the government's answer to mass unemployment was for Britain to become a nation of window cleaners, Brown said caustically. 'When the Prime Minister talked regularly during the election about ladders of opportunity, I had not realised that the next Conservative Government would have something quite so specific in mind,' he joked. 'Perhaps the minister is to do for ladders what the Secretary of State for Employment has done for bikes. Perhaps the exhortation "Up Your Ladder" will become as intellectually compelling as a solution to Conservatives as "on your bike" was in the previous parliament.' The shaft went home. Years later, Boyson wrote in his memoirs that Gordon Brown, had made 'the most effective speech' in that debate, despite being a new boy.[5] Brown was scathing about the reality facing the unemployed: 'The truth is that if there are no real jobs to be found, to cut unemployment benefit is not, as the Chancellor was trying to imply, a necessary act of economic policy. It is an act of vindictiveness to the

poorest in our community.' And he was sharply critical of proposals that the unemployed should be put to work on roads,
municipal parks, clearing waste land and even the beaches
(though this idea was a prescient version of the 1997 Labour
government's environmental task force). He went on to quote
approvingly Winston Churchill, who had said that the state
must concern itself with the care of the sick, the aged and the
young, and assume the position of the reserve employer of
labour. In his peroration, Brown said, 'The House was told in
1948 that the welfare state was created to take the shame out of
need. Is that principle to be overthrown by an ever-increasing
set of government assaults on the poor that are devoid of
all logic, bereft of all morality and vindictive even beyond
monetarism?'

He sat down at 7.05 pm. The speech was a *tour de force* for a
new member, combining authority, wit and a sense of passionate moral outrage, and it marked him out as a serious figure in
the Commons and potential high-flyer in the Labour Party.
The impression was not lost on the next speaker in the debate,
Alan Haselhurst, Tory MP for Saffron Walden, who congratulated Brown on his 'force and fluency, and the wit he introduced into a powerful political speech', and predicted that 'He
will undoubtedly be a worthy opponent.'

Just how worthy became clear in the ensuing months, as
Brown pressed his claim to speak for the forgotten folk of his
constituency: the unemployed, the disadvantaged and those in
fear of losing their jobs. In November 1983, speaking after the
Queen's Speech outlining new curbs on trade unions, he excoriated the government for doing nothing to combat low pay in
Fife. A new study by Aberdeen University showed that six out
of seven women doing manual work in the county earned less
than £85 a week. He challenged Employment Secretary Tom
King to explain why so many employers avoided their legal
responsibility to pay the statutory minimum rates laid down by
the Wages Councils. King admitted that one in four employers
checked by inspectors were evading the law. His own

department had uncovered more than £2 million in illegally underpaid wages. Brown thundered: 'It is scandalous that in 1980s we should have so many Victorian employers.' The Tories' answer would be to attack the wages councils, not the exploitative employers. The following month, he took on the defence procurement minister, John Lee, demanding in the Commons to know what new work the government had for Rosyth naval shipyard. The minister promised refits for the Navy's Type 42 and Leander-class frigates. Brown was re-assured, but promised 'continuous vigilance' to ensure that the yard got the best deal. At the back of his mind was the threat of privatisation hanging over the dockyard.

In February 1984, Brown was sharply critical of government plans to use Cowdenbeath in his constituency as a test-bed for DHSS officials to investigate jobless eighteen- to 25-year-old men and women to persuade them to accept the lowest-paid job available, and to identify school-leavers whose benefits could be cut by 40 per cent if they refused to accept a training place. This strategy was contained in a leaked DHSS policy paper, which Brown naturally used to best political advantage. 'These rules are an insult to the workless,' he told his local paper. 'Essentially, the papers say that DHSS officers are to inculcate good working habits in the unemployed. What the government would be better doing is bringing new jobs to the area.'[6]

His high profile on issues affecting the world of work natu-rally brought Brown to the attention of Labour's new leader, Neil Kinnock (also a TGWU-sponsored MP), who was im-pressed by the political grasp and incisiveness of the new mem-ber for Dunfermline East. Brown was put on the Commons Select Committee on Employment, and the Commons com-mittee debating the passage of the government's Trade Union Bill, the Conservatives' latest series of measures to humble 'the enemy within'. Not only did the proposed law further dimin-ish rights at work, but it put in jeopardy the unions' support for the Labour Party by requiring them to conduct ballots of their members to see if they wished to discontinue paying the political levy. In this field, Brown was working under a close political friend, John Smith, the shadow employment secretary and MP for the Scottish seat of Monklands East, who lived in the south Edinburgh constituency that Gordon had fought in 1979. Fortune had once again smiled upon Brown. Eric Varley had been Kinnock's original (if reluctant) choice for employment, but he suddenly announced he was quitting Parliament to become chief executive of the Coalite Company, and Smith took on the demanding portfolio.

Brown quickly made his mark, impressing the adroit employment minister, Alan Clark, with his Commons performances. 'Labour has a very tough team,' Clark confided to his diary on 8 December 1983. Apart from Smith ('rotund, bespectacled Edinburgh lawyer') there were two bright boys named Brown and Blair. 'I got into difficulty almost immediately. They were bobbing up all over the place, asking impossible, spastic questions of detail – most of them, as far as I could make out, to do with the fucking Rule Book.'[7]

Outside Westminster, events were taking a rather less agreeable turn. The craft print union NGA was embroiled in a bitter dispute with the newspaper owner Eddie Shah at his Warrington printworks, which degenerated into violent scenes of mass picketing. The union was eventually sequestrated and fined more than half a million pounds. At the same time, pressure was building up in the mining industry for an all-out strike over pit closures. Brown was in no doubt about the aims behind the Trade Union Bill. He told a meeting of Cardenden and Kinglassie Labour Party it was nothing more than 'a disguised attempt to cut wages'. He pointed out that Chancellor Sir Geoffrey Howe had let slip that the real objective of trade union 'reform' was to lower wages by curtailing workers' bargaining power. A precise example had just occurred in Brown's own constituency. Cleaners working on HMS *Cochrane* at Rosyth yard had been sacked, and then rehired at lower wages. 'The government say they want to hand the trade unions back to their members. In fact they are handing them over to the courts. The Bill is designed to cause the maximum disruption and confusion within the trade union movement,' Brown argued. He contrasted the different treatment of employers and unions: companies could give as much as they liked to the Tory party without consulting their shareholders, whereas unions would now be forced to undergo the most complex procedure before they could pay a penny to the party they had founded.

Practical politics aside, Brown and Robin Cook found time to collaborate on what might be seen as a rewriting of *The Red Paper*, a collection of essays entitled *Scotland: The Real Divide* and subtitled *Poverty and Deprivation in Scotland*, in which academics, writers and public-service professionals pooled their analysis of poverty, its causes and possible solutions, north of the border. Brown wrote the introduction, drawing heavily on the social and political assessment he had put forward in his maiden speech. He was now making use of the 'confidential government document' trick to lend an extra air of authority to his pronouncements. It was to become the hallmark of his style, and make him a sought-after property among political reporters.

On this occasion, he cited a confidential government document which made clear that redistribution of income from the rich to the poor 'is not among the government's objectives'. Instead, Brown argued, 'The real incomes of the poor have simply been cut.'[8] Most of his contribution was an unrelentingly-bleak parade of figures portraying the plight of the Scottish poor, together with an equally dire set of predictions about what the second-term Thatcher government would do. Some, but by no means all, of these warnings were justified. But Brown did also signal a shift in his thinking. Making the case for social justice was not the same as solving the problem of poverty, and 'If life is more complex than it seems to the ideologists of the new Right, changing circumstances force the Left to reassess its social strategy,' he conceded.[9] In the past, it had been assumed that, as the British economy expanded, there would be sufficient resources to meet rising public expenditure needs. The welfare state would expand, and improve measures for the poor. In short, the state would make up the difference for those who did not benefit from a successful market economy. Experience of periods of economic growth had disproved this comfortable theory. Inequality of wealth and income in Scotland was as pervasive as ever.

Brown was gloomy. 'The era of automatic growth is not only over but unlikely to return in the near future,' he said. 'New principles for social security in a low-growth economy are badly needed. The first prerequisite for eradicating poverty is the redistribution of income and wealth from rich to poor.' Yet, as the need for redistributive policies had grown, the consensus required to achieve them had withered. Social solidarity had given way to a new ideology favouring inequality. This clear-eyed, if pessimistic, analysis was a virtual admission that Thatcherism had prevailed. Indeed, he conceded that 'the new Right have consistently won the argument that further moves towards equality are absurd, impossible and undesirable.' He exhibited understanding – if not respect – for the right's argument that inequality is inevitable, and issued a clarion call: 'It is time for the Left to argue the case for equality.'[10]

He proposed a five-point programme for radical reform of the tax, social security and welfare systems:

1. An end to mass unemployment and the poverty it creates. To begin with, benefits for the unemployed must be at least as good as those going to others who depend on state help.
2. A legal minimum wage.
3. A more generous definition of the state's minimum 'safety net', enabling the poor to participate more fully in their communities.
4. More public spending, targeted on areas and groups most in need.
5. Restoration to the tax system of two basic principles: that

those who cannot afford to pay tax should not have to;
and that taxation should rise progressively with income.

'What is needed is a programme of reform that ends the current situation where the top 10 per cent own 80 per cent of our
wealth and 30 per cent of income, even after tax,' he suggested.[11] As a panacea for all social ills, this vision could not be
faulted. As a political strategy, it was lamentably deficient,
rooted in the Labour Party's traditional tax-and-spend, govern-
ment-knows-best philosophy, which continued to hold the
ascendancy, particularly in Scotland. Of course, Gordon
Brown was still only 32. His exposure to national politics
remained limited, but his readiness to accept that the new right
was winning the argument marked him out as a politician
ready to inject fresh thinking into the party's internal dialogue.

   The miners' strike broke with full force in March 1984, as
the Trade Union Bill was completing its journey through the
Commons. There was no secret pit-head ballot, as required for
a national stoppage under NUM rules, but Mick McGahey fulminated that the miners would not be 'constitutionalised out of
action'. In Scotland, the walk-out was initially sporadic, but
within a week militant miners had 'picketed out' the collieries
that remained open for work. So began the most disastrous dispute in Scottish mining history.

   Brown sympathised with the men and their families, faced
with the impossible choice of meekly accepting pit closures or
engaging in a do-or-die struggle with the most hard-line
Conservative administration in living memory. He gave
unstintingly to the strikers' hardship funds – £100 a week, at
his own estimate. But he was critical of Arthur Scargill's conduct of the dispute, which had the NUM executive – including
three Scottish members – in thrall. His refusal to entertain a
ballot (having lost two similar previous votes) was not only
undemocratic, robbing the dispute of legitimacy in the eyes of
the public, but subversive of Brown's own efforts in Parliament
to limit the impact of the Tory 'anti-union laws'. He said later,

'We said we would not allow the miners and their families to starve in Fife. And that was right. But it was tragic, the way the strike was led. They could have settled in the summer. These were people who wanted to believe in their leaders, because they were desperate.'[12]

Friends at the time confirm Brown's misgivings over the pit strike. 'Privately, Gordon confided that it was madness to bring the men out at that time of year, particularly without a ballot. He knew the miners were beaten from the start,' recollected Jonathan Wills.[13] Yet the new MP's surgeries were soon thronged with striking miners and their wives undergoing the most appalling hardship and appealing for help. He had promised to be their friend, and they turned to him in their hour of need. The government had already taken away social security payments for strikers, and automatically deducted £15 from benefits payable to their wives and children in lieu of (often fictional) strike pay from their union. From start to finish of the year-long dispute, the NUM gave no strike pay – only a meagre daily cash allowance for those who took part in picketing.

However, the DHSS in Fife began deducting from benefits not only the £16 notional strike pay, but small cash loans given by the county council. Brown met Rhodes Boyson, the social security minister, to protest that this practice was not only cruel but illegal. It inflicted hardship on families twice over. Families in which no benefit was paid to the striker and only £6.45 a week to his wife lost all benefit if they accepted a £10 loan from the council's social work department – yet the loan still had to be paid back. 'The state, having minimised its responsibility for the relief of poverty, now seeks to nullify assistance from other sources,' he argued. 'The matter is urgent, because hundreds of families, already impoverished, are being subjected to even greater misery, uncertainty and destitution. Children are hungry, worse off than they would be if their fathers had deserted them, or were in jail.'[14] The government ignored his appeal to reverse the ruling.

Brown kept up the pressure at Westminster. In a Commons debate called by the Opposition on 26 November to protest at the further curtailment of social security benefits to miners' families, he pointed out that a miner's wife was expected to live and meet all her household needs – food, heating and clothing – on 92p a day. 'Members should recall that even the Conservative government of 1926 were so worried about the destitution that they had created in the mining communities that they ordered the local authorities to break the law to alleviate at least some of the suffering that they had created,' he told the House. Yet in 1984, the Thatcher administration issued new DHSS regulations, orders and instructions almost week by week to make impoverished families subject to even greater misery and destitution. A new deduction of £1 a week had just been announced, through a late, written answer. 'At every point during this strike, the government have had a choice. When ministers should have shown compassion to the wives and children of miners, they have chosen vindictive cuts,' he raged. 'When they should have relieved suffering, they have increased it. When they should have prevented destitution, they have sought to worsen it. When they should have mitigated hardship, they have sought, for the narrowest of ideological reasons, to intensify it.' A hapless Tory backbencher tried to halt the flow of real – not synthetic – anger, but Brown refused to give way. The government might win the vote that night (they did, by more than a hundred votes), 'but on this issue, as on many issues affecting the benefits and rights of ordinary people, they have lost all moral authority to govern.'[15]

The miners set up ten strike centres in Fife, equipped with soup kitchens. These also became the base for the women's support groups that sprang up in the coalfield. Picketing the pits was unnecessary. The strike was solid for the first six months. But the men also picketed an open-cast mine at Lochgelly, where there were 'pretty rough' scenes, according to Brown's election agent, Dave Stoddart. Within three days, more than two hundred men were arrested. Brown was asked to lend his support to union moves to get arrested pickets released from jail. 'He said, "Go ahead, I trust you." I got them out on the promise that they would not go back on the picket line,' recalled Stoddart. 'It was Gordon's name that got it done. He always supported them. He was always there when he was required. He was always loyal. He would toe the line whether he agreed with it or not. There was criticism of the party leadership, but there was never criticism of Gordon.' Stoddart toured the strike centres every Friday, sometimes with his MP, and sometimes not. 'When he was here, he was around too. He was always there and always prepared to speak and encourage them.'[16] Wills concurs: 'He never said a word in public against the Scargill donkeys who led the lions of the NUM to destruction. He stood on the picket lines in freezing dawns. He marched in the rain. He went the rounds of the Miners' Welfare Centres and Wives Committees. He spent hours agonising over speeches to pointless, triumphalist rallies like the famous one in Cowdenbeath Stadium where Dennis Skinner railed against the scabs. But, a long time before it was all over, he and the ailing Jimmy McIntyre knew things had to change, not just in the unions but in the Labour Party.'[17]

As the struggle took its toll, miners began to go back to work: in some areas, the trickle turned into a flood. When an NUM delegate conference in London called off the dispute on 3 March 1985, the union was in a state of utter devastation. The industry they had fought to save was in little better shape. Brown spoke at a 'victory' rally in Lochgelly Town Hall, where McGahey was heckled by die-hard militants who wanted the strike to continue. 'Gordon ignored the procedural and tactical mistakes of the strike, but delivered what sounded very like a eulogy for the mining communities of Fife. He got the biggest cheers of the night. Doctorate or no doctorate, he had earned his place as one of them. The crowd loved him,' said Wills.[18] The miners showed their appreciation in the way they knew best. He was presented with two miners' lamps, and several inscribed certificates that adorn the walls of his North

Queensferry home. And, most coveted of all, he was made an honorary member of the Scottish Mineworkers' Union, a rare privilege. They knew whose side he was on.

The men returned to work exhausted, without an agreement on pit closures and in no condition to insist on the re-employment of thousands of strikers dismissed by the National Coal Board for offences ranging from the grave to the trivial. In Scotland, 206 miners were been sacked, fifty-four of them in Fife. NCB managers north of the border took an exceptionally hard line. Not one of the dismissed men was offered reinstatement, and only a handful were offered a job – and then only if they withdrew any claim for unfair dismissal to an industrial tribunal and waived their previous service entitlement to pensions and redundancy pay. Brown said the move was 'wholly unethical and probably illegal'.

Brown persuaded the Tory-dominated Employment Select Committee to interrogate Arthur Scargill and Ian MacGregor, the industry's Scottish-American chairman. Brown quizzed MacGregor on Coal Board procedures. He asked why the Coal Board had given dismissed men no right of appeal, and was told that the unusual circumstances of the strike prevented the industry's procedures being used. He then got MacGregor to admit that, but for the strike, he would have adhered to the procedures. At that point Brown asked how many had been sacked – without appeal – since the strike had ended. In fact, most of the dismissed men fell into this category, he conceded. MacGregor had thus been forced to admit that his reasons were merely a pretext. The Employment Select Committee condemned the policy, and urged a rethink. The government was unmoved.

For Brown, the plight of the sacked men, and the savage contraction of the industry in his constituency, would be a problem for years to come. In Scotland, he secured the support of police chiefs and the churches in his campaign to win justice for dismissed mineworkers. Eventually, most men returned to work, but by the end of 1985, he reported glumly that two thousand mining jobs had been lost since the onset of the strike. The workshops at Cowdenbeath were gradually cut back, and then closed. Seafield colliery closed, with the loss of seven hundred jobs. Rosyth also cut back, with the result that, for all Brown's efforts, unemployment in Fife was rising three times faster than in the rest of Scotland and ten times faster than in the rest of Britain.

Tory strategy offered no hope. In November 1984, as the coal strike neared its end, Trade Secretary Norman Tebbit introduced the Regional Policy Bill, whose objective was to reduce state aid to the regions. Brown protested that it would plunge Scottish industry into its worst crisis for twenty years. His own constituency would lose all development grants despite unemployment which stood at 16 per cent and was rising. The measure, passed in the teeth of Labour opposition, cut £80 million from Scotland's regional aid budget.

Brown spoke most often in debates on industry, employment and social security issues. He also asked hundreds of written questions, building up a small library of expertise on the subject. In the debate on the Queen's Speech in November 1984, he was scathing about the government's industrial record. They were losing manufacturing jobs at the rate of 5,000 a month, and all they could do was appoint a minister without portfolio, Lord Young, without powers, without policies or a programme, and without the faintest possibility of anything other than a few pounds to spend. 'The recession will last until Doomsday if the Minister without Portfolio is all that confronts it,' he taunted. 'How can the Chancellor call an economy healthy when four million who want to work in it are producing nothing, when teenagers born in the 1960s, at school in the 1970s, are condemned to the dole queues in the 1980s and beyond?'[19] The chancellor, Nigel Lawson, had said that the real problem was not unemployment but the unemployed. Yet wages in the UK were about the lowest in Europe. Having, as a matter of policy, made people poor by forcing them out of work, the chancellor now said that even if they found work, they must remain poor.

'How much poorer have people to become to secure true prosperity for all?' Brown demanded. 'There are women in my constituency whose wages have been halved over the past few years, without the creation of a single job. There are women in manufacturing work in my constituency who are earning only £1.56 an hour, who were told last week that their jobs were to go because the company was refusing to invest in the area. People cannot price themselves into jobs where no jobs exist. We must ask the government how much poorer they think people have to become, how much spending power must be taken out of the economy, how many more lost producers and lost consumers must there be in Britain before true monetarism arrives?'[20] The following speaker, Tory MP Charles Morrison, conceded that government policies were not reducing unemployment and that Brown had raised questions to which the government was duty bound to reply.

Ministers found that their duty lay elsewhere, but the new member for Dunfermline East had made his mark as a thoughtful and coruscating critic of Thatcherism and of the impact of her government's dogmatic outlook on jobs. His Commons performance, always competent and sometimes with flashes of brilliance, brought him to the attention of the party's talent scouts. Neil Kinnock offered him a front-bench spokesman's job in November 1984, but Brown turned it down. 'I felt it was better for me to stay on the backbenches and do more there,' he said later. 'I said that I wasn't ready.'[21] Kinnock had him in mind as a social security shadow minister, or possibly spokesman on Scottish affairs. Tony Blair leaped at the chance when he was offered a frontbench posting on City matters at about the same time. Brown bided his time, consolidating his parliamentary position. In February 1985, he shone in a clash with the government on severe-weather payments. Opening the late-night adjournment debate – it began at 11.43 p.m. – he mounted a howitzer assault of statistics, arguing that as many as 900,000 old people could be at risk from hypothermia. Yet the government had reduced the qualifying temperature by 5.5 degrees celsius – 'for some people the difference between life and death'. Only Brown could contrive to make a deadly serious issue also entertaining. 'I am not accusing ministers of lying about the weather. But they are, to say the least, guilty of meteorological inexactitude when, no matter how cold it is, the sun shines out of their statistics – and for one reason only: to cheat pensioners and other poor families out of a few pence by way of allowance.' He called for special payments for every low-income family to help with crippling fuel bills. In his reply, Ray Whitney, the social security minister, casually dismissed Brown's fiery speech as 'a farrago of misrepresentation' adding complacently that pensioners were better off than under Labour.[22]

Brown did not lose sight of his commitment to bread and butter constituency issues. In July 1985, he called for the abolition of DHSS 'snooper squads' operating in his area, making early-morning calls on young mothers 'to check for the presence of male items'. It was, he argued, a campaign to make the young and healthy feel they should be able to get a job, though in practice it was an infringement of personal liberty and a further penalty on the poor and unemployed. (Two decades later, he would be arguing that staying at home in bed and drawing benefits was 'not an option' for the young jobless.) That same month, he complained that deprivation of Wages Council minimum rates for the under-21s was 'scandalous. Under this government, the already rich are to become richer and the poor are to become poorer.' In August, he lambasted Defence Secretary Michael Heseltine for proposing the privatisation of Rosyth shipyards. He said the official unemployment figures were 'fabricated', and demanded health warnings for children on Skoal Bandits, an American chewing-tobacco product. He demanded better roads around Rosyth, eventually securing the £1m Hillend bypass for local residents through pressure on the government.

All this industry was finally rewarded in November 1985, when Kinnock appointed Brown a frontbench spokesman on trade and industry, with special responsibility for regional policy. He was delighted. Shadow minister for regional affairs sounded perfect. He would again be working with John Smith, now the shadow trade and industry secretary. 'It is a major job,' he told his local paper, 'my part of which will be to try to stop the destruction of industry.' In particular, he would keep up the fight to forestall the privatisation of Rosyth: 'I have an agreement with Neil Kinnock that will allow me to keep in the dockyard campaign.'[23] Brown had emerged as 'the obvious choice' to understudy Smith, according to Smith's biographer.[24] For a rising MP with only two years' experience in the Commons to secure a place on the Opposition front bench was not unique, though it was unusual. Tony Blair had made it after only seven months, to the job of looking after Labour's relations with the City. The rivalry between the two now began in earnest. Kinnock was generous about both: 'Both he [Blair] and Gordon shone. Gordon I knew much better before he came into Parliament. I got on particularly well with both of them. Not in any clubby sort of kitchen-cabinet way, but simply because they were friendly, lively, younger members who were serious about the job they were doing and virtue has its own rewards.'[25]

Unemployment dominated Brown's 1986 New Year message to his constituents. He promised that the fight for jobs would dominate Labour's campaigning that year. In Dunfermline East, 1,643 people had joined the dole queues in the year the coal strike ended, making a total of 4,700. He gave his constituents a sneak preview of what his party's new policy document would contain. Labour would promise to create a million jobs when it came to power. Fife would benefit greatly, particularly in housing and environmental schemes.

That year was destined, however, to be dominated by three quite different issues: the Westland Helicopters row, which looked briefly as if it might bring about Margaret Thatcher's downfall; the ill-fated poll tax, which actually did set in train her eventual political demise; and the expulsion from the

Labour Party of the ultra-left Militant Tendency, which greatly accelerated the party's 'modernisation' and made it once again electable.

On 9 January, Defence Secretary Michael Heseltine quite literally walked out of the Cabinet after a furious row with Thatcher over who should buy Westland, the ailing military helicopter manufacturer. Heseltine favoured a European consortium, Thatcher an American buyer, Sikorski. The row exploded in the Commons on 15 January, when Brown's boss, John Smith, put the government on the rack for sacrificing the public interest to an ideological obsession with market forces. Leon Brittan, the trade and industry secretary, was forced to quit over the leaking inspired by Thatcher, of a private ministerial letter, designed to undermine Heseltine. The prime minister had repeatedly to defend her 'innocence' at the despatch box, and her premiership was seriously wounded.

The poll tax, or 'community charge' as its promoters preferred to call it, replaced local property taxes ('the rates') with a per capita charge for council services levied on all adults, rather than just householders, based on property values. It was to be introduced in Scotland a year earlier than England and Wales. This was a fatal error. Not only was the tax unpopular because of its unfairness – the laird living alone in his castle paid less than a single parent and her eighteen-year-old son living in a council flat – but the Scots naturally resented being used as a test-bed for a Thatcherite tax experiment. A 'can pay, but won't pay' campaign got under way north of the border, and while Labour officially dissociated itself from the affray, the party benefited everywhere from hostility to the tax. Brown attacked the tax on two grounds: it would hit the poorest families most, and it would hit local services.

Finally, there was the affair of Militant. Kinnock's devastating speech to the party conference in October 1985, in which he tore into Militant Tendency leaders in Liverpool for the 'obscenity' of sending redundancy notices round to council workers by taxi, signalled the start of a purge of the ultra-left infiltrationists during 1986. That speech, argued his deputy, Roy Hattersley, 'began to nudge the Labour Party back into the mainstream of politics'.

John Smith and his new deputy took the jobs and industry campaign on a highly professional roadshow round Britain. Each region was treated to a well-organised presentation of how Labour could revive the local economy and improve employment prospects. Invitations did not go out only to the party faithful; businessmen and chambers of commerce were invited too, in an unprecedented bid to diminish business suspicion of Labour's industrial policies. In a tour of the north and north-west, Brown promised regional development agencies for England. It was not the easiest message to sell. The CBI sent out letters with awkward questions for Labour, trying to diminish the impact of the campaign.

At home, the shadow minister for regional affairs told his constituents that 'at least' 7,500 jobs in construction, community services and economic regeneration would be created in Fife if Labour could win back power and implement its emergency jobs programme. 'The programme would mean a 30 per cent reduction in unemployment as a first priority of the Labour government,' he argued. 'And this would mean a substantial reduction in Fife's depressingly high unemployment figure which now exceeds 22,000 men and women.'[26]

Not everything in 1986 was heavyweight politics. In late October, Brown's biography of his icon James Maxton appeared under the imprint of Mainstream, the Edinburgh publishing house, headed by his old varsity friend Bill Campbell, which had published Brown and Cook's *Scotland: The Real Divide* three years previously. *Maxton* was a genuine labour of love; it had taken three years to write. Brown had unique access to his hero's unpublished letters and personal papers. As a result, the book reads like the diary of a spiritual and political journey, as though Brown is torn between heartfelt admiration for the most charismatic socialist of his generation, and intellectual frustration with Maxton's compelling –

but ultimately self-defeating – integrity. Maxton, MP for Glasgow Bridgeton from 1922 until his death in 1946, was to the end an unapologetic ILP left-winger. He never held ministerial office, yet Churchill described him as 'the greatest parliamentarian of his day' and he was often spoken of as a potential Labour Party leader. Brown, whose speeches are crafted with immense care, praised him as 'the polemicist and the populariser, the man people came to hear and the man they listened to'. He argued that the rightness of Maxton's proposals for solving unemployment 'cannot now be doubted'. He was 'a man with a mission', whose job was to convince people that his vision was attainable.[27]

How much of Brown can be read into this portrait? Maxton's father was a headmaster who was an elder in the Presbyterian Church. He emphasised social responsibility and the improving role of education. The young Maxton was active in the Glasgow rectorial election of 1902 – ironically, as a Tory. Within two years he was an active socialist. He fought for a Scottish Parliament. He supported minimum wages in industry. He went into politics with the purpose of 'trying to free the world from poverty'. Yet being right was not enough. Maxton was a man to be admired, but not emulated. Brown's verdict was: 'If a successful socialist politician is one who advances the fortunes of his or her political party and progressively uses political power to transform society, Maxton had little success . . . The party whose cause he championed for forty years could, with justice, be accused of committing political suicide for the sake of ideological purity.'[28] It was not a mistake that Brown intended to repeat.

Brown spent much of 1986 working on the party's jobs campaign, culminating in a Commons speech on shipbuilding in which he condemned the Tories for ending a thousand years of shipbuilding tradition in the UK. His speech attracted the attention of ex-premier Lord Callaghan, who gave every appearance of watching his career with a benign, fatherly eye.

Labour began preparing in earnest for the 1987 general

election in January, with a 24-hour brainstorming session at the trade-union college in Bishop's Stortford, followed up by a joint meeting of the Shadow Cabinet and the National Executive Committee in mid-February. Kinnock argued at this meeting that Thatcher was the government's biggest weakness. She was 'hateful' and the party's best slogan would be 'Get her out!' Labour had hired Peter Mandelson, a former researcher with LWT's *Weekend World*, as its director of press and public relations. He revolutionised the party's public image, ditching the red flag for the red rose and importing a slick presentational style from television. Brown approved. He had brought with him from STV quite a few similar tricks of the trade, and he shared Mandelson's reformist zeal. The two became friends and political allies. Labour was doing badly in the opinion polls, trailing the Tories by around 8 per cent – a lamentable performance for an Opposition facing a government in power for seven years. The long-running dispute at Rupert Murdoch's News International plant at Wapping, just drawing to a close, had not helped. Then, Labour found itself faced with a critical by-election in Greenwich, caused by the death of its sitting MP, Guy Barnett. Brown was among the shadow ministers who trekked down to south-east London for the campaign, but to no avail. To Kinnock's fury, Labour lost the seat to the SDP, a grim omen for the forthcoming election.

Brown took the jobs gospel to the country, but there were doubts within Labour's high command about the value of the party's jobs policy statement, *New Jobs for Britain*. Bryan Gould, the shadow chief secretary to the Treasury, thought Labour's pledge to create a million jobs within two years at a cost of £6 billion 'ridiculous'. He thought it 'reeked of the mechanistic approach to economic issues' – that so much public investment will yield so many jobs – that had dogged Labour for too long. Kinnock agreed that it lacked credibility, and suggested that the party was in hock to the public-sector unions. It was tightened up and rewritten, giving greater emphasis to jobs coming from economic expansion. In May,

Thatcher named election day: 11 June. Labour was still trailing in the polls.

In Dunfermline East, Brown faced a four-cornered contest, two men and two women. The Tories once again put up Clive Shenton, now 41, the Sandhurst- and Edinburgh University-educated advocate whom Brown had seen off in 1983. Mrs Elizabeth Harris, a 30-year-old Dunfermline teacher and a member of the local council, stood for the Liberal–SDP Alliance. She was definitely on the Liberal end of the Alliance, being, despite her youth, a member of the Scottish party's national executive, and its housing and employment panels. The quartet was completed by Mrs Alice McGarry, a civil servant aged 35, standing for the SNP. Like Brown, she had been educated in Kirkcaldy, and she was a member of Fife Regional Council. Brown romped home, lifting his majority to 19,589 – exactly 50 per cent of all the votes cast. In a 76.6 per cent turnout – up nearly 5 per cent – he received 25,381 votes, or 64.8 per cent of the total votes cast. The Tory vote fell by 4 per cent to 5,792, and the Alliance slumped almost 10 per cent to a risible 4,122. The SNP were breathing down the Liberals' neck, up nearly 3 per cent on 3,901, an omen of political shift north of the border.

The Dunfermline East result was a personal triumph for Brown, but Labour had done exceptionally well all over Scotland, winning the Western Isles from the SNP, Edinburgh South (where Brown had stood in 1979) and Central from the Conservatives, and a clutch of other government marginals in Glasgow and the west of Scotland. In all, the Tories lost eleven seats, cutting their representation in half. Several ministers had gone, and Labour could claim with some justice that the government no longer had a mandate to rule Scotland.

Brown had a good election campaign, touring the country on regional visits. He launched the party's blueprints for the regions, and for the first time gave a number of national press conferences, exposing Tory privatisation plans as ill thought-out. But he was still not quite in the upper echelons. He was not on the key election committees. He saw the campaign at first hand, and observed its weaknesses, but, not being at the centre, could do little about them. Scotland's good results were not mirrored south of the border. The government lost thirty-nine seats, but Thatcher swept back into Downing Street for the third time, with an overall majority of 101. Labour licked its wounds in private, its leaders consoling themselves that at least they had put paid to the Alliance challenge. For Brown, it was the second disappointment in a row. He had not expected Labour to win nationally, but its bravura performance in Scotland made his party's position doubly anomalous. In a massive majority north of the border, they ought to be the party of government. Yet the political arithmetic locked them into five more years of Opposition. Something had to be done.

CHAPTER 7

SHADOW CABINET

THE INQUEST ON THE FAILURE OF LABOUR'S ELECTORAL campaign came to some brutal conclusions. Neil Kinnock, agreed Gordon Brown and his fellow soft-left Tribunites, had fought a good election, and deserved another chance. They ridiculed the right-wing Solidarity Group's tentative moves to have him replaced, either by Roy Hattersley or by John Smith. Kinnock bounced back quickly from the disappointment of polling day, insisting, 'The next campaign starts now.'

But first, there had to be changes. There was widespread dissatisfaction with the way Hattersley had handled the economic portfolio as shadow chancellor. The party's strategy had sunk into muddle and presentational nightmare that allowed a hostile tabloid press to trumpet Tory claims of 'Labour's hidden taxes' in an election manifesto absurdly costed at £35 billion. The voters were confused about the party's tax and national insurance proposals, a perplexity only increased when Hattersley denied on live radio an admission by Kinnock during the election campaign that people earning less than £25,000 might be worse off under Labour.

Brown concluded long before polling day that Labour had lost. 'I never thought we were going to win in 1987,' he disclosed later.[1] 'All these seats were won in Scotland, but you could see what was happening nationally. We were up-ended by tax. It goes back to people's view of Labour. I always said that people should and did think that Labour is on their side. Taxes and other things were holding them back. Labour was supposed to be the party of aspirations. But it became a party that put a cap on people's aspirations.'

Shadow Chancellor Hattersley had also been criticised for his rather laid-back style. It was clear that he would shoulder much of the blame for the party's poor showing in a critical area of policy, and this might open up opportunities for Kinnock's Young Turks. Brown and his allies pondered their prospects. Chief Whip Nick Brown recollects that: 'Gordon Brown and Tony Blair were easily the outstanding two individuals of the 1983 intake. We discussed whether they should stand for the Shadow Cabinet after the 1987 election. I was very strongly of the view that they should. A lot of the new blood was on our side. We organised a very thorough campaign for them – which was frowned upon by the leadership, who saw it as a threat.'[2] Both MPs appeared on the Tribune 'slate' of preferred candidates. (This cumbersome and potentially divisive system was, incidentally, on its way out. Soon afterwards, Kinnock abolished the practice of lists.) With the help of the substantially enlarged group of Scottish MPs, Brown was successful in the elections held after the state opening of Parliament on 25 June. With more than forty hopefuls standing, he came eleventh in the poll with a very creditable eighty-eight votes – denying a place to veterans Peter Shore and Tony Benn. Blair had to wait another year.

There was a brief hiatus as Kinnock sorted out his Shadow Cabinet. Hattersley was resigned to giving up his post of shadow chancellor, but fought a determined rearguard action – even threatening to resign – to prevent the job going to Bryan Gould, shadow chief secretary to the Treasury and Labour's popular campaigns co-ordinator during the election, who had topped the poll in the parliamentary committee elections. John

Smith made it abundantly clear that he regarded himself as the natural heir-apparent for the job, and Kinnock duly appointed him. The Labour leader also boosted the role of the Treasury team in the Opposition line-up. With the presentational débâcle of Labour's tax plans still acutely fresh in his mind, Kinnock decided that the shadow chief secretary to the Treasury should also be a member of the Shadow Cabinet. He would act as a politically sensitive sieve, examining all press statements and briefings to ensure that other frontbench spokesmen did not commit Labour to reckless spending proposals.

Who better to fulfil this role than Gordon Brown, who had made such an impact as Smith's deputy as shadow DTI secretary? At the age of 36, Brown succeeded Gould in a key frontbench role – shadowing future prime minister John Major. He was the youngest member of the Shadow Cabinet, yet he was entrusted with a senior role. 'I was surprised but pleased that I am going to have a role in shaping the financial, economic and industrial approach of the Labour Party in the coming years,' he told his local paper. It was, observes Smith's biographer, Andy McSmith, the fastest rise through the Opposition ranks since the 1950s. But it was not as surprising as the man himself suggested. 'As well as being extremely able, Brown was a team player, slightly shy and famously workaholic, without the brittle, sensitive ego often found in politicians. He could be trusted not to use the number two post in the team for some private enterprise to advance himself at his boss's expense.'[3]

Immediately after the election, Kinnock said there had to be a fundamental review of policy. He urged party officials to think of voters rather than blocks of trade unionists or members of other pressure groups. They had to be told that socialism was the answer for them because socialism looked after the individual. Kinnock insisted it would not be a bonfire of everything Labour had stood for at the general election. But he also said 'Any political party which did not undertake the assessment, that did not undertake the review – that party would be betraying its principles, its policies and its people.'

Brown was already working on reforms embodying this principle, both in public policy and for the internal structures of the
party. He shared Kinnock's view that Labour had to show that
it could change, before the electorate could be convinced that
Labour could change society for the better. Soon after the election, he published a *Tribune* pamphlet, arguing the case for a
mass-membership party, with greater input from individual
members. He also backed Kinnock's plans for reforming the
ways in which parliamentary candidates were selected, extending the principle of the electoral college used for electing the
leader to constituency level. This was seen as a half-way house
to one member, one vote. The cumbersome compromise gave
individual members the majority voice, 60 per cent of the total
vote, with trade-union delegates having the remaining 40 per
cent. The clear intention was to send a message to the electorate
that Labour was serious about reducing the power of the unions
in the constituencies. In practice, nothing very much changed.
The system was too complex, and never operated properly. But
it was the first step to Brown's stated goal of one member, one
vote.

The review began in earnest on 21 October 1987, after the
party conference, at which unilateral nuclear defence had once
again been adopted as policy. However, Kinnock made it clear
that there were no no-go areas in the review. Defence would be
an integral part of it. Bryan Gould was appointed joint convenor of a review group on economic policy in which Brown
would participate. John Smith was convenor of a separate
group on taxation and social-security issues, in which the
shadow chief secretary also had a deep political interest. In all,
there were seven policy-review groups.

Bryan Gould, perhaps the most self-assured member of the
Shadow Cabinet, had an ambivalent view of Brown. He
admired the way Gordon had made his name as the recipient
of a regular number of leaked documents from various parts of
Whitehall, and recognised that he was also a formidable

speaker and debater. Yet he played down his role in the review process. 'He played, however, virtually no part in the work of my policy review committee. He attended only rarely, and spoke, as I recall, on only one occasion.' Nevertheless, Gould got the distinct impression that he 'was not fully supportive' of the line the committee was taking on various issues but that he did 'either not dare or know how to put a contrary view'.[4] This sounds most un-Brownlike. Indeed, Brown was biding his time. When Gould had finally finished his draft, he got the document through his policy-review group and was about to send the paper to the printers when Brown and Blair, plus John Eatwell, a Cambridge economist and Neil Kinnock's economic adviser, who attended the policy-review meetings as an observer, went as a delegation to the shadow DTI secretary's office at Westminster. They told him the document could not go to conference as it stood. They could not accept the compromise formula on public ownership, in particular a commitment worked out with the telecommunications union, the National Communications Union, to buy a 2 per cent shareholding in British Telecom to give a Labour government a majority share-holding. All mention of state ownership had to go.

Gould was furious. 'I was extremely irritated at this last minute *démarche*,' he said later. He was further angry at the presence of Blair, who was not even a member of his review group, but was clearly in on the act. He pointed out that Brown and Eatwell had had every opportunity to make their views known, but had chosen to keep their own counsel. The draft had been agreed by everyone involved, including the unions, and it was too late to change the text. On this occasion, Brown did not get his way. 'They left empty-handed,' said Gould, 'but no doubt, as subsequent events have demonstrated, uncon-vinced.'[5] The review document, rather portentously entitled *The Productive and Competitive Economy*, was approved by the National Executive Committee (NEC) on 25 May 1988.

Brown was on good form when Lawson presented his first budget of the third Thatcher government in March 1988.

Speaking in the budget debate on 21 March, he attacked Lawson head-on. The budget would transfer £2,000 million to the 5 per cent at the top who were already extremely rich. It would award £200 million more in inheritance-tax relief to the 35,000 people who paid that tax. It would provide an extra £40 million for the small number who benefited from the business expansion scheme. And £290 million would go to institutions and individuals who stood to gain from relief on capital-gains tax. But fully 95 per cent of the population would gain nothing from the changes.

He contrasted this largesse to the well-off with the problems of the poor. Social-security changes to be implemented alongside the budget would make an estimated 9 million people worse off. Child benefit for 7 million mothers and 12 million children frozen. One million to lose housing benefit. The statistics rolled like gunfire. 'The only conclusion we can draw is that the tax cuts that have gone to the few at the very top are to be paid for by the withdrawal of benefits and the misery that that will cause to the poorest of our country.'[6] Brown rehearsed the themes that would become familiar in his own budgets: policies for the long term, investment in training and education that would do most for social justice. He even invoked the ghastly memory of 1960s property racketeer Peter Rachman, who, had he still been alive, would now be subsidised by tax breaks for property development.

Rejecting Lawson's claim to have balanced the budget, he quoted an article by the chancellor written some years previously. This was too much. 'When was it written?' demanded Lawson. Brown was 'happy to concede' that it had been penned in 1962 – more than a quarter-century earlier. But it was still relevant: the chancellor had attacked then the school of economic commentators who 'see mystical significance in an overall budget balance, since this is a muddled amalgam of Gladstone and Keynes without the logical consistency of either'.[7] He had repeated the same view in the intervening years. 'Although he may claim to have balanced the budget, just about everything else in the economy and society was left unbalanced.' Lawson kept to his seat, but rose, infuriated, when Brown concluded with the charge that no budget had so offended the decent instincts of the majority of British people. 'The truth is that this country can no longer afford the price that it is paying for this government.' After half an hour on his feet, Brown had clearly got under Lawson's skin. The irritated chancellor accused him of 'impertinence' in saying that the government had done nothing for the poor, the sick, the disabled and the needy, when the Tories were spending more on social security than Labour had.[8] But the mud stuck. Lawson, an astute parliamentary performer, was rattled.

The shadow chief financial secretary was also busy harrying John Major that month, asking sheaves of written questions about government debt interest (£16 billion, but planned to fall), the borrowing of public corporations, the sales of public land and buildings (almost £4 billion), the tax payable by a 51-year-old married man earning £1 million a year who took full advantage of government scams (nil), and the number of working families too poor to pay tax (almost two million). The figures he gained by this relentless drive for information about the real impact of Conservative fed directly into his speeches and Labour's policy-planning.

Labour's fortunes appeared to be on the mend. With the good publicity emanating from Kinnock's policy review, the voters were coming back. The opinion polls showed Labour only one point behind Tories in February 1988. Even when Tony Benn launched his bid for the party's deputy leadership in March, with the self-important left-winger Eric Heffer announcing a forlorn campaign for Kinnock's job, the Opposition continued to gain ground as the government's poll tax began to bite. Labour was one point ahead in April. The following month, Smith took his policy-review paper, *Economic Equality*, to Labour's NEC. It promised not to increase the highest levels of taxation above those in the rest of Europe. 'We must persuade the rich of the need for fairness,' he argued. His tax manifesto was carried by twenty votes to three.

In the meantime, political jockeying at the top continued. Smith and Gould were locked in a bitter rivalry (which would eventually culminate in a battle for the leadership) over economic policy. On 27 June, the Economic Committee of the Shadow Cabinet discussed Labour's policy on the European exchange-rate mechanism (ERM). It was clear to Gould, a convinced Eurosceptic, that 'powerful forces' – Kinnock's economics adviser John Eatwell, strongly supported by Smith and Brown – were unhappy about the credibility of the party's counter-inflationary policy. Their line, according to Gould, was that Labour had to assuage City fears of a Kinnock government being soft on inflation. Giving a commitment to go into the ERM, it was argued, would avert that danger, because monetary policy would be determined by an independent mechanism. Gould, as shadow trade secretary, vehemently opposed any such change, and carried the day. 'No one dared really take me on in argument since, I assume, they realised that they would not get the better of it,' he boasted later.[9] But it was, as he acknowledged, a pyrrhic victory: Brown was to have the last word.

The leadership campaign proved to be the distracting influence that Kinnock had warned it would be. In the opinion polls, the party's positions were reversed. The gains of the policy review were soon dissipated. By August, Labour had slid to a ten-point deficit in the polls. But Kinnock and his allies dominated the NEC, and his firm grip on the leadership was confirmed in the electoral-college leadership poll held on the eve of the 1988 conference. Kinnock saw off Heffer, taking 88.6 per cent of the votes, while Hattersley beat the combined challenge of Benn and John Prescott, polling 66.8 per cent. Unlike his early mentor Alex Falconer, by now MEP for Fife, Brown voted for both incumbents.

The 1988 party conference carried the first version of *Meet the Challenge, Make the Change*, which emphasised the need for a 'real or productive economy'. There was a commitment to managing interest rates and the exchange rate in the interests of investment and production. It combined a rejection of monetarist emphasis on financial measures with substantial reservations about joining the ERM. On the awkward issue of renationalisation, the paper shied away from taking gas, water, electricity and telecommunications back into state control, talking instead about 'some form of public ownership', a deliberately vague formula that did not commit a Labour government to spending billions on a buy-back.

John Smith had a good conference, although he displayed his impatient side with a BBC radio interviewer, walking out of an interview when presented with what he thought were impertinent questions. At home in Edinburgh that weekend, he complained of a headache, and his GP sent him straight to hospital for a check-up. A cardiogram failed to find any problems, but as he was getting dressed Smith suffered a serious heart attack. By his own admission, the shadow chancellor lived an unwise lifestyle. He ate too much, drank too much, stayed up too late and worked too hard. Like Brown, he could not say no to invitations, and spent much of his time clattering round the country to political events that really did not require his presence. Like many physically and intellectually robust men, he thought he was invulnerable. Having a heart attack while bending down to tie his shoelaces proved he was not. Smith's doctors instructed him to take at least three months' complete rest from politics. Brown was shocked at the scale of his heart attack, but not totally surprised that he fell ill. 'I had been with him at the party conference, and he clearly wasn't a hundred per cent,' he said later.[10]

In Smith's absence, the responsibilities of shadow chancellor devolved on to Gordon Brown's ample shoulders. Kinnock asked him to take over. It was an awkward juncture. 'We had just started to get public spending sorted when John had his heart attack,' he recollected. 'I was trying to find a solution to the problem of poverty that was quite different to what we had done before, because I knew our tax and spend policies were not popular – and they were not tackling the problem of poverty. The difficulty was to find a new way forward. It was quite important to me in the years I was shadow chief secretary to get Labour attuned to the global economy, but to make sure in the global economy we didn't create a nation of people who were marginalised and lost out. I was thinking all the time about a way forward.' Globalism, having done away with the old national boundaries for business, had made redundant the old policies of exchange controls, capital controls and national- ist corporatist strategies. 'The issue is not how to divide up the national cake, but how to win a greater share of the interna- tional cake.'[11]

But first, there was the more pressing problem of how to con- front the government in the absence one of Labour's most able frontbenchers. On 1 November, Chancellor Nigel Lawson pre- sented his autumn statement, in which he claimed that public spending would fall below 40 per cent of national income for the first time for over twenty years. He promised an extra £1.25 billion for the NHS in 1989/90, and another extra £1.5 billion the year after, plus almost £500 million for new roads and repairs, and £720 million for prison-building. Spending on the police and defence would also rise, but National Insurance con- tributions would rise. He forecast growth of 4.5 per cent, increased investment, falling inflation and debt repayment: in short, 'economic transformation'.

It sounded too good to be true, and it was. Brown fell on Lawson like a wolf on the fold. He pointed out that inflation would rise beyond 6 per cent, and the nation's balance of pay- ments would be an unprecedented £13 billion by the end of the year. 'Does the Chancellor recall his objective, set out in 1984 and 1987, of zero inflation? Does he think that that promise is still credible when, after five Budgets and six Autumn state- ments, inflation is now higher than when he became Chancellor?'[12] Because of higher inflation, there was a £5 bil- lion shortfall in real terms in public spending, which would mean a real deterioration in essential public services. The extra sums given to the NHS would be swallowed up by rising costs, and the UK would still be spending less on health than its major competitors.

Then he was back to fairness. 'Is there anything more revealing of the Government's priorities,' he asked, 'than the fact that in the month when the Chancellor went to the Conservative party conference to affirm a new round of top rate tax cuts for those who are already rich, he still refuses to find even the tiny amount that would save free eyesight tests and free dental check-ups, even for pensioners?' Increases in pensions and family income support announced the previous week were now shown to be below the rate of inflation, and therefore the standard of living of millions of citizens would inevitably fall. 'This is an autumn statement which compounds rather than corrects the errors of the Budget.' It condemned an already congested Britain to further deterioration in public services, and through neglect of investment and high interest rates 'leaves the British economy ill-equipped and ill-prepared for the challenges of the 1990s'.

Brown's reward for his impressive performance against Lawson came swiftly in the recognition of his fellow MPs. In the Shadow Cabinet elections later that month, he zoomed up from eleventh place to top, taking 155 votes – practically double his first showing the previous year, and unheard-of in modern Labour politics. Somewhat sheepishly, Brown telephoned the results through to his mentor, John Smith, convalescing in Edinburgh. The shadow chancellor too had done very well, increasing his vote by 33 over the previous year to 144, which was 15 ahead of the next contender. But he was still in second place to his brilliant protégé.

For the first time, Brown began to be talked about seriously as a possible leader of the Labour Party, and prime minister of his country. Hitherto, his hard work on trade and industry issues, his sedulous efforts to master the intricate links between tax, social security and the world of work, and his passionate denunciation of the impact of untrammelled Thatcherism on the unemployed and the working poor, had marked him out as a competent and caring politician of the new, Kinnockite school. Now, his name was bracketed with that of John Smith himself as a potential successor to Kinnock. An *Observer* profile noted that Brown was unfamiliar to the British public, though he was admired by Westminster analysts, and that his name had even been canvassed by the *Economist* as a possible successor to Neil Kinnock in the event of a centre-left rebellion. 'Now, at 37, his unforced debating style and natural authority have projected him into the national consciousness,' the anonymous profile-writer added.

There was much more in the same vein elsewhere. Suddenly, people sat up and took notice of the son of the Kirkcaldy manse. 'It was a very important moment,' says Nick Brown. 'He had arrived, and from there he went from strength to strength with the management of the Treasury brief. He was always the first person in and always the last to leave, always working his heart out. He was a huge engine of ideas, and yet he was incredibly decent. He was the only member of the Shadow Cabinet who would type out your press releases for you. There is no side to Gordon, or edge, or feeling of rank. He is a very democratic character.'[13] Given the erratic nature of Gordon's typing, it must be assumed that Nick Brown cannot type at all, but his personal assessment was shared by others.

An issue of conscience emerged later that month. David Alton, a Liberal Democrat MP, who had campaigned long and hard against the liberalising 1967 Abortion Act, brought forward another Bill to amend – in fact, to limit sharply – the rights of women to have a pregnancy terminated. Brown had no hesitation. He voted against the proposed legislation, arguing to a constituent who asked for his views, 'I support the framework of the 1967 Act. I feel unable to support the fundamental changes in the Alton Bill. Prior to the vote I received many letter from both sides of the fence. What I said to them is that I understand the feelings of both viewpoints, and I am willing to discuss the Bill with them. But I would also stress that it was a free vote, and I voted by my conscience.'[14]

After a holiday in the sun in the Gambia, John Smith returned to Westminster in the last week of January 1989. Generally, the media welcomed his comeback, but 'Cross-bencher' in the *Sunday Express* noted mischievously that, in his absence, Brown's star had risen considerably. 'How quickly the spotlight moves on,' wrote the columnist. 'How quickly friends and colleagues forget. Almost every day of his absence, he has heard glowing reports of the brilliant way in which his deputy, Dr Gordon Brown, has stood in for him . . . Suddenly nobody is talking about Smith any more. And everybody is talking about Brown.'[15]

Labour's policy-review documents were brought together in May 1989 and published under the overall title of the conference slogan, *Meet the Challenge, Make the Change*. It was probably the most comprehensive set of proposals ever assembled by any political party half-way through the term of a government in Britain. From being the party of state-owning socialism, Labour had now moved to embrace, in the words of one commentator, 'the responsible social market model', and extolled the virtues of individualism. Kinnock wrote in the Introduction of maximising 'the self-reliance which flourishes on opportunity and security'. At an NEC meeting to endorse the policy package, Tony Benn and his few remaining allies had tried vainly to amend what he regarded as 'by far the most right-wing policy during my time in the party'. But the work of the modernisers, including Brown, was carried, mostly with overwhelmingly majorities.

It broke much new ground. A Labour government would introduce lower starting rates of tax, beginning with a target of 20p in the pound, and would cap the higher rate at 50p. There would be improvements in child benefit, and a new charter of employee rights at work within a framework of refashioned labour legislation – but many of the Tories' 'anti-union' law reforms, including pre-strike ballots and secret elections for union leaders, would stay. Labour's new path, explicitly reject-

ing nuclear unilateral disarmament and outright nationalisation, and charting a closer relationship with Europe, proved
immediately popular with voters. The party's standing in the
polls shot back up to 40 per cent. At the October 1989 party
conference Kinnock secured support for a multilateralist
defence policy, for his limited changes in union law and for his
proposal to review the trade-union block-vote system. The
voters signalled their approval in an opinion poll that gave
Labour a nine point lead over Tories.

Scarcely had the conference season closed, when Chancellor
Nigel Lawson finally gave up the unequal struggle for
Thatcher's ear with her private economics adviser, Sir Alan
Walters, and resigned after six and a half years in office. On 26
October, he had given the prime minister an ultimatum: her
Rasputin must go, or he would. She refused to fire him, and he
quit the same day. Walters followed suit soon after. In the economic policy debate that followed Lawson's resignation, Brown
was caustic. Thatcher did not seem to know why her chancellor had gone. Could anyone be in any doubt? 'It was not a personality clash, some wayward gesture or a spur of the moment
decision: it was a fundamental question of exchange-rate
policy, right at the heart of government economic strategy – a
matter that has not yet been resolved.' Lawson had told the
House that he believed in exchange-rate management, that the
European monetary system and its exchange-rate mechanism
were the best vehicle for such a policy and 'the sooner we were
able to join rather than later, the better for this country'.[16]

Since this was essentially Labour policy too, Brown was on
firm ground. He pilloried Thatcher for finding excuses, year
after year, for not joining the ERM. In 1985, it was the strength
of the dollar. In 1986, it was variously because the British
economy was 'different', or because of the special status of
sterling, or the potential drain on UK reserves, or speculation.
In 1987, it was the deflationary impact of links to the
Deutschmark, while in 1988 the excuse was inflation. In 1989,
the conditions for entry multiplied still further. 'She is looking

for action that she expects others to take so that we can stay out,' he taunted.

Brown welcomed the new chancellor, John Major, but there was a sting in the tail. 'He has had the right training for the job over the past few weeks when he was Foreign Secretary – private humiliation, public repudiation and instant promotion. They say that the Chancellor is ambitious. I cannot believe that.' Had he been truly ambitious, he would have gone for Sir Alan's part-time, back-stage job. Brown observed of Walters's position, 'It was the most damaging appointment of an adviser by a head of government since – I was going to say, since Caligula's horse, but at least the horse stayed in Rome and worked full-time.'[17]

The following week, Gordon Brown topped the poll in the Shadow Cabinet election for the second time in succession, taking 165 votes, thought to be a record. Smith again came second, with 153 votes. Brown was clearly ripe for promotion, and it duly came. Kinnock sacked Gould from his post as shadow trade and industry secretary, and gave the portfolio to Brown. It was a well-orchestrated move, for not only did it reward Brown, but it removed Gould from the arena of economic policy-making to the relatively marginal post of shadow environment secretary. It was also a signal that Labour policy on the ERM was about to change. Gould certainly saw it that way. 'It seemed to me that those who could not win the argument had nevertheless contrived to have me removed from a position of influence,' he noted sourly.[18] Brown was more polite. 'I am delighted to have been given the challenging job of Shadow Secretary for State and Industry,' he told the *Dunfermline Press.* 'And I am very much looking forward to playing my part in the new Front Bench team. I am particularly pleased to be one of four Scots in the new Shadow Cabinet.' Tony Blair also performed well in the election, coming fifth, and Kinnock appointed him shadow employment secretary. He was still a long way behind Brown in political esteem, but he was closing the gap.

In early 1990, Kinnock outlined plans for further reform. The unions' vote at conference was to be reduced to 50 per cent, and he wanted MPs to be reselected on basis of one member, one vote. The work of the policy reviews continued, and on 15 May the NEC and the Shadow Cabinet agreed a new five-part document including a section on 'Creating a Dynamic Economy', which insisted that economic development depends on confidence of business – interpreted as a further signals to Brussels that Labour would take the UK into the ERM and, ultimately, monetary union. The document was published as *Looking to the Future*, a 20,000-word draft manifesto with a distinctly pro-European tinge and clearly designed to ditch traditional images of Labour. 'We will not spend, nor will we promise to spend, more than Britain can afford,' it promised. Spending commitments were qualified by the addition of 'as resources allow'. The 1987 commitment to full employment was dropped, and a pledge inserted that the poll tax would be replaced by a property tax based on ability to pay. In June 1990, Shadow Chancellor John Smith said fourteen out of fifteen taxpayers would not pay more under Labour.

That summer, a row raged inside the Shadow Cabinet and the parliamentary Labour Party (PLP) over the wisdom of embracing British membership of the ERM. Kinnock was by now convinced of the merits of making a commitment to join, not least because the Tories were divided over the issue and Mrs Thatcher was deeply hostile to entry. Gordon Brown and John Smith were urging him to take this radical step. Brown advanced his arguments in favour of joining at a PLP meeting, and was warmly received. His claim that membership would disarm the speculators went down well. Every Labour MP knew that every previous Labour government from 1964 onwards had been beset by sterling crises, often within weeks of taking office. They would listen sympathetically to anything, however radical, that might prevent a Kinnock government being blown off course as all its recent predecessors had been. Gould fought a desperate rearguard action in the Shadow

Cabinet against what he regarded as monetary necromancy, but lost. He recorded later that he was 'obliged to sit silently in the PLP while Gordon secured the agreement of his largely ignorant colleagues to a step which I knew would be disastrous from every point of view.'[19]

Events were going Brown's way. The 1990 party conference agreed a compromise deal over one member, one vote at constituency level. The local electoral college was scrapped, but unions still had the right to nominate candidates. However, not even John Major's deal to take the UK into the ERM during October 1990 at the unsustainable rate of 2.95 DM to the pound could keep Thatcher politically afloat. On 13 November, her deputy prime minister, Sir Geoffrey Howe, resigned over the issue of her attitude to Europe. Following a clear signal from her MPs in the leadership election that ensued, she went soon after him, and two weeks later the ambitious chancellor, John Major, did indeed become prime minister.

This was bad news for Brown and his colleagues. They were convinced that under Thatcher the Conservatives could not win a fourth consecutive term of office. With a new leader in place, the government's opinion-poll fortunes started to mend. Deep unease set in at the top of the Labour Party. There was talk of a coup. An opinion poll in late 1990 suggested that John Smith could turn Labour's deficit into a lead over Major. Leading figures rallied to Kinnock, insisting that it would be political folly to replace him so close to a general election. Inevitably, given his astonishing rise to prominence, Gordon Brown's name came into the frame as a possible contender. But he rejected the idea out of hand. 'My only ambition is to serve in a Labour government under Neil Kinnock,' he declared.

The tension subsided as Major played a long game, scrapping the poll tax and preparing the ground for an election in two years' time. In the spring of 1991, Labour relaunched its policy review yet again, this time as *Labour's Better Way Forward for the 1990s*. John Biffen MP, former Tory Leader of the House and a Westminster wiseacre, acknowledged that Neil Kinnock had done more than Hugh Gaitskell to bring Labour back into the centre ground of British politics. 'After so many years in the margins, Labour now looks distinctly electable,' he said.

At the annual party conference in Blackpool, Gordon Brown made a dramatic speech on jobs and 'the four great industrial evils of our time': the failures to train, to innovate, to invest for jobs and the failure to attack regional economic inequalities. It was a speech designed to put Labour's policies – and his own political ambitions – in a pre-election showcase. Brown now intended to stand for the NEC: not this year, but next. It would not have escaped the notice of his colleagues and potential rivals that all the party leaders of modern times have served a spell on the NEC.

In the Monday afternoon debate, opened by John Smith, on the party policy paper *Building a World Class Economy*, Brown lashed John Major and offered a vision of life under Labour. 'The unemployed have not failed the government. John Major's government has failed the unemployed,' he declared. 'That is why an emergency jobs and training programme, the best in Europe – real jobs to end mass unemployment – will be the first act, not in the first hundred days, but in our first few days as a new Labour government.' He promised 'economic powerhouses' for Scotland, Wales and the regions of England. If the nation could raise billions of pounds to fight the Gulf War, or overcome the embarrassment of the poll tax, it was within the power of the government to attack the evils of unemployment, under-investment and inequality. He was in cracking form. What had John Major achieved in three hundred days? 'In his first hundred days, President Bush told him what to do. In his second hundred days, President Bush told him what to do. In his third hundred days, the photographers told him what to do. No Opportunity Britain under John Major, just photo-opportunities for John Major around the world.' The jokes came thick and fast, and so did the applause. The Tories now depended on dubious financial donations, 'most shamefully of all, on a Greek billionaire moving his money out of colonels and into majors'. Never mind that the dictator colonels were long gone from Athens: the wit worked. He lambasted the Conservatives' reverse investment policy, which was 'not that the Tories should invest in business, but that business should invest in the Tory Party'. First a privatisation write-off, then a City sell-off – and then a Tory Party pay-off. 'Not so much the old Tory magic circle, more the new Tory magic roundabout of City, Cabinet room and boardroom.'[20] The delegates loved it. He had found their G-spot.

Labour might have abandoned old-style nationalisation, but Brown outlined a shamelessly interventionist strategy of a different kind: a national investment bank, tougher takeover controls for the City, a British investment decade, a long-term modernisation programme, a new venture bringing together business and the universities to upgrade people's skills, and a European Technology Trust for every region so that companies could benefit from innovations as quickly as possible. There were echoes of Harold Wilson's 'white heat of technological revolution' speech of the early 1960s that caught the popular mood then. Brown certainly caught the mood of the audience, pulling them out of their post-lunch torpor. They applauded him eight times. The next speaker, Ali Syed, of the Socialist Health Association, was ecstatic: 'What a speech! What a commitment! This is the sort of commitment the country is looking for . . . Here we are, we have not fallen yet. We are going to rise again.'[21] The delegates knew that this would be the last conference before the general election, and were inclined to give the leadership what it asked for. Kinnock was given fresh powers to require a one member, one vote mandate before a sitting MP was obliged to go through the re-selection process, a further step towards the aims of reformists like Brown.

At the European Union summit at Maastricht during December 1991, Major won a opt-out for the UK on the social chapter and European single currency, putting more 'clear blue water' between the Conservatives on Labour. But it was on tax

that the real political battle would be fought. Labour's policy
review was relaunched for the third time early in 1992, as *Made
in Britain*. It included proposals to abolish the upper limit on
National Insurance (NIS) contributions which the Tories
immediately seized on as a £1,000 tax rise. John Smith refused
to alter course: the money from higher NIS contributions was
needed to pay for public-spending pledges on higher pensions
and improved child benefit. Labour leaders knew they were still
vulnerable to the 'tax and spend' charge, even though the
impact of their changes had been grossly inflated by the government. A MORI poll in March still put the government eleven
points ahead on economic competence. In his 10 March budget, Norman Lamont cut taxes again in a clear bid to buy the
forthcoming general election.

Labour entered the election campaign marginally in the lead,
on 41 per cent to the Tories' 38 per cent. Central to Kinnock's
bid for power was a proposal to introduce fair taxes. The
Labour manifesto, *Time to get Britain Working Again*, promised
an attack on poverty, arguing, 'The most effective way to
reduce poverty quickly is to increase child benefit and pensions
and take low-paid people out of taxation.' Child benefit would
go up to £9.95 a week for all children, benefiting 7 million
families. The basic retirement pension would be increased by
£5 for a single person and £8 for a married couple, benefiting
12 million people. The 'anomalous' ceiling on National
Insurance contributions would be abolished. Labour would
take 740,000 taxpayers out of taxation altogether by increasing
allowances. The basic rate of 25 per cent – introduced by the
Tories – would stay, as would the 40 per cent rate. A new top
rate of 50p in the pound would be applied to those earning
£40,000 or more. The manifesto claimed that this package was
self-financing, and everyone earning up to £22,000 a year
would be better off. The programme had been tested on the
Treasury forecasting model by the respected Institute for Fiscal
Studies, and pronounced sound. It was well known to the electorate, having been part of John Smith's 'shadow budget' for

many months.

The Tories had launched their attack on Labour's 'fair taxes' manifesto earlier in the year, claiming it would cost families £1,000 a year more. As the campaign intensified, they simply relaunched the same simple slogan of Labour 'double whammy' on taxes. The Tory tabloids took up the hue and cry, emblazoning the '£1,000-hit' across their front pages. The relentless propaganda worked. Barbara Castle, meeting elderly residents in sheltered accommodation, heard piteous complaints from pensioners who didn't know where they would find the money, though in fact they would have been better off under Labour. Middle-class voters were put off by the prospect of paying more tax via the NIS increases. A typical remark was made to an *Observer* reporter in a Hampstead wine bar: 'I didn't realise it was *my* income that was going to be redistributed.' Opinion polls suggested that voters wanted to pay higher taxes for education, the NHS and better pensions, but in the privacy of the polling booth the allure of tax cuts promised by the Conservative proved stronger.

Neil Kinnock opened Labour's campaign at the Scottish party conference in March 1992. The Opposition started in pole position, ahead of the Conservatives in the opinion polls by up to 5 points. North of the border, the election was dominated by the constitutional issue. Labour offered an elected Scottish parliament with limited tax-raising powers, the Nationalists fought for the principle of independence, while the Tories campaigned strongly on retention of the Union with England.

On his home ground, Gordon Brown once again faced a four-cornered fight. Mark Tennant, aged 44, the bagpipe-playing, old-Etonian director for Scotland of the Chase Manhattan Bank, and treasurer of the Scottish Conservatives, carried the government's banner. John Lloyd, a 40-year-old modern studies teacher who was also a freelance journalist and writer, stood for the SNP. The Liberal Democrats chose another teacher, Teresa Little, aged 43, a former Fife regional councillor who had contested Fife Central at the two previous elections. The outcome was a small swing – 2 per cent – to the Tories, partly at the expense of Labour but more so at the expense of the Liberal Democrats. The overall swing masked an improvement in the fortunes of the SNP, whose vote went up by more than 5 per cent. The result was not in doubt, however. In a marginally lower turnout than 1987, Brown held on to his safe seat with a majority reduced by just over two thousand to 17,444.

Scotland showed the fewest changes of seats of any region of the UK. The Tories gained one, winning eleven. Labour lost one, and won forty-nine. The Liberal Democrats and the SNP were unchanged on none and three respectively. As in Dunfermline East, these raw figures did not tell the whole story. The Nationalists saw their share of the popular vote rise sharply by more than seven points to 21.5 per cent, while Labour's share slipped by more than 3 per cent to 39 per cent and that of the Liberal Democrats by six points to 13 per cent. The Tories' share increased by just under 2 per cent to 25.7 per cent – still uncomfortably close to the SNP's performance, and John Major promised to 'take stock' of the constitutional position, while rejecting any substantial change to the 285-year-old Union. Events in Scotland, however, were totally overshadowed by the national disaster. Labour had failed for the fourth time to dislodge the Conservatives. John Major, the 'grey man' who had been the butt of so many well-aimed Opposition shafts, was back in Downing Street on 10 April 1992 with an overall majority of twenty-one seats – down from the 102 of 1987, but still a working majority for a full Parliament.

CHAPTER 8

TWO STURDY OXEN

WHEN THE AWFUL TRUTH OF A FOURTH CONSECUTIVE disaster began to break, late on polling day, Gordon Brown was at the count for his constituency in Lochgelly Town Hall. He was apprehensive, not about his own result, which was beyond peradventure, but about the national outcome. The opinion polls had shown a detectable swing to the government in the final few days of the campaign. Brown had confided to close political allies his fears that Labour would fail yet again. His brother John was at the count too in Fife too, working as a producer for ITN's election-night special. He had signed up a reluctant Gordon to do what the television people called a 'matchmaker', a three-way live link-up of politicians in different places. The shadow trade secretary (as he still was) was lined up to go live in conversation with Kenneth Clarke and Alan Beith, the Liberal Democrats' Treasury spokesman. The technicians got the complicated links in place, and then put the matchmaker on hold until the first result was declared soon after 11 p.m. This was Basildon, Essex, where the Conservatives, seemingly against all the odds, held on. And if they could retain the loyalty of Essex Man, the archetypal new Tory of the 1980s, they could hang on to power nationally.

Brown was bitterly dismayed, and stumbled through his lines about it being 'too early in the evening' to come to any firm conclusions and similar platitudes. 'But he knew,' said John Brown. 'He had known in his heart for several days. He was quite angry that he was the first Labour politician to come in, but it was just as circumstances had it. The programme said, "We are coming now to Gordon Brown." He was trying to be as polished as possible, but was quite depressed that night. He had told me earlier he knew we weren't going to win.'[1] There were no further interviews.

Others shared Brown's misgivings about Labour's prospects in the 1992 election. The shadow budget, centrepiece of the party's manifesto, was necessary to pay for commitments entered into three years earlier, long before the process of policy modernisation had reached its present pitch. Nick Brown, then a junior member of the shadow Treasury team, said the programme had become 'a tail wagging the dog'. It had been agreed by John Smith at a time when the modernisers were fighting off pressure from the left to tax more and spend more. 'As the election got closer, of course it got clear that the fact that these big decisions had been cast in stone was limiting our room for manoeuvre – and was probably an error. Everybody privately recognised it, with varying degrees of force. John's view was that he had to live with it because we couldn't change it. He had gone through a fight to get it down to that level.

'The shadow budget was constructed around these commitments. It was socially just, defensible and clear-cut – better than the policy we had in 1987. The tax burden fell on those most able to pay, and the money was being spent in a redistributive way. Gordon always had reservations. His private view, even before the election, was that we had allowed ourselves to be boxed in. In retrospect, he was clearly right, and it is to his credit that he didn't say publicly what he thought privately. He was tremendously loyal to John Smith.'[2] Brown himself admits that this was the case. 'I was always loyal to John Smith in public, but in private I had disagreements about the

1992 proposals. They weren't tackling the real problems. We were putting up pensions. That was fine. But we had to deal first of all with the causes of poverty – which are unemployment, a welfare state that isn't working and poor skills.'[3]

The shadow budget may have been defensible on grounds of logic and social policy, but the Tories did not address its intellectual merits, relying instead on reviving bad folk memories of Labour as the 'tax and spend' party. They were also able to capitalise on apparent divisions within the Opposition. At an informal dinner party at Luigi's restaurant in London in January, Neil Kinnock had suggested to political correspondents that the National Insurance changes could be phased in over several years to mitigate the impact on middle-class voters. This looked like nervous back-tracking in the face of the Conservative 'tax bombshell' onslaught. Smith had refused to be diverted from his programme, and Brown loyally supported him. But disaster at the polls now relieved him of all necessity to support policies with which he disagreed.

First, however, there was the immediate issue of the party leadership. Having lost twice in a row, it was assumed that Neil Kinnock would not wish to continue. 'It became clear very early on that he was going to go. He was upset at the result, and felt personally responsible for it,' said a senior party insider. 'He had decided to stand down as leader.' Brown felt there was no time to lose. He telephoned Tony Blair, and arranged a meeting with him and Nick Brown. His brother John drove him to Edinburgh Waverley station to catch the train south, noting his sombre mien. Over the ensuing days, the three men had a series of meetings: the first at Blair's home in Trimdon, in his Sedgefield constituency, when they went for a walk in the Durham countryside; the second, at Nick Brown's home in Heaton, in his Newcastle East constituency; and the third at County Hall, Durham, in a room made available by the council leader. This last gathering was attended by Peter Mandelson, the newly elected MP for Hartlepool, a key figure in the modernising process.

It was plain that they would play a critical part in deciding the direction that Labour would take. They had long discussions about what they had to do. On one objective they were unanimous: the leadership must go to John Smith. Brown had to discourage speculation that he would run against his mentor. Alastair Campbell, political editor of the *Daily Mirror* (he later became Blair's press secretary) wrote, 'Although Smith is convinced Gordon Brown won't challenge him, the trade spokesman, 41, is coming under intense pressure to persuade Labour to "skip a generation". But Brown has been damaged by some roughing up by opponents who felt he was getting too big for his boots. He was once Kinnock's chosen successor, but would be unlikely to get his backing now.'[4] Brown concedes that the loyalty factor came into play once more. I asked him why he did not stand, when the tide of his popularity in the party - he had topped the poll for the Shadow Cabinet three years in succession – was running at its highest. 'Because I felt I owed a debt of gratitude to John Smith. I felt I had to be loyal. It was for no other reason. I had worked with him for almost eight years on the front bench, and it was right for me to be loyal. I thought the Labour Party was more ready for change than people imagined, but I never thought for a minute of standing against John Smith.'[5]

The plotters then turned to the issue of the deputy leadership. Blair clearly fancied his chances. 'Tony wanted to stand for deputy leader, and some thought was given to getting him to stand,' recalled Brown. 'I had also been asked by people to stand for deputy leader. But I felt that two Scots could not stand together.'[6]

Mandelson and Harriet Harman, another rising moderniser, urged Blair to stand. Roy Hattersley, the outgoing deputy leader, sought to dissuade him, on more machiavellian grounds. 'I urged him not to stand for deputy because I believed he should be leader of the Labour Party one day . . . I believed he was John's natural successor, more than Gordon.'[7] Nick Brown, the 'fixer' with long experience of the labour movement, was strongly against Blair running for the deputy leadership. 'I thought he would never make it, because of the method by which the election was done,' he said.[8] At that time, the leader and his deputy were still chosen by the electoral-college system introduced during Labour's fundamentalist period, which gave the unions 40 per cent of the votes, with the rest evenly divided between the constituency parties and MPs. The leadership election system was top of the modernisers' agenda for change. 'In retrospect, it was right for Tony to decide not to stand,' said Nick Brown. 'But it was a close call. Clearly, there was a huge case for him on merit.'[9]

In any event, Smith had other ideas. Nick Brown travelled to Westminster to offer him the backing of the triumvirate, only to find Margaret Beckett leaving Smith's office in 1 Parliament Street as he went in. Smith announced without further ado that Mrs Beckett would stand, and he would back her. And, oh, would Nick Brown help her campaign? Robin Cook also entered the room at this point and heard the news. 'He didn't take it well,' recollected Nick Brown, with some amusement. 'John Smith would have been happy with Tony Blair, but the party would have found it difficult to elect him in preference to Margaret Beckett or Bryan Gould.'[10] The great virtue of Mrs Beckett – who also got Gordon's firm support – was that not only did she have street-cred with the unions and Labour traditionalists, but she was not Bryan Gould either. Gould, who had scant respect for Gordon Brown's judgment, was nevertheless Kinnock's preferred option for deputy leader. As it fell out, Gould ran for both jobs, though with no serious prospect of winning either. The Smith–Beckett partnership romped home in the election on 18 July. Smith scored a ten to one margin over Gould, and Beckett easily saw off the combined challenge of Gould and John Prescott.

The Shadow Cabinet election had taken place two days previously, and Brown had again topped the poll with 165 votes, sealing his political ascendancy. Smith was quick to offer him his heart's desire – the shadow chancellorship – though Robin

Cook had let it be known that he would like the post, indeed was better fitted to occupy it. 'Most people, in retrospect, would say I had been preparing for the Shadow Chancellorship by doing the DTI job,' Brown recalled.[11] He had arrived.

Brown's manifesto for a modernised Labour Party was delivered at Central Hall, Westminster on 9 July. Giving the annual *Tribune* lecture, he set out a strategy for 'power in the mid-1990s'. It was an unashamed demand for reform. 'We must assert our basic values in a new crusade for change,' he argued. To meet the challenges ahead, Labour had to ensure that its policies reflected its values 'by preparing a programme for a modern economy, a modern society and a modern constitution'. To achieve that goal, 'we must create a modern party with membership roots in every community in Britain', in which 'not only is there one person, one vote, but every member feels they can contribute to policy making'. The code is not difficult to break. 'Modern' means different, politically more mainstream and acceptable to that elusive, but critical, constituency, Middle England.

Next, the individual. Brown rejected 'Basildon Man – the selfish, indeed self-centred, individual' who feels held back by both government and the community around him. Yet he believed that Labour must refashion its appeal to take account of the resurgence of individualism. 'Our task is about helping each other to help ourselves,' he said. 'And the distinctive message of socialists is that while individuals on their own do not have the power to tackle and control vested interests, the power of all of us can advance the good of each.' In some respects, this is the classic pitch of a trade union organiser trying to explain why workers should join the union, an old-fashioned collectivism: the more we are together, the stronger we shall be.

But Brown was looking to a wider audience. 'The truth is,' he declared, 'that our natural constituency is far broader than what our commentators call our traditional constituency, and there is no contradiction between them. Our natural constituency is the majority who benefit from a just society.' He could see 'no clash' between individual freedom and the advancement of the common good, but he did discern a paradox. The need for Labour had never been greater, yet people had not elected it as a national government, even if they agreed with its purposes and values. 'We have to do more to convince people that Labour reflects these values in a way relevant to the challenges of the modern world.' 'Relevant' is another encryption. Brown pointed out that Labour's constitution - Clause IV and all – was written in 1918 and grew out of a series of ethical principles applied by socialists to the challenges of the time. The inference, surely is that the constitution is not 'relevant' to the 1990s, even though the party's ethical principles are 'more relevant than ever before'.

In the early twentieth century, collective action was necessary to ensure liberation from exploitation, and essential to promote individual well-being. 'Now, at the end of the century, it means much more.' Brown sought an examination of how the community could organise its affairs, 'breaking out of the one-dimensional view of government that all too easily assumes that where there is a public interest there must always be a centralised public bureaucracy always directly involved in provision'. Is this not a quietly spoken embrace of the market?

He concluded that Labour must recognise the attractions of a world of new aspirations and diverse needs, 'in new circumstances where every individual has become a decision maker'. In a new, interdependent world where individuals had the highest expectations, Labour had to apply its values in a political programme whose priority was to face up to such challenges. Just as it had done for the generation of 1918 and 1945, it was time for the party to 're-establish the importance of the individual in a community and to show how individuals can advance with and through the community'.

Since Gordon Brown takes such infinite care over writing his speeches, certainly more than any other politician of his generation, it is worth pondering what he said in that speech. The buzz-words 'new', 'modern', 'relevant' and 'individual' were

repeated remorselessly through the text. He was nowhere specific (he does not say, 'Clause IV must go') but he was everywhere directive. He suggested that what Labour offered in the
past had been fine for 1918 and 1945, but it was not appropriate for 1992 and beyond. He was firm about bedrock
principles, but policies must be attuned to what the voters want
today, hence the accent on individualism. The Thatcher years
had made people more self-reliant, whether they wished it or
not, and that 'dimension' must be accommodated in Labour's
approach. Broadly stated, Brown was signalling that Labour
had to live with the changes of the 1980s, and that meant an
accelerated pace of reform, in the party's constitution and its
policies.

Unsurprisingly, Brown's first act was to slough off the tax
strategy that had helped lose the election. 'I scrapped the
Shadow Budget,' he said simply. 'I told John Smith we were not
going back to it, and we then had to tell the party we had to
change our whole economic policy.'[12] It was easier said than
done. His erstwhile comrades in the Tribune group were on the
point of publishing a pamphlet attacking him for his radical
remaking of tax and spend. It was stopped. At first, 'people were
very resistant to change', he admitted.

But then a full-blown sterling crisis supervened, putting
Labour's internal arguments into the shade and testing Brown's
mettle when he had been shadow chancellor for less than three
months. The Major government's political credibility was
blown away, but Gordon Brown also suffered from the back-
wash of the crisis. He, with John Smith, had been the architect
of Labour's change of policy to favour British membership of
the ERM, and he was inevitably identified with its manifest
failure.

Brown had seen the crisis coming, but refused to soften
Labour's opposition to 'unilateral devaluation'. With memories
of forced Labour devaluations of the 1970s still fresh, Brown
did not want the party of the 1990s to be thought of as the
party of devaluation. He said later, 'I walked into a big storm,

because I said devaluation should not be the way that we should be judged. And I certainly was not going round shouting the odds for devaluation. People were annoyed, because they wanted me to call for devaluation.'[13] For 'people', read rivals and opponents in the Shadow Cabinet, who saw Labour's shadowing of Lamont's failing policy as a useful opportunity to take the shadow chancellor down a peg or two. Brown stuck to his guns, proposing instead on 29 July, at the launch of a new Labour 'summer campaign to harass ministers' that European finance ministers should get together and discuss collective action. He hoped, against the evidence, that Germany would ease the pressure on sterling by revaluing the Deutschmark. His tough stance created friction with John Smith, but Smith accepted that his shadow chancellor was right to avoid any suggestion that Labour was the party of devaluation.

Intriguingly, though the leadership election was well behind them, Brown and Blair now had to contend with fresh speculation about their future. As Parliament went into recess, political commentator Charles Reiss, a former party staffer, wrote in the London *Evening Standard* of the 'coming war' between these two bright young stars of the Shadow Cabinet. With remarkable prescience, he observed, 'We know, and they must know, that this happy friendship cannot last.' By the very nature of politics, they would become deadly rivals. 'In five years' time or, who knows, even earlier, they are likely to become contenders for the greatest prize in politics – the leadership of the Labour Party, and then, they hope, the premiership of the country.'[14] They also knew that only one of them could make it – and only at the expense of the other.

Conjecture about the next leader had begun the day after Smith's coronation on 25 July, when the *Sunday Times* colour magazine published a five-page article on Tony Blair, 'Labour's leader in waiting'. Reiss's article indicated that such speculation would now be a continuous feature of Smith's tragically-brief period as leader. The *Standard's* political editor compared Brown and Blair to two earlier stars in the Labour firmament,

Roy Jenkins and Anthony Crosland – an uncomfortable omen, as their friendship was tested to destruction in the 1960s, yet neither ever took the ultimate crown. 'In one way,' mused Reiss, 'Labour is extraordinarily fortunate to have two such outstanding heirs apparent. Some MPs, including Tories, can still be heard to mutter that the party would have been more fortunate still if it had picked one of the princes rather than the current king.'[15]

As the crisis deepened, there were serious divisions in the Shadow Cabinet. Bryan Gould, semi-detached from Cabinet responsibility by his defeat and demotion, David Blunkett, John Prescott and Michael Meacher all demanded a comprehensive realignment of the ERM – effectively, a devaluation of the pound. Brown denied the divisions existed, insisting at the TUC conference in Blackpool that 'There is no policy for devaluation on the part of the Labour Party.' Writing in the *Guardian* the day before Black Wednesday, he argued that to say 'there is no alternative but devaluation' was to deny the potential of government. He called instead for an emergency plan for jobs, to reduce the fear of unemployment; a new industry policy involving government-coordinated investment in manufacturing; initiatives to help the housing market; and a joint European package of fiscal and employment measures to expand economies and get interest rates down. 'Quite overwhelmingly, the recession has made the case for intervention,' he concluded.[16]

On 16 September, despite having spent billions propping up the pound, the UK was forced out of the Exchange Rate Mechanism, after two interest rate-hikes in one day – to first 12 and then 15 per cent – failed to halt speculation. Making his first Commons speech in his new post during the debate on economic policy that followed on 24 September, Brown was unrelenting in his criticism of Major and Chancellor Norman Lamont. Economic failure had been compounded by the humiliation of withdrawal from the ERM, he said, which they promised they would never do. To the intense discomfort of

Tory backbenchers, he reminded the House of repeated statements by the chancellor that devaluation was 'fool's gold', and
he ridiculed him as a man on the brink of departure from high
office: 'There is no point in the Chancellor setting monetary
targets other than in negotiations of his memoirs.' He heaped
scorn on John Major, who had boasted that membership of
ERM was one of his greatest achievements. In a peroration that
was to become the central theme of Labour's bid for power five
years later, Brown said, 'The Conservative Party ran a general
election campaign on the slogan "You can't trust Labour" and
has shown itself completely unworthy of trust. The party that
already for years has been the party of unemployment and of
poverty is now the party of devaluation . . . Ministers who continue to hold responsibilities now cannot command respect.
They may hold office for five years, but even after five months
they have lost all authority to govern. They have failed the
country and they will never be trusted again.'[17]

His words were to prove prophetic, but Brown's standing still
came under pressure from colleagues for holding the line
against devaluation right until the eve of the Labour Party conference in Blackpool. Blair's biographer John Rentoul suggests
that 'when the pound was devalued, Brown's reputation went
down with it'.[18] But the policy he propounded was the policy
of the whole Shadow Cabinet, not simply his own, and the
taint of being identified with Norman Lamont's disastrous
clinging to the ERM did not affect his performance in the elections for the NEC. Standing for the first time, he polled
523,000 votes in the constituency section, coming third after
Neil Kinnock and David Blunkett. Blair also stood, and
scraped in at seventh place.

Making his first appearance before the party conference as
shadow chancellor, Brown pinned the blame for the sterling
crisis where it belonged. 'Let us be clear: the weakness of the
currency is the result of the weakness of the economy, which is
in turn the inevitable result of the weakness of this government.
I say to Norman Lamont: spend your energies pursuing the

useful goal of creating jobs for others rather than the futile goal of clinging to your own.' Delegates relished his joke about John Major's stewardship of the economy: the recession started when he became Treasury secretary, worsened when he became chancellor and intensified when he took over as prime minister. 'Every time he changed jobs, thousands lost theirs,' he declared. 'I say there was never anything more to Majorism than monetarism . . . he has retreated from the challenge of Europe to the squalid pursuit of Thatcherism in one country.' Only the Kremlinologists in his audience would have recognised his reference to the Stalin's policy of 'socialism in one country.'[19]

To win the election, Brown argued, John Major had pronounced the recession over. 'They said you can't trust Labour. Let every billboard round this country tell the truth: you can never trust the Tories.' He was applauded for that sally, which was to become Labour's slogan for the next four and a half years. From the ruins of the ERM fiasco, the shadow chancellor plucked a critique that undermined the Conservatives' most potent weapon: that they could be trusted on the economy, whereas Labour could not.

The *Financial Times* praised Brown's 'combative' performance, while noting that he had not committed Labour to support UK re-entry to the ERM, calling instead for a 'new internationalism' in economic strategy designed to limit the power of speculators. The shadow chancellor told reporters that Labour support for sterling's eventual return was contingent on reform of the system.

Members of the NEC are normally limited to one appearance on the rostrum during conference week, but Brown had a second bite at the cherry when he was asked to present a brief statement on the economy from the national executive. The statement demanded that John Major replace his discredited chancellor, and make a full personal statement on the handling of the financial crisis. Naturally, he did neither.

However, Brown's introduction of the statement enabled him to recover some of the credibility he had lost. Two weeks after the devaluation of sterling, the withdrawal from the ERM and the squandering of billions of pounds of public money, the government still had no economic policy in place, no explanation for the failure of past policy 'and shamefully no apology either'. He called on Major to face up to his duty, answer 'serious allegations' about his conduct of economic policy and sack his chancellor 'for the good of the country'.[20] The delegates loudly cheered Brown for his sharp words, but in politics there are few unalloyed pleasures. Three days later, 'Black Dog', the gossip columnist of the *Mail on Sunday*, said he was not alone in finding Brown's oratory at Blackpool 'nauseating'. Despite the media plaudits for his performance, the newspaper claimed that eight members of the Shadow Cabinet were 'decidedly underwhelmed' by his performance, and named John Prescott, Jack Straw, Michael Meacher, David Blunkett and Robin Cook as five of them. 'They are furious at how he threw away the party's great chance of plunging the knife into the Tories,' the column went on. Brown's crime was to have 'slammed the door' on a policy option to realign the pound in the event of a crisis, banging on instead about maintaining current exchange rates at all costs.[21]

Gossip columns are often close to the mark. The gossip is safe behind ironclad anonymity, and can conduct a whispering campaign against real or imagined enemies, sometimes prompted by individual envy and at other times as part of a concerted campaign to bring down a politician. On this occasion, it is almost certainly true that other Shadow Cabinet members (or their gofers) were privately 'briefing' against Brown, though their criticism was wide of the mark. They shared collective responsibility for the agreed policy of no unilateral devaluation.

The shadow chancellor shrugged off the sniping, publicly confirming on 9 November 1992 that he had scrapped the election manifesto tax-and-spend plans. Launching Labour's policy document *Campaign for Recovery*, he said the situation had deteriorated so much since the election that 'we are not proposing to raise tax and national insurance at this stage'. He demanded immediate interest-rate cuts and an emergency jobs programme. At a meeting of the parliamentary Labour Party that evening, he was asked by an energetic new MP, John Denham (Southampton, Itchen), why he had abandoned, so soon after the election, the key policy on which it had been fought. He replied, courteously but firmly, that Labour had not actually won in April.

Brown aroused interest in one new tax that eventually found favour right across the spectrum of the party: a 'one-off public dividend' on the 'excess profits' of the privatised utilities. This idea, which became popularly known as the 'windfall tax', had initially been proposed during the Blackpool conference economy debate by John Edmonds, leader of the GMB general union. Brown quickly latched on to the public distaste for the massive profits made by the telephone, gas, water and electricity companies since privatisation, and the lavish share options and salaries – often exceeding £400,000 – that industry chiefs paid themselves, while making redundant tens of thousands of their employees. A windfall tax, similar to that imposed on the gargantuan profits of the high-street banks by the Conservatives in the early 1980s, would bring in at least £2 billion. Brown took the proposal to the leader. 'John Smith backed me. He thought it was a good idea,' he said subsequently. 'Most of my Shadow Cabinet colleagues were against me.'[22] The policy first appeared in *Campaign for Recovery*, and survived to become the basis of the Blair government's ambitious welfare-to-work programme, financed by an even more productive £5.3 billion levy on the privatised utilities.

In the debate on the government's autumn statement during November, Brown teased the Tories with the charge that 'the Opposition are speaking for the country'. Contrary to what the chancellor had said the previous year, national output was down, not up; consumer spending was flat, not increasing; investment had fallen, not risen, along with manufacturing output; and unemployment was half a million higher than predicted at 2.9 million, after rising for the thirtieth month in succession. His speech was a long succession of rhetorical questions, and Lamont dismissed it is 'a pretty feeble showing'. But as the year drew to a close, the chancellor provided Brown with some much-needed light relief. He was obliged to admit that the taxpayer had paid £4,700 legal fees incurred in the eviction of a 'Miss Whiplash' sex therapist renting the basement flat of his home. The shadow chancellor sought to get an emergency debate on the issue, demanding that Lamont come to the House and answer questions about the 'questionable circumstances' surrounding the payment of Treasury funds to Peter Carter-Ruck, the noted solicitor. 'The Chancellor must explain why secret arrangements were such that the public would not know that this payment was made,' he said.[23] Infuriated MPs accused Brown of muck-raking, but the National Audit Office took up the complaint.

There was not much to laugh about in a confidential report on voter research handed to John Smith by party officials in mid-December. In-depth interviews with selected lower-middle- and skilled working-class people aged 25–40 and living in the south of England, who had contemplated voting Labour nine months previously but switched to the Tories, showed only too clearly that Labour's double-digit lead in the polls was chimerical. None of the focus group would vote Labour if there was an election the next day. Labour was seen – still – as untrustworthy, inexperienced, a 'party of the past' in favour of minorities rather than ordinary men and women. On top of this bad news, a leaked report prepared for the soft-left Labour Co-ordinating Committee, unfavourably compared the Labour Party to US President-elect Bill Clinton's Democratic Party. It praised Clinton's 'total repackaging' of the Democrats, which rejected the tax-and-spend, altruistic approach and appealed to Middle America.

In fact, Brown and Blair had already made plans to study the US model. They flew to Washington in the first week of January 1993 for talks with Clinton's staff, arranged by

Jonathan Powell, political secretary at the British Embassy there. They also met Larry Summers, a key figure at the World Bank who was just about to become deputy secretary at the US Treasury, and Robert Reich, Clinton's newly appointed labor secretary. These last two meetings were fixed by a little-known journalist at the *Financial Times*, Ed Balls, who was to figure substantially in Brown's new economic order.

On their return, Brown and Blair presided over a private meeting in London at which the new president's campaigners were introduced to members of the influential Labour leader's committee, the inner circle of Shadow Cabinet members. There had been some previous contacts between Brown's aides and the Clinton campaign team. Yvette Cooper, who had worked for John Smith while he was shadow chancellor (she later became Ed Balls's partner and a Labour MP in the party's Yorkshire heartland), and Geoff Mulgan, an adviser to Brown, collaborated with Democratic Party staffers on an exhaustive report comparing the US and British elections. This paper was sharply critical of Labour's 'all things to all people' image and its inability to hit back against the Tories' distortions on taxes.

Smith's office denied that the US initiative was about turning Labour into another Democratic Party, but accepted that some things could be taken on board. 'We will not win by one last heave,' said a source. 'We have got to prepare the ground so that people will say it is perfectly safe, sensible and attractive to vote Labour.' Traditionalists in the Shadow Cabinet were alarmed. John Prescott complained of an obsession with image, while Clare Short linked the activities of the 'secret, infiltrating so-called modernisers' who wanted the Clintonisation of Labour, to Gordon Brown's rejection of the 1992 tax-and-spend agenda. 'The hint we get is "dump the poor". That appears to be what they are saying. "Labour is seen as the party of the poor. You can't get the mainstream. Dump the poor." That would destroy the party,' said Ms Short.[24] Brown would no doubt have argued that Labour could not help the poor without winning power, and it could not do that without making itself acceptable to Middle England, much as Clinton had broadened the Democrats' appeal to Middle America.

They returned from the US even more convinced of this message, and determined to remodel Labour. Soon afterwards, Brown raised some eyebrows by confessing a sneaking admiration for Margaret Thatcher. 'The one thing you can say about the Conservative Party in the Thatcherite era was its belief that things had to change.'[25] He was busy refashioning Labour's economic strategy. He looked at the possibility of adopting the Tories' move towards indirect taxation, but rejected it. Then, before he could complete his reforms, John Major unceremoniously sacked Norman Lamont and installed Kenneth Clarke, the beer-swilling, cheroot-smoking Home Secretary, in his place. Brown dismissed the Cabinet reshuffle in late May as a botched job, 'no more than the political equivalent of a change in the cast of *The Mousetrap*'. By locking Clarke into his predecessor's policies, Major had missed the opportunity to bring in a new economic agenda, he argued.

Perhaps so. But Kenneth Clarke was one of the few remaining heavyweights (in every sense of the phrase) in the Cabinet, and he would be no pushover for Brown. His first appearance at the despatch box confirmed that. 'For the first time,' observed commentator Philip Stephens of the *Financial Times*, 'Gordon Brown, the Shadow Chancellor, found himself facing an opponent with the self-confidence to fight back.'[26] In the debate on the government's economic and social policy that followed Lamont's dismissal, Brown congratulated Clarke on the fact that 'in only nine months he has made the transition from Chancellor in waiting to Prime Minister in waiting'. Not quite, though Clarke did have ambitions to fill Major's shoes. He reminded the House of the chancellor's frank view of the previous month that the government was 'in a dreadful hole'. Yet Major's response was merely to 'refresh' the government by bringing arch-Eurosceptic John Redwood into the Cabinet as Welsh secretary. 'A Cabinet that needs to be refreshed by the inclusion of the new Secretary of State for Wales is indeed a

Cabinet in need of refreshment,' he remarked, plainly eager to outdo Clarke's public-bar style. He spoke at length on his favourite subject of long-term strategy, and called for a change of government. Clarke was not to be put down. 'I have heard that speech before, and I have no doubt I shall hear it many times. It is the speech he always gives.' He called it 'an extremely good foil' to John Smith's speech. 'I put them both into the same category: good on jokes, very weak on content.' He observed Brown's intriguing and forceful style. 'He does great damage to the Despatch Box, but it is certainly a very vigorous delivery. He has a particular technique of launching into lists – there is a strategy for this, a strategy for that and a strategy for something else, all rapped out in rapid Scottish tones. He has about as much policy content as the average tele-phone directory . . . and if I may say so – it is a modest claim, given the competition it faced – I thought the best parts of the hon. Gentleman's speech came when he was quoting me.'[27] He had a point. More important, he had a majority of twenty-four when the vote was taken an hour later. For all the fine rhetoric, Brown was banging his head on a brick wall unless Labour could confront the Tories at the polls.

From early summer, Brown was intimately involved in John Smith's battle to push through his reforms in the party. They were determined that the October 1993 conference in Brighton would change Labour's constitution so that MPs and the party leader were chosen on the basis of one member, one vote (OMOV), dispelling for ever the image of trade-union domination. The campaign got off the ground at the first meet-ing of Labour's new National Policy Forum in the Ark, an appropriately futuristic building in Hammersmith, west London, on 8 May. Smith insisted that the individual members were the lifeblood of the party, providing much of the energy and enthusiasm that had always been the hallmark of Labour's historic mission. 'That is why we should modernise our inter-nal democracy on the basis of the principle of one member, one vote,' he urged. Unfortunately, he had to convince the trade unions of their duty to vote for a form of political hara-kiri. Some did not need much persuasion, but others, like John Edmonds's GMB, the National Union of Public Employees and the National Communications Union, threw out the proposals. Tom (now Lord) Burlison, a GMB leader and the Labour Party treasurer, predicted defeat for Smith, and denounced senior members of the Shadow Cabinet for arrogance and inflexibility.

Brown's union, the Transport and General, led the search for a face-saving compromise, but it, too, demanded retention of a 'collective input' in the choice of prospective MPs. Many of the unions did not consult their members on this key issue, but the moderate Amalgamated Electrical and Engineering Union (AEEU) conducted a MORI poll among two thousand voters and found that only 21 per cent of trade unionists believed the unions should have a role in deciding who should stand for Parliament. Brown and his allies argued that it was only fair that the franchise should be confined to those who were actually members of the party, though he welcomed suggestions that trade unionists should get a cut-price membership. He denied that OMOV was a distraction from Labour's bid to win the election, whenever it came. 'Widening our membership and making the party more democratic are part of John Smith's strategy to win,' he said.[28]

The AEEU's opinion poll, clearly timed to influence the tide of opinion in the trade unions, brought to Brown's notice a potentially useful labour movement spin-doctor: Charlie Whelan, the engineering workers' press officer. Whelan, a 39-year-old Londoner, was something of a contradiction – a former public schoolboy, who became a Communist while a student at the City of London Polytechnic, and had been employed briefly as a foreign-exchange dealer in the City before going to work for the labour movement. For most of the previous decade, he had handled media relations for leading AEEU figures, most notably Jimmy Airlie, the Clydeside Communist who, with Jimmy Reid, masterminded the 1971 Upper Clyde

Shipbuilders work-in, which had so fired the imagination of young Gordon Brown. Whelan's cheerful extrovert style – he was much given to dismissing rival efforts to spin stories as 'bollocks' – belied a serious professionalism that was influential in building up a coalition of support for Smith behind the scenes.

On the eve of the Brighton conference, Whelan and 'Big Nigel' Harris, the AEEU's man on the Labour Party national executive, met the author over dinner in a seaside restaurant to review the prospects for the vote on OMOV. Most commentators predicted that it would be very close, and some believed that Smith could lose. Somewhere about the fifth or sixth bottle of wine, Harris, a genial ex-foundryman with a strong Black Country loyalty to Labour, blurted out that, at a private meeting with the union barons in his Westminster office, Smith had threatened to resign if he lost the vote. Harris immediately regretted his volubility, but agreed to let the story run. It was the front-page lead in the *Independent on Sunday* on 26 September. Inevitably, it was denied (though officially confirmed months later), but the impact was undeniable. The story contributed to the pressure building up on delegates to back Smith, though the leader himself was unimpressed. Accosted on Brighton seafront that Sunday morning, he growled that he was going to church 'to say an extra prayer for Nigel'.

That night, Brown joined Blair, Prescott and Kinnock on the stage for a fringe meeting to mobilise backing for the OMOV package of reforms, which would give one member, one vote for choosing parliamentary candidates. Under what became known as the 'levy-plus' scheme, trade unionists could take part in the vote if they paid an extra £3 to the party on top of the political levy they paid through the union. There would be individual voting in all three sections of the electoral college in leadership elections. The college itself was now divided equally three ways between the unions, the MPs and constituency parties. At party conferences, delegates from the unions would also vote as individuals, an end to the infamous 'block vote' – technically, at least. In practice, the unions still voted en bloc.

The package, regarded by some as a 'classic fudge' in finest Labour tradition, had the approval of the national executive, but was still opposed by the big unions. The vote was on a knife-edge.

Amid scenes of tension unknown for decades at conference, delegates first cast their votes for the NEC. This time, Brown fared less well. In the constituency section, he took 414,000 votes and slipped to seventh – bottom – place below Tony Blair who came sixth with 421,000. The shift reflected rank-and-file dissatisfaction with Brown's difficult start as shadow chancellor. He had courted unpopularity by unceremoniously ditching not only Labour's 'tax and spend' election strategy, but the philosophy that underpinned it. And the party activists punished him for doing so. It was a penalty he had to pay, but finishing behind Blair was slightly galling. Blair had performed well as shadow home secretary – the portfolio for which Brown had recommended him to his leader, not least because of his brilliantly pitched soundbite promising to be 'tough on crime, and tough on causes of crime'. Ironically, the phrase was written by his friend Gordon Brown.

Inevitably, the switch in fortunes prompted more speculation that Blair was the coming man, eclipsing the shadow chancellor who seemed obsessed with a 'Year Zero' programme of reform in policy and constitution, and who peppered his speeches with dreary statistics and long lists. At Brighton, Brown consciously brought a human element into his conference speech, welcoming Wendy Cobb, 'shamefully dismissed' from the strike-hit Timex factory in Dundee, who was sitting in the public gallery. Fifty jobless men and women were chasing every vacancy in her city, he declared. And he also greeted pensioners George and Lily Haines, two of the 10 million old folk who would be hit by the imposition of VAT on domestic fuel the following April. 'Pensioner poverty is not just an evil, it is a crime,' he asserted. Sounding rather like an Old Testament ranter, he went on, 'Friends, I am here in Brighton today to preach the gospel of discontent about the evils of unemployment, the gospel of discontent about poverty, and the gospel of discontent about the abolition of wages councils'.[29] There was more hot-gospelling about home helps, nurses, firefighters, speculators, tax evaders and greedy ex-ministers in privatised boardrooms. He used the word 'social-ist' three times, and touched the sacred hem of full employment: 'That is our aim. Work for all who want it, opportunity for all who need it, security for all denied it: our aim is a fundamental and irreversible shift in favour of work and opportunity and against the privilege and abuse of power under Conservative governments.' This formula was an echo of previous manifesto commitments to 'an irreversible shift' in wealth and power to working people, but subtly rewritten to reflect Labour's changing perspectives. 'Work' and 'opportu-nity' were Brown's new watchwords.

After some sleight of hand by the white-collar union MSF, whose delegates abstained, the modernisers won the vote two days later, scraping home by a margin of 3 per cent. Smith opened the debate, but it was John Prescott's bravura perfor-mance – 'joined-up shouting' in support of the leader, unintel-ligible but perfectly understandable – that caught the mood of conference and projected him into the role of unofficial deputy leader. Brown and his allies had scored a famous victory, but he was left wondering if this was the furthest point to which reform could be taken. In his view, it ought not be. The 'pro-ject' had still some way to go. A supporter gave his view in the *Sunday Times* that weekend: 'Gordon and Tony are like two sturdy oxen pulling an occasionally reluctant plough. They get an occasional flea-bite on their backsides from Peter Hain [the Tribunite MP] and Bryan Gould, but they are still ploughing in the same direction.'[30]

In the debate on the Queen's Speech in November 1993, Brown was heavily barracked while attempting to put the government on the rack. Tory backbenchers, mostly on the party's right, interrupted time and time again when he tried to deliver the Opposition's view. Betty Boothroyd, the Speaker, had to stop MPs shouting at him 'from a sedentary position'. It was not the first time. The Tory bovver-boys at Westminster had identified him as the Labour politician they had to get by any means possible. In that, they were less successful than Kenneth Clarke, whose cutlass was more effective than their knouts. He sneered at Brown's use of a 'most impressive pile of books' that simply made it easier for him to read 'photostats of sales of raffle tickets in Hornchurch, which he was using as his principal authority to attack the government'.[31] He must have known that Brown's sight with his one good eye is so limited that he has to rest his notes on a stack of books in order to read properly. The thrust was below the belt.

Shortly after the budget, Labour made discreet overtures to Charlie Whelan, the spin-doctor whose tireless efforts had helped deliver the OMOV victory. Would he, asked Peter Mandelson, be willing to leave the trade-union movement and come to work for the Labour Party – in fact, for Gordon Brown? Few would disagree that Brown could handle his own press relations well, though he sometimes leaned rather heavily on individual correspondents. He demanded assurances that his exclusive story would get front-page exposure, and bargained hard to get his way. The copy was usually worth it. But as shadow chancellor, he could not be in day-to-day, hour-to-hour even, contact with the legion of political journalists at Westminster. He needed someone who knew the field and could place stories – and shoot the breeze in the Press Gallery bar through which filtered all the Commons gossip and intrigue. Whelan's friends urged him to take the job. The opportunity would not come again. His partner, Philippa Clark, a devout socialist and head of research for the Fire Brigade Union, was unenthusiastic. But he took the plunge, and joined Brown's staff. At about the same time, Brown also recruited Ed Balls, the brilliant young leader-writer at the *Financial Times*, who had smoothed his path with the US Treasury, as his economics adviser. Balls, 27, was a Young Financial Journalist of the Year. Before joining the *FT*, he had been a Kennedy Scholar at Harvard, where he co-authored an academic paper on unemployment in Britain with Larry Summers, later deputy secretary at the US Treasury. He also met Larry Katz, who became chief economist to Robert Reich, Clinton's Labour Secretary. These contacts proved very helpful in the reworking of Labour's economic policy. Balls came from a strong Labour family in Nottingham where his father was an academic in the university and an expert on alternatives to using animals for medical experiments. Young Balls joined the party at 16, and worked privately for Brown for more than a year prior to his full-time appointment.

Nothing was likely to sting Gordon Brown into action more than the calculated jibe of 'intellectual apathy' hurled by Sir Norman Fowler, chairman of the Tory party, early in 1994. He let it be known that, after several months of seeming inactivity, he and Blair were preparing to take the initiative, in speeches and articles that would dispel any false impressions that the modernisers were resting on their laurels simply because Labour was enjoying a double-digit lead in the opinion polls. On 6 January, Brown published a dossier of election tax promises broken by more than 150 Tory MPs, part of his 'you can't trust the Tories on tax' campaign. Five days later, he produced evidence that direct taxes had risen since 1979, contradicting every Conservative tax pledge. Picking up John Major's ill-fated 'back to basics' theme, he said, 'If back to basics means anything, it means telling the truth. This is an act of hypocrisy, broken promises and deceit unrivalled in the history of taxation.'[32] He spelled out the message again in a leader-page article in *The Times* on 14 January, arguing that 'Tax is the cash nexus between people and government. Trust is therefore essential. The Tory deception is therefore betrayal of a central trust.' Finally that month, the clincher – from Stephen Dorrell, the financial secretary to the Treasury. He admitted in a written reply to Harriet Harman, shadow chief secretary in Brown's team, that a typical family would, from April, pay more in direct and indirect tax under Kenneth Clarke than under

The Brown family with John, Gordon and baby Andrew, autumn 1956. (above)

Gordon and John with their mother, 1954. (left)

John (far left), Gordon (2nd left) & Andrew (bottom) hold a charity sale in the garage of their parents home in Kirkcaldy, 1960. (below)

Gordon Brown celebrates his first election victory for the rectorship of Edinburgh University, 1972.

Gordon Brown the student politician standing for the Edinburgh University rectorship against industrialist Sir Fred Catherwood, November 1972.

With the Lord Provost of Edinburgh, Jack Kane.

University rectors meet at
The Old Quadrangle.

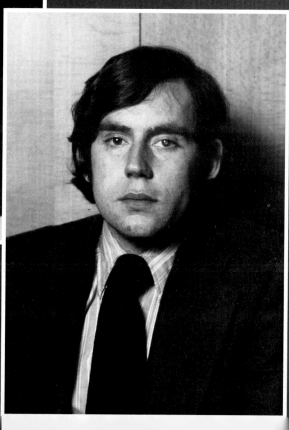

Gordon Brown with his
father after collecting his
PhD from Edinburgh
University, 1981.

Brown in 1977 when he
was elected Labour PPC
for South Edinburgh.

Partners in beating crime: Tony Blair and Gordon Brown at the launch of plans to involve young people in the fight against crime, May 1996.

Gordon Brown 'relaxing' on holiday in Cannes, South of France.

In Central Park, New York, with brother John. (left)

Triumvirate of power. Brown, John Prescott and Tony Blair meet in the Opposition leader's office in the run-up to the 1997 general election.

'Believe me . . .' Shadow Chancellor Gordon Brown explains the tough economic policies he will follow in government, Jan 1997.

Gordon Brown and Treasury team January 1997: including (from left) Sue Nye, Alastair Darling, Dawn Primarolo, Ed Miliband and Ed Balls.

Cover story: Gordon makes it to the front cover of the *Economist* in his first week as Chancellor of the Exchequer.

Pain at the top: Shadow Chancellor Brown keeps fit in a Westminster gym.

ELECTRONIC COMMERCE A survey after page 72

The Economist

MAY 10TH - 16TH 1997

The amazing Mr Brown

JACQUES SANTER ON BRITAIN
pages 40-41

THE COMING CRASH FOR CARS
pages 14 and 21-23

£2.20

A new style: Chancellor Brown wears a lounge suit to the Mansion House dinner in London in June 1997. The Lord Mayor, Roger Cork, wore traditional court dress, trimmed with ermine.

We are the masters now? Gordon Brown meets Bank of England governor Eddie George (right) and his assistants David Clement (left) and Mervyn King (far right).

Gordon Brown breakfasts with his Treasury team in Downing Street, Helen Liddell, Dawn Primarolo (right) and Geoffrey Robinson, on the day of the first Labour Budget for more than 18 years.

The picture that started the rumour of an engagement, Gordon Brown and girlfriend Sarah Macaulay in an Italian restaurant just before his 1997 Budget.

Chancellor's Press Secretary, Charlie Whela[...]

Whelan is caricatured as His Master's Voice durin[...] the row that preceded Labour's announcement stay out of the Europea[...] Single Currency, October 1997.

Labour's last chancellor, Denis Healey: 35 per cent of their income, against 32.2 per cent. Coming so soon after Clarke's dismissal of Brown's analysis as 'piffle', this was a bombshell. Harman commented, 'These figures destroy the Conservatives only political claim. Never again can they say they are the party of low taxation.'[33] Brown's new spin-doctor had a hand in the dissemination of this story, his first front-page coup. But the sedulous hard work that went into it was Brown's. Of the Treasury team, he was always first in in the morning, and always last home to his third-floor flat in Great Smith Street, Westminster.

The Tory 'wobble' that followed Dorrell's disclosure boosted Brown's standing. Commentators agreed that he had landed a heavy punch on the Tories and had made some headway in his campaign to establish a new trust on tax between the voters and Labour. Smith backed him up with an instruction to Shadow Cabinet members not to make random, unauthorised spending pledges that would undermine the party's new-found credibility on tax. Brown laid down the line clearly: 'There is no commitment to spend money on anything,' he said on Radio 4's *Today* programme on 26 January. 'We will only spend what we can afford to spend.' This was the first hint – not properly grasped at the time – that in government, he would not spend more than the outgoing chancellor. The policy was implemented rigorously. After a row between the shadow health secretary, David Blunkett, and Brown's team, a policy paper on the NHS was rewritten to remove pledges that Labour would restore funding cut by the Tories.

Labour's parliamentary left soon realised what was happening. Tony Benn and thirty-three other MPs signed a Commons early day motion demanding 'massive public investment,' but the fact that only just over 10 per cent of Labour backbenchers put their names to the motion indicated that Brown was winning the battle for hearts and minds in the parliamentary party. Or that they knew what had to be done if Labour was to win the election, which amounts to the same thing. They cheered the shadow chancellor's soundbite victory during Treasury questions on 3 February, when he said the only people who had benefited directly from fifteen years of Conservative rule were those on £64,000 or more a year. 'Isn't that the £64,000 question the Chancellor must answer?' he asked. He scored another hit with the Treasury's second damaging admission: that a typical family would pay £1,160 more in tax from April 1995. This real figure contrasted sharply with the Tories' bogus election claim that Labour would increase a family's tax bill by £1,000 a year.

In the propaganda war, at least, Brown was winning. Inside his own party, he was also making progress. On 20 February, he disclosed a further fundamental shift in policy, abandoning Labour's traditional commitment to state ownership. A 6,000-word policy paper, ponderously titled *Financing Infrastructure Investment*, drawn up with Shadow DTI Secretary Robin Cook and John Prescott at shadow employment, envisaged an ambitious programme of public–private partnerships extending even into schools and the NHS. The remaining state-owned undertakings would be turned into 'public interest companies' operating under the same financial regime as the private sector. Effectively, Clause IV, the Labour Party's constitutional commitment to nationalisation, which Neil Kinnock was openly demanding should be abolished, was now a dead letter. Brown was even more heretical. 'Historically,' he said, 'there has been a battle between public and private, as if it is a matter of territory. The real issue is how you can have private and public sectors working in the public interest.'[34]

Unfortunately, the leak of the policy document sparked a major row in Labour's high command. Prescott, reported to be 'spitting tacks', called off a press conference amid thinly veiled charges that Brown's aides did not understand the document. In the absence of an official Labour launch, the Tories stirred the pot, welcoming the paper as 'exactly the kind of thing we could have written'.

Undeterred, Brown pressed on with his unveiling of a new

University for Industry, modelled on the Open University established by the Wilson government thirty years previously. It would do for workplace education what the OU had done for tens of thousands at home. He also drew up plans for Labour to reduce VAT on domestic fuel to the European legal minimum of 5 per cent, from the 17.5 it was due to reach in 1995. The political outlook was good. His Treasury frontbench team – Harriet Harman, Alastair Darling, Andrew Smith and the one-time star of the left-wing Campaign Group of MPs, Dawn Primarolo – worked well together. Their suite of offices on the third floor at 7 Millbank, facing the Thames across the road from Westminster, was a powerhouse of activity. Brown did not allow strong signs of economic improvement – good news for the government – to cheer him up, in public at any rate. 'The recovery is not only weak and feeble but for millions of people, as the March unemployment figures show, there is no recovery at all,' he said.

Labour went into the April campaign for the spring local government elections in good heart. For the first time, opinion polls began showing that voters trusted Labour on tax, not the Conservatives. It was an astonishing breakthrough, and Brown crowed over his good fortune in the *Sunday Mirror*. 'The plain fact is that the Tories will NEVER be trusted on tax again,' he wrote. '"Open" John Major won the last election by telling lies. I want Labour to win the next election by telling the truth.' He published a Fabian Society pamphlet promising that fairness would be his guiding principle in government. 'We have unfairness in plenty, and precious little to show for it,' he said. 'The fairness we seek for reasons of social justice is also essential for economic growth and prosperity.'

Gordon Brown is not the kind of man of whom it is said that he is 'on a high'. His natural reserve precludes such talk. But he was clearly in good spirits, batting Kenneth Clarke around the field for publishing the minutes of his private meetings with the governor of the Bank of England. In January, the chancellor was saying in public that the recovery was robust, it was now plain that in private he was telling the governor it was feeble. 'How can this country ever trust you?' he taunted Clarke. He gleefully seized on a gaffe by Michael Portillo, the Treasury chief secretary, who publicly aired his ambition to succeed John Major. The government's Treasury team, Brown told a Labour Party youth meeting on 23 April, 'are no longer under Major's orders, but under starters' orders'. The government was in disarray. Labour had finally learned to live with financial discipline. Everything was going so well.

On the evening of 12 May, Brown attended a lavish fund-raising dinner at the Park Lane Hotel in London. His long-time mentor and friend, John Smith, was on sparkling form, cracking jokes and enjoying himself as if there was no tomorrow. Hours later, Smith was dead.

CHAPTER 9

DEATH OF A HERO

JOHN SMITH SUFFERED A MASSIVE HEART ATTACK IN THE bathroom of his flat in the Barbican, in the City of London, just after eight o'clock on the morning of Thursday, 12 May 1994. He was rushed to nearby Bart's Hospital, where doctors he had met only two weeks previously to campaign for their accident and emergency section fought to save his life. But the Labour leader was pronounced dead at 9.15 a.m. He was 55.

It was a devastating blow not just to his family and Gordon Brown, his protégé, and the Labour Party, but to British public life as a whole. There was a spontaneous outpouring of grief. Members of the public laid flowers outside party headquarters in Walworth Road, where staff cried and clung to each other for comfort. The Queen sent a message of sympathy to his widow, Elizabeth, and their three daughters. The Commons was suspended. The Conservatives halted their annual Scottish conference in Inverness, their chairman, Struan Stevenson, saying that 'a great dark cloud has descended over us'. Flags flew at half-mast all over Scotland. Neil Kinnock resorted to Shelley for the appropriate simile, describing his successor as the man who 'burst the icy chains of custom and shone, a day star of his age'. It was the most dismal of days.

Brown heard the tragic news from Murray Elder, his friend
from schooldays in Kirkcaldy, who was John Smith's chief-of-
staff. Brown then contacted Tony Blair on his mobile phone as
he disembarked at Dyce airport, Aberdeen, where he was to
campaign in the European parliamentary elections. Brown is
also said (by Blair's first biographer, Jon Sopel) to have been
contacted by a 'close personal friend' to ask if he had heard the
news. 'Yes', said Brown. 'What are you doing?' she went on.
'I'm thinking. I'm thinking,' he was quoted as replying.[1] They
were both thinking, furiously. In the midst of the shock and
grief the critical question had to be asked: who would succeed
Smith as leader? Just as much as nature, politics abhors a
vacuum.

Gordon Brown had long been seen as John Smith's natural
heir-apparent. He was cut from very similar cloth: a thoughtful, committed Scot with a sound base in the party and the
unions, but utterly dedicated to the cause of modernising
Labour. Brown's name was invariably linked with that of his
fellow-moderniser Tony Blair because they came into the
House at the same election, shared an office and often operated
together. They were both seen as rising stars in the Shadow
Cabinet and as potential leaders of the party. However, Brown
had always been thought of as the senior of the two – indeed,
that is how Blair himself viewed the relationship for many
years.

There were sound reasons for his deference. Blair was a rela-
tive latecomer to Labour. He had none of Brown's experience
of university politics or the Labour machine. Unlike Brown,
whose political instincts were stirred in his teens, Blair had
shown little interest in politics until he met his wife-to-be, the
lawyer Cherie Booth, who encouraged him to get involved. At
this stage, to be 'a party man' was vital. Brown was a party man,
with a real flair for knowing how to identify the levers of power
and the routes of advancement. He had burned the midnight
oil in committee rooms and trade-union seminars. He had
shaken hands with people with whom he had little or no

political affinity, but who could ease his way forward. In this context, Blair was less practised, and less trusted. He was seen as a creation of Labour's smart new image-makers, rather than a natural son of 'this great movement of ours'.

So close were the two that a secret pact existed between them, according to Brown's closest advisers. In the event of a leadership contest being called in the tragic circumstances now facing the party, they would not split the modernising vote by running against each other. Gordon Brown would be the candidate. That was the understanding. It was based on a recognition of Brown's fitness to succeed, as well as on hard calculation of the support each could hope to gain in Labour's reconstituted electoral college.

It was a proper assessment. The party's traditionalists were far from throwing in the towel. They had lost the one member, one vote battle at the 1993 conference by only a whisker, and the wearying experience of that drawn-out conflict had virtually persuaded John Smith that the modernisation process should be put on hold. He had privately threatened to union leaders he would resign if he lost, and he could not deploy this ultimate deterrent every year. Margaret Beckett, the deputy leader, who now took over as acting leader, had been noticeably lukewarm about the whole modernisation project. She was certain to stand for the leadership, and could expect the backing of left-wing unions like the powerful TGWU. On these grounds – that it was the right and proper thing to do, and that it would command wide support in the party and the unions – Brown was the man to succeed.

But few things are as they should be in politics, and the sequence of events that now unfolded could have come straight out of a Michael Dobbs novel. As Blair's car sped down the Great Northern Road in Aberdeen, his thoughts were elsewhere, with his family, and with his future. As he admitted later, 'What was so awful was that however much you were grieving for John, the plain fact is that within minutes everyone was saying: "Who's going to be the next leader?" I was sitting in the car having heard the news, thinking: "This is going to move to me very quickly." I felt terrible about John. At first I just knew that he'd had a heart attack. I didn't actually know he'd died until about an hour later.'[2] He carried out his Euro-election engagement, caught the next plane back to London and went home to meet Cherie in Islington. She told him, 'You didn't ask for this, you didn't plan it. But it's here, and you've got to do it.' Soon after, she urged, 'You'll never be happy again if you don't do it.'[3]

This version is a 'myth spun into profile-writers' fact', according to a rival interpretation of events said to originate with Peter Mandelson. In the *Spectator* three years later, the journal's deputy editor, Anne McElvoy, known for her private contacts with Mandelson, insisted, 'In fact he [Blair] had always intended to fight Brown.'[4]

He was certainly off the starting block in a hurry. He drew back from forming a campaign team that day – though a capable group headed by Shadow Cabinet minister Mo Mowlam had already offered their services – but he did signal to David Blunkett, then the Labour Party chairman, that he would run for the leadership. Blunkett, who under party rules was in charge of the election, told Blair the job was his if he went for it. 'But you've got to make your mind up now.' Blair responded, 'Yes, I suppose I have.'[5] Chris Smith, the culture secretary in Blair's first Cabinet was under no illusions: 'There was never any doubt in his mind that he had to be the candidate. And what Gordon decided about whether he was or wasn't going to stand was irrelevant.'[6] His use of words is interesting. It was assumed that the party's modernisers would not split their vote by fielding more than one standard-bearer. The process of reform within the party may have been well advanced, but it was not irreversible.

Against this conspiratorial backdrop, Brown was behaving more like a grieving friend than an ambitious politician. He telephoned Charlie Whelan and Ed Balls with the news, swore them to secrecy (not all Smith's family knew the awful truth

yet) and summoned them to his Millbank office. His aides were
not exactly in prime condition. They had attended Labour's
glitzy fund-raising dinner the night before, and then gone on
to Sue Nye's flat for more champagne, getting home at 5 a.m.
By the time they got to Millbank, the word was already spread-
ing. Journalists harried them, asking, 'Is he dead? Is he dead?'
They left for Brown's flat in Great Smith Street.

There, Brown wrote for the next day's *Daily Mirror* a deeply
felt tribute to the 'great leader' Labour had lost.

> The shock we felt when the news came through was sud-
> den and profound. Now, as it sinks in, a terrible sense of
> loss is added.
>
> I was at the dinner John Smith hosted and addressed on
> Wednesday night. He was at his best. Hospitable, witty
> and, in what was to be his last-ever speech, passionate
> about his beliefs. He took a large view, dealing with mat-
> ters of principle that had concerned him all his political
> life – education, our political values and the future of
> Britain's economy.
>
> I remember the first time I met John Smith after he had
> become a Cabinet minister in 1978. He was modest,
> approachable and as interested in listening as talking. I
> know now he was always like that.
>
> John never forgot his roots in Ardishaig and the values
> he learned there. He treated everyone as his equal because
> he believed everyone was equal. And on the solid rock of
> his belief he lived his whole political life. He was driven by
> his sense of what had to be done. He had enormous talent
> for both law and politics, but he sacrificed the opportuni-
> ties of a glittering legal career because he put service to
> others first . . .
>
> His fearless sense of duty drove him on. He was never
> afraid. To the end and at the height of his political career
> he remained what he always was, an essentially humble
> man from a small town in the West of Scotland. His

talents took him to the brink of leading a government of which we could all be proud.

All his life he was a committed Christian. He was an elder of the kirk to which he went regularly to worship. Like [those of] so many Scottish socialists before him, his politics were shaped more by kirk and community than by ideological theories.

He was a good man, and, unlike some good men, he was also good company. He was fortunate in his friends and blessed in his family life. The strength of his marriage was there for all to see – John and Elizabeth walking hand in hand to Wednesday night's dinner. Elizabeth and their three daughters must face a dreadful loss. We all mourn with them.

He leaves a legacy of duty done and an aching sense of what might have been.

Brown was 'shattered', recalled Whelan. 'He only seemed interested in writing obituaries. We spent the whole day doing that. He didn't feel up to doing any interviews. Everybody was asking "Where's Gordon Brown?" But he wanted to calm himself, collect his thoughts. He wanted to write things down, rather than speak. We didn't have any clue while this was going on that people were plotting for the leadership. It didn't register at that stage.'[7]

This may sound naïve, and in some respects it was. Brown's aides were newcomers to the hothouse of Westminster politics. Gordon knew how events would unfold. He alerted his staff to watch the Sunday papers and Peter Mandelson. He was aware, from a steady flow of information from an aide in Blair's office that 'the succession' was already a constant topic of gossip and intrigue. Blair's people thought their man was ahead. They said that Brown had 'lost his place'. It was also clear that Alistair Campbell, assistant editor of the now-defunct *Today* newspaper and confidant of Neil Kinnock, was jockeying for position. Sidelined under John Smith, he was nevertheless regularly to be seen in Blair's Commons office, briefing him on the state of play inside John Major's government. In return, he was kept informed of developments in the Labour leadership. On the night of Smith's death, Campbell went on *Newsnight* on BBC TV to air his view that 'it will probably be Blair'. And another Blairite media figure, Sarah Baxter, fashionable ex-political editor of the *New Statesman* piped up in the London *Evening Standard* on the theme of 'why it should be Tony'. 'They didn't leave much to chance,' said one Brown staffer sourly.

Amid the sorrow, the succession battle began. Within two hours of Smith's death, traditionalist MPs were plotting at Westminster to avert the inheritance of Brown – or Blair. At about the same time, the lunchtime edition of the London *Evening Standard* was already weighing up the prospects of the front-runners. The paper described 'wily Brown' as 'among the most serious challengers', citing the wide variety of Shadow Cabinet posts he had filled, his experience and his power base in the party. However, even at this early stage Blair was named as 'the heir apparent – the man most likely to succeed against the Tories'.[8]

This might reasonably be described as wish-fulfilment journalism. The article was by Charles Reiss, a former Labour Party insider, who two years previously had written a feature on 'the coming war between Gordon Brown and Tony Blair', in which he said: 'We know and they must know that this happy friendship cannot last. By the very nature of politics, they are going to become deadly rivals . . . No matter how much they may say they wish to remain friends and work together, only one of them can make it to the top – at the expense of the other.' The 'build-up to the fight', he had argued, had already begun.[9]

The theme was picked up the following morning. *The Times* devoted three inside pages to John Smith's life and tragic death. Its second lead on page one reported that Tony Blair had emerged as favourite to succeed, but immediately qualified this judgment with the observation that Blair and Brown 'face the most difficult decisions of their lives', clearly indicating that it was not a foregone conclusion. Labour MPs were said to be wondering aloud whether the unspoken pact between the pair would hold. 'The prize is so great that each may genuinely believe he has the better chance of winning.'[10] In the *Independent*, Donald McIntyre wrote that there were 'strong signs' that Blair and Brown would not both stand, though they had not yet decided which one would. These rapid assessments were not plucked from thin air. Tory MPs – unnamed, naturally – were happy to be quoted as saying that Blair was the man of whom they were most frightened. More serious was the comment by Lord (Denis) Healey, a former deputy leader and the man widely regarded as the best prime minister Labour never had, that Blair should become leader, with John Prescott as his deputy. That idea drew a rebuke from David Blunkett, Labour health spokesman, but it struck a chord in the Westminster lobbies, and appealed to some prominent backbenchers on the Tribunite left who were restive at the prospect of a Brown leadership, claimed the *Independent*.

Clearly, the briefers were already at work, chief among them being Peter Mandelson. Although initially closer to Brown he had discreetly gravitated to Blair, the man most likely to advance his ill-concealed ambition. On 15 May, the *Sunday Times* led its front page with the story of a 'secret pact' between Blair and Brown that they would not stand against each other. It was written by Andrew Grice, the paper's quiet-spoken political editor, who was known to be particularly close to Mandelson. The clear inference was that Brown would stand down. His suspicion that the Sunday press and Mandelson would break cover first had been confirmed within three days, despite the official party moratorium on campaigning. Mandelson had trailed his move in an appearance on Channel Four television's *A Week in Politics* on Saturday night, when he said that, before putting themselves forward, contenders had to consider 'who will play best at the box office, not simply appeal to the traditional supporters and customers of the Labour

Party'. This was a shaft aimed directly at the heart of Brown's leadership hopes. Mandelson then asked, 'Who would fully maximise support for the party in the country?' He did not need to answer his rhetorical question to get the message across. He must have been aware of the result of three opinion polls carried out by ICM for the *Sunday Express*, by Gallup for the *Sunday Telegraph* and by MORI for the *Sunday Times*. All made Blair the public's favourite to succeed John Smith, and he enjoyed a lead of between eleven and fifteen points over John Prescott and Gordon Brown.

At this critical stage, Mandelson showed his hand to Brown, in a personal letter that superficially offered him support but was plainly freighted with subversive intent. He argued that if Brown stood for the leadership against Blair, it would inevitably damage Labour and Gordon would be blamed for splitting the party. Nonetheless, Mandelson offered to front Brown's campaign should he decide to run, but the offer was a cleverly-worded invitation to stand aside for Blair. It was a well-crafted letter. It also gave the game away. Understandably, Brown did not reply.

Mandelson's not-very-discreet activity angered some Labour MPs, who felt it was an insult to John Smith's memory. Brown came under swift pressure not to stand down, to keep his options open. His close ally Nick Brown, MP for Newcastle East, wanted him to stand, as did a number of other MPs who made clear their support. They queued up to tell the Scottish edition of the *Sunday Times* that his claims on the leadership could not be overlooked. The ban on electioneering compelled them to request anonymity. One west Scotland MP argued, 'There is a lot of support for Gordon. People believe he is authentically Labour, a suitable successor to John with a similarly impressive intellect and the kind of gravitas needed for a party leader. I have also to say there has been a slight backlash against the prominence of Tony Blair so quickly in the race.' Another Scots MP said, 'Gordon naturally wants to canvass support in order to gauge his position. Although I don't think

Gordon Brown

Gordon and Tony would stand against each other, whoever stands aside would lessen his chances of becoming party leader in the long run. It's only fair he should have the opportunity to test the water.' Backing also came from his constituency agent, David Stoddart, and many other members of his local party.

There were countervailing pressures, almost racist in nature, and certainly anti-Scot. Peter Shore MP, a veteran former Labour cabinet minister, had a few months previously provoked controversy by arguing that Scots were 'over-represented' in the party's high command, particularly in the Shadow Cabinet. The so-called 'McMafia' was held partly responsible for Labour's poor showing in England, particularly the prosperous south. English MPs rallied to Shore's support, and the argument played into the hands of Blair – a Scot by descent, who attended Fettes public school in Edinburgh, but was now an 'adopted son' of County Durham, where his lawyer father had made his home. A Scots academic, Dr Jack Brand, of Strathclyde University Politics Department, weighed in with a prediction that the new leader would have to be popular in England. 'Smith wasn't aggressively Scottish, but it did seem difficult for him to understand what people in the south-east have been through in the last couple of years. Scotland has been Labour's stronghold,' he said. 'There will be a new emphasis if Tony Blair wins.'[11]

The pressure continued into the week of John Smith's funeral. Brown's brothers, Andrew and John, urged him to stand, as did more members of the parliamentary party. The common message was: 'You have to let it be known that you are going to stand so we can get down to business. Blair has made it absolutely clear he will stand.' Still he hesitated, while his supporters begged him to give a clear indication of his intentions. A 'shadow' campaign team was taking shape. Nick Brown, shadow deputy Leader of the House (later to become Blair's chief whip), was the boss. Other MPs ready to serve included Andrew Smith, MP for Oxford East and a member of Brown's shadow Treasury team; Nigel Griffiths, a frontbench spokesman on trade and MP for Edinburgh South; and Eric Clarke, MP for Midlothian and former general secretary of the Scottish miners' union, by now a Labour whip. It was a formidable group. They would have given Blair a serious run for his money, and he knew it.

To a degree, Brown's 'dithering' unnerved Blair. Was it a sign that his campaign was under way, sotto voce? The pair met several times at Westminster before Smith's funeral at Cluny church, in south Edinburgh on Friday 27 May, and they spoke on the phone 'permanently', but the widely predicted pact did not emerge.

Instead, Brown let it be known that he would use the opportunity of a long-arranged appearance at the Welsh Labour Party annual conference in Swansea during the coming weekend to make a major speech. The media immediately assumed that the gloves were now off. *The Times* said the shadow chancellor 'will inevitably be seen as firing the first shots in the campaign', despite denials from his camp that he was making a leadership speech. Blair had also been invited to the conference, but he pulled out – officially because of other engagements. The ubiquitous 'friends' said the shadow home secretary was staying away because he did not want to set up a media 'circus' of competing potential leaders. However, in private, he also asked Brown not to speak either. Brown demurred, and took his speech-writers up to Edinburgh with him. 'All the people who went up to work on the Wales speech didn't think we were writing an "I'm pulling out of the race" speech,' said one speech-writer. 'It was written more as an "I'm running" or "I'm a formidable figure" speech.'

In the days before Smith's funeral, tempers became frayed. Nigel Griffiths, Brown's most loyal supporter but possessed of an excitable nature, could not suppress his irritation that Mandelson was canvassing for Blair. He aired his wrath in the *Evening Standard*, claiming that Labour MPs were upset by Mandelson's tactics. Brown went ballistic, and ordered Griffiths to apologise. He did so, but the incident exposed tensions bubbling just beneath the surface. Brown attended an emotion-charged Shadow Cabinet meeting with Blair, before travelling up to Edinburgh on the eve of the funeral.

At his home in North Queensferry, Brown held a strategy meeting with his closest advisers. Ostensibly, it was one of those barnstorming sessions that always precede one of his major speeches. Balls attended, with Andrew Brown and Dr Colin Currie, a consultant in geriatric medicine who had got to know Brown in his student journalism days. Currie, also a successful writer of thrillers under the pen-name Colin Douglas, describes the business of speech-writing with Brown as 'an intellectual wrestling match, going at the problem until the problem becomes clearer. That's fun.'[12]

There wasn't much amusement on that evening. They worked into the early hours, discussing how to play what was becoming an increasingly difficult hand. Brown did not agree that the Blair bandwagon was unstoppable. He would not throw in the towel. If he pulled out of the contest, he would have to do so from a position of strength, not weakness: for his own sake certainly, but also for the sake of those who saw in him a political dimension that distinguished him from Blair, a commitment to fairness and democratic socialism derived from a life in the Labour Party. Blair was quintessentially the candidate of the 'London establishment', of which Brown had never been – and never wished to be – a part. The Swansea speech that emerged from this exhausting session was to be Brown's personal political credo.

On the day of the funeral, 27 May, with the blue and white saltire of Scotland flying everywhere at half-mast, they paid tribute to John Smith's life in the Victorian gothic kirk at Cluny where he had worshipped. Blair and Brown entered the church five ranks apart. James Gordon, now Lord Gordon, a fellow-student of Smith at Glasgow University and now managing director of Radio Clyde, delivered the eulogy, arguing that the late party leader was 'one of us, not one of them'. Donald Dewar, the shadow Scottish secretary, agreed that 'the people

have lost a friend, someone who was on their side'. John Smith
had wanted high office 'not for himself, but for what it would
enable him to do for others.' Much the same theme ran
through Brown's obituaries of his mentor. Alexander 'Derry'
Irvine, a Labour peer and close friend of Smith since the late
1950s and also the head of Blair's legal chamber, paid tribute to
'a Labour party family man'. Lord Irvine of Lairg, lord chancellor in Blair's first Cabinet, was discreetly backing another
'family man' for the leadership.

Blair and Brown met again after the funeral in a suburban
Edinburgh hotel on the road to the airport. Blair's line was
uncompromising: he was the one who could win – not just the
leadership election, but a general election, too. So many people
were urging him to stand that he could not step down. The
unarticulated, but clear, inference was that Gordon Brown
should be the one to withdraw. Blair returned to London, and
Brown to North Queensferry for further consultations with his
inner circle. A new blow added to the pressure on Brown.
Because of the formal prohibition on campaigning until the 9
June European elections were over, the contest so far had been
played out in the media. The way that television and the newspapers behaved was critical. Overwhelmingly, the chattering,
metropolitan classes favoured Blair, and so did their newspapers, such as the *Independent*. Brown had the support of the
Glasgow *Herald*, Scotland's biggest-selling heavyweight broadsheet, but the Edinburgh-based *Scotsman* opted for the former
Fettes boy rather than the city's best-known former student
politician. The newspaper ran a poll of Scots Labour MPs, con-
tacting all but six of the forty-eight. The results were published
on 27 May. Fifteen MPs said they would back Brown if he
stood. Only six said they would back Blair in any circumstances. Six others said that although they felt a 'personal oblig-
ation' to support Brown, they hoped he would stand down and
back Blair. Furthermore, several MPs declared they would not
be urging Brown to enter the contest because they believed that
the 'charismatic' Blair was more likely to win a general election.

Although Brown had the backing of far more MPs – 21 out of the 42 polled – than Blair, who had only six from commitments, the story was written as a setback for the shadow chancellor, 'proving' that he did not even have the support of a majority of Scots MPs.

Charlie Whelan, who is himself not averse to guiding the facts, was livid at the 'spin' put on the poll, but the damage had been done. Some MPs later said that they had not been approached, and those close to Brown thought they detected the hand of Peter Mandelson in the operation, which was part of a strategy to neutralise the Scottish support that the shadow chancellor might have got. His elder brother John disclosed that 'Gordon said to me that was the finish. It was the key issue in coming to a conclusion, that poll in the *Scotsman*.'[13]

Then came a further complication. On Saturday, 28 May, Margaret Beckett, the acting leader of the party, signalled that she was preparing to stand in the contest. Speaking at the Communication Workers' Union conference in Bournemouth, she made an impassioned plea to the party to remain true 'to John Smith's vision'. Mrs Beckett had already called for an election for her existing post of deputy leader, and it was clear she envisaged a double poll: for leader and deputy leader. She would stand as the candidate of unity and continuity, and she could almost certainly count on the votes of the left-wing unions – including Brown's own, the TGWU. Her intervention made the task of assembling the right coalition of support for Brown practically insuperable.

The Brown team talked throughout Saturday at his North Queensferry home. Whelan fielded dozens of queries about the shadow chancellor's intentions. Some media outlets said that Mandelson was still claiming to speak for Gordon. An infuriated Whelan shouted down his portable phone, 'I'm speaking for Gordon! I'm right here in his house!' He talked up Brown's prospects of staying in the race, building up speculation in the Sunday papers that a leadership bid could not be ruled out. Adrian Lithgow, the hard-nosed political editor of the *Mail on Sunday*, was happy to run with the idea. 'Brown set to take on Blair' was the headline on his story, which predicted that Brown had 'reconsidered' his position, and would signal his entry into the race by quoting party icon Nye Bevan on 'the passion for unity'. The story also quoted an unnamed senior Labour MP who said, 'To stop Gordon standing you'd have to put him in a straitjacket with twenty people sitting on it.'

On Sunday, 29 May, Brown flew to Birmingham, and travelled to Swansea by car. Sheena Macdonald, the television presenter and sometime girl-friend, was on the plane. His speech was a brilliantly crafted claim for the political succession to John Smith, but it was not an overt bid for the leadership, more a demand for recognition that he still carried the late leader's torch. 'The flame still burns, the work continues, the passion for justice endures and the vision will never fade: the vision of Labour in power' he said. The hour had come for Labour. 'For us now, more than ever before, this is the time to unite. Because we have travelled too far, too many miles together, for us to lose sight of our destination. Together we have climbed too high for us not to achieve the summit. Labour is the party that, itself united, is ready to unite this country.' He went on to outline policies for trade unionists, women, young people and pensioners. Labour's goal was 'full and fulfilling employment', a national minimum wage, equal rights for working women and social justice. Brown also pledged to implement a strategy for the coal industry, and promised wide-ranging reform of the welfare state to ensure it became 'not just a safety net against failure, but also a springboard for success'. He was rewarded with a standing ovation, and delegates talked freely about Brown's chances of winning votes from the trade unions and his prospects of uniting the party better than Tony Blair. Some, however, believed that Blair was more likely to win a general election, and achieve the summit of which Brown spoke so lyrically. *The Times* thought it was an attempt to test the waters, but predicted that the weight of support building up for Blair within the Labour leadership would prompt the shadow chancellor to step down 'over the next three weeks'.

In fact, the big decision was much closer. Commentators have always assumed that Brown made up his mind not to run over dinner with Tony Blair in Granita's, an upmarket restaurant in trendy Islington on the night of 31 May. Not so. It was agreed with his closest associates the night before, at an altogether more brash and entertaining basement restaurant in Covent Garden, Joe Allen's, in Exeter Street, haunt of the theatrical set. Brown called together his shadow campaign team for the last time to put together the terms on which he would withdraw from the contest. Around the table at this 'Last Supper' were the shadow chancellor, Murray Elder, his friend since nursery-school days and ally in the long march through the Scottish Labour Party; Nick Brown MP, his most loyal fixer and Margaret Beckett's deputy; and Charlie Whelan, the public-relations man least likely to use PR language.

They considered Brown's position at length. Speculation has raged ever since the 'Last Supper', but the full truth is divulged for the first time here. Privately, Brown's friends believe Blair let him down, and there can be little doubt that they represent his feelings accurately. Blair had repeatedly promised Brown he would not stand against him in a future leadership election.

Indeed, while Brown revolutionised Labour's economic policy-making, taking the flak from the press, he had relied on Blair and his supporters to defend him with the London media establishment. Brown spent little or no time in London at weekends, and had a great deal of disdain for the weekend party circuit that took in the Alastair Campbells, the Harriet Harmans, the Peter Mandelsons, the Tony Blairs and some journalists from the *Guardian*, the *Independent* and a few other papers. Instead of Blair's supporters defending him, he found them promoting their man at Brown's expense.

Brown genuinely believed – and still believes – he could have won the leadership. But he knew that because of Blair's position as early runner, he would have to take Blair head-on, something he did not want to do. His alliance against Blair would have included not only Scots MPs – from the right, Donald Dewar, George Robertson and Alastair Darling, all supporting him across to the left, made up of John McAllion, Jimmy Wray, Ernie Ross and Jimmy Hood. Even the 'biased' *Scotsman* poll found 21 out of 42 MPs north of the border supported him, while only six backed Blair. His support also went across the centre and left of the Parliamentary Labour Party in England and Wales as well.

Nick Brown told the 'Last Supper' that Brown would win if he was prepared to stand. He had a list of 120 supportive MPs, and he believed that would just be the starting point. There were more to be harvested. Other influential figures agreed that as soon as the 'upper class, public school educated' Blair came under serious fire from Brown's more conventional Labour credentials, then he would be in trouble. Brown's dilemma was that he knew *how* to defeat Blair, but he did not want to damage him.

Brown has always refused to say much, if anything, about the leadership race. But he did break his silence to tell me: 'The newspapers, with a few notable exceptions, did not back me – not least because I was out of fashion. I was never part of the London scene anyway. But that did not in my view mean much, once the campaign started among ordinary Labour Party members and indeed backbench MPs.'

So, for Brown, the decision was not based on calculating whether he could win – he always believed he could – but to accept that winning would mean damaging an indispensable ally in Labour's revival: Tony Blair. Brown felt that an increasingly edgy contest between him and Blair would harm both, and the modernisation process that they were leading. The press would argue that if the two could not agree among themselves, what chance would there be of the party ever uniting properly?

Accordingly, Brown was reluctant to begin even the softest press campaign against Blair. No such considerations, Brown was aware, motivated Blair's top advisers, including Mandelson and Alastair Campbell who were briefing heavily and continuously against Brown. And it would have been a dirty war. Some anti-Brown campaigners were insinuating allegations about his private life. They also completely distorted Blair's previous promise to Brown that he would not stand against him.

In the end, Brown felt he had to make a choice between his owner leadership claims and the needs of the party. A damaging contest would help no one. He would support Tony Blair. There was no overt 'deal' between the two, only a recognition on Brown's part that while he could win, the contest would damage Labour's chances for the future.

However, his own position would be consolidated. Gordon Brown would remain shadow chancellor, and be the real thing in a Blair administration. He would have full charge of economic policy and a powerful influence across the range of social policy. A joint policy statement would be agreed by Blair and Brown, acknowledging that the latter would be the driving force on the economic side, with full approval for his 'fairness agenda' broadening employment opportunities and improving training schools as the centrepiece of Labour's social and economic programme.

Even before the Joe Allen's 'Last Supper', Brown had hinted that he would not stand in Blair's way. On BBC Radio on Bank Holiday Monday, he insisted, 'I will make my decision, as I believe my colleagues will make the decision, on what is necessary for Labour to win the next election. I don't think anybody's personal interests should come before what is the greatest public endeavour that the Labour Party is engaged in – that is, to return a government to power that is interested in creating the economic efficiency and social justice that this country needs.' Nick Brown was feeding to political correspondents 'private soundings' suggesting that support for Blair and Brown in the parliamentary party was evenly balanced. Each was said to have the support of about six members of the Shadow Cabinet, and each had the backing of about eighty MPs. Opinion among trade-union leaders was also evenly divided, while the constituencies, with one-third of the electoral college that would eventually decide the winner, favoured Blair.

Brown agreed to have dinner with Blair at Granita's at 8 p.m. on Tuesday, 31 May. For a man about to give away, perhaps for ever, his chance to become prime minister, his sang-froid was admirable. Brown, Whelan and Balls sat drinking in the Atrium, a marble-floors-and-potted-palms restaurant in the basement of 4 Millbank, home of the BBC Westminster staff, until 7.50 p.m. Then Brown and Balls took a black cab up to Islington, several miles away, through heavy London traffic. Anji Hunter, Blair's secretary, paged Balls anxiously. 'Where's Gordon?' she asked. 'You won't be late, will you?' They were. Neither of them had ever been to Granita's before; it was not exactly Brown territory. The cab cruised up and down looking for the sign, 'but it was so trendy it didn't have one', remarked an aide. When they finally found it Blair was already there, seated alone at the back, looking a little nervous. He had not expected to see Balls. Gordon said, 'What about a drink?' That broke the ice. They all had drinks, and called for the menu. Brown wasn't impressed with the minimalist food on offer, being more of a prawn-cocktail and steak man than a fan of char-grilled aubergines and polenta. They made small political talk, chiefly about the European elections. 'It was all a bit tense,' says Balls.

The uneasy calm was shattered by the arrival, unannounced, of a young woman journalist, Allison Pearson. According to Balls, 'She came over and shook hands.' Pearson remembers the scene differently. Writing in the *Telegraph Magazine* two years later, she recollected introducing herself to Blair – whom she did not know – and 'stammering condolences' about the death of John Smith. 'At that moment, a familiar dark, burly figure approached the table. "Allison, do you know Gordon," asked Blair. No, I did not know Gordon Brown. But I knew enough about the state of the Labour leadership campaign to beat a blushing retreat. How could I make small talk with Muhammed Ali while George Forman was stepping into the ring?'[14] It matters little whose memory is better, for Pearson seems to have eased the tension. Blair became casual and friendly, his body language saying, 'This is just us having dinner.' For Brown, it was a serious piece of business: he was desperate to get it over and get out. Balls left after the first course. The shadow chancellor ate little more, and, having made clear the price of his withdrawal from the contest, went back to Rodin's restaurant in the Atrium, arriving there about 10 p.m. – for dinner with his chums. They went back to his flat for 'celebratory' champagne until 3 a.m. The party was a bit gloomy, but they all felt that 'a great weight' had been lifted off their shoulders.

All that remained was to tell the world, and put on a good face. Brown travelled up to Nottingham on 1 June to carry out an engagement in the European election campaign, taking Balls with him. It was just as well that they had three mobile telephones, because the news of Brown's self-sacrificing gesture got out during the morning. He handled dozens of calls, some from bewildered members of his constituency party asking why he had stood down, and begging him to reconsider. When the pair arrived back at St Pancras station, there were television crews and photographers on the platform, and Brown knew he had to go public.

Shortly after 3 p.m. on 1 June, a fax went out from Brown's Westminster office 'For immediate release' to all media outlets. It read:

> As I said in speeches in Wales ten days ago and in Luton on Sunday, the Labour leadership election should be conducted with one consideration and one consideration only in mind – to ensure the election of a Labour government to improve and regenerate our country.
>
> There should be no confusion in the public's mind about our utter determination to achieve this objective. And nothing must be a diversion from the unity and the team work necessary to do so.

> While I had planned to wait until after June 9 before announcing the decision I had made, I now believe that the speculation and confusion about my position should be swiftly brought to an end so we can concentrate on victory in the European Election campaign.
>
> When nominations open on June 10 I will encourage Tony Blair to stand and if he should stand I will give him my full support to become not only the Labour Party's next leader but the next Prime Minister of our country.

The briefing note giving Brown wide responsibility for Labour's social and economic agenda was agreed with Blair's office, and the two friends, no longer rivals, then staged an amiable walk round New Palace Yard, the cobblestoned square below Big Ben with a fountain, trees and a severely trimmed pergola. They chatted for the television cameras, and posed again on the balcony of 1 Parliament Street, the modern office block built in traditionalist style where many MPs have their offices. Nobody was fooled by the smiles and the bonhomie. It was a day of doing one's duty to the party.

The tributes poured in, as though Brown had laid down his life for a friend. Neil Kinnock said on Channel Four News that 'this is the bravest act of any politician'. Donald Dewar accepted that the decision would disappoint friends in Parliament and in the country, adding, 'But it has been taken in the best interests of the party. It enhances his position and his stature.' The *Daily Mirror* effused, 'Gordon Brown will be a key player in the new Shadow Cabinet and in the next Labour government. He deserves no less. Greater loyalty hath no man than to lay down his ambitions for his party.'[15] Brown squirmed at the gushing nature of some of the coverage of his unselfish act, writing in the *Mirror* that 'Nothing was to be gained by me standing against my friend Tony Blair.' He was comforted by a letter from James Callaghan, urging him not to worry. 'I was 65 before I became party leader,' pointed out the former prime minister.

Brown quit London that night for yet another Euro-election round of campaigning in the north-west of England. He then returned to Scotland to muse on what might have been, and what might now be done. With Brown's campaign-that-never-was out of the way, Blair had a easy run. When nominations closed after the Euro-poll – which went hugely well for Labour – John Prescott and Margaret Beckett had entered the lists for leader and deputy leader. There was never any doubt that Blair would win, and on 21 July his victory was proclaimed at Westminster Central Hall. Blair won all three sections of the electoral college, taking 57 per cent of the total votes cast, with Prescott on 24 per cent and Beckett on just under 19 per cent. She went on to lose the deputy leadership to Prescott, and with it her ex-officio seats in the Shadow Cabinet and the NEC. She had not lost the powerful support of Gordon Brown, however. Brown greeted the result warmly. 'It's not just a new beginning for the Labour Party but a fresh start for Britain,' he declared.

CHAPTER 10

A NEW TREASURY

TONY BLAIR'S VICTORY, AND THE DECISIVE POLITICAL SHIFT it represented, threw John Major's government into complete confusion. Ministers could not decide whether to argue that Blair had no policies, or that his policies were really bad 'old Labour' ones that would plunge Britain back into a socialist nightmare. Kenneth Clarke emerged as the least muddle-headed. He warned fellow members of the Cabinet that New Labour's appeal to middle-class voters was potentially fatal for the Conservatives. A Gallup poll for the *Sunday Telegraph* of 24 July underscored his point: Major was rated by only 23 per cent of respondents as the best choice for prime minister, with Blair on 61 per cent. Voters put Labour ahead on every area of policy – including tax, where Gordon Brown's long march to reality was now producing results. Fifty-five per cent of voters thought Labour had better tax policies.

Brown's theme, hammered home at every opportunity, was 'fairness'. Shortly before John Smith's death, he had written a pamphlet, *Fair is Efficient*, in which he challenged the idea that the role of government was simply to compensate people for poverty. This was not enough. Poverty had to be tackled at source, by equipping people with better skills, and by reforming the welfare state. He embraced the idea of loans for students in higher education. His 'fairness agenda' was an intellectual advance in Labour thinking, but, appearing the week before the leader died, it 'got lost'. However, the theme was revived in Blair's leadership manifesto, which Brown helped to draft. His ideas were also floated in Labour's Economic Commission, a talking-shop or a useful policy forum depending on one's political point of view.

In late August 1994, when most ministers and members of the Shadow Cabinet were still on holiday, the shadow chancellor used an appearance on BBC TV's *Breakfast with Frost* to set out his stall. Labour's election campaign strategy, he promised, would be based on an appeal for fairness over taxation, the welfare state, employment and issues such as bank charges. 'Fairness will be the theme, indeed the agenda, of a Tony Blair administration. What people want in this country is a restoration of a sense of fair play and fair dealing. It's something that has gone missing,' he argued. Behind this simple message lay much hard work and thought: during the previous weeks, Brown, Ed Balls and Ed Miliband, a bright young member of the team, had put in long hours to get the words right. Brown recalled Blair's leadership acceptance speech the month before, in which he had talked of the need for a new political language of 'social justice, of what is just and what is unjust, fair and unfair, right and wrong'. He expanded on this idea. 'People want to see social cohesion. That's why Tony Blair's theme about rebuilding Britain as a community has struck a chord right across British society.'

The shadow chancellor refused to be drawn on the awkward question of just how far 'fairness' would require redistribution of wealth, and avoided committing Labour to outdoing the Conservatives by cutting income tax to 15p in the pound – though his mind was working on these lines. Tax rates as low as 10p in the pound could work, it was thought. Brown simply pounded home at his message of fairness. 'The issue at the next election will be between fair taxation under Labour and unfair taxation under the Conservatives.' VAT on domestic fuel was one example. He would relaunch Labour's campaign to prevent the second-stage rise in tax on gas and electricity to 17.5 per cent, due in the autumn budget.

In the meantime, Brown had to clear up a little matter of unfairness in his party. In late August, the newspapers carried reports that 'pressure' was coming from unnamed Shadow Cabinet ministers and members of Labour's NEC for Brown to be dropped as shadow chancellor, to be replaced by Robin Cook, the ambitious shadow trade secretary. Cook had made no secret of his wish to take over the Treasury brief; he had hoped for it when John Smith became leader. The whispering campaign began again. Cook was having a good summer, impaling Lord Archer, a Tory peer close to John Major, on his admission of 'grave error' in making a handsome profit on shares in Anglia TV shortly before a takeover bid. Archer's wife, Mary, was a non-executive director of Anglia, but she denied passing inside information to her husband. The mini-scandal ran for several weeks before running into the sands.

Now, 'senior members' of the party were said to be looking for changes at the top when Tony Blair reshuffled his minister- ial team in October. The 'pressure' for promoting Cook came not only from 'Shadow Cabinet colleagues' – assumed to be Deputy Leader John Prescott, who shared Cook's estimate of his economic grasp – but also from the NEC, 'including the trade unions'. Prescott had not forgiven Brown for nominating Margaret Beckett for the deputy leadership four months previ- ously. He also had an inordinate desire to get his hands on the levers of economic power, and Brown was equally determined that he should never do so. Among the unions, John Edmonds, general secretary of the GMB, who fancied himself as a mover and shaker in the party, was suspected of being one of the chief whisperers. He had long been urging a massive increase in state spending to attack unemployment. The *Independent* reported that Labour's left believed Brown was 'too cautious', adding: 'They want more radical plans to tax the rich and spend more on measures to create employment and alleviate poverty.'[1] Brown shared their objectives, but not their means to achieve them. Blair was unequivocal: Brown must stay. They had a deal, and it would stick.

Events began to go the shadow chancellor's way. The government was forced to put up interest rates, and Brown insisted this was 'our big moment'. On the telephone from France where he was on holiday in the first week of September, Brown instructed Ed Balls to go on the offensive on the economy. Balls attended discussions in Blair's office on how Labour should shape its reaction. 'We realised this was an opportunity to break out of the old caricature. In the past, if interest rates went up we complained, and if they went down we said they should have gone down more. This time we said, "This is the right thing to do. It is right for them to increase interest rates. But what an indictment that they have raised them so early in the economic cycle. The reason is that the economy is unable to sustain growth."'[2]

The aim was to demonstrate Labour's conversion to monetary rectitude. 'That was the moment when we showed we would be disciplined on the macro-economic front,' recollected Balls.[3] The policy was spelled out in an article by Blair for the *Financial Times*, which made damaging comparisons between Britain and the USA. These first signals of the revolution to come were to be firmed up in a mould-breaking speech by Brown some weeks later. This is characteristic of his style. For only too many politicians, making speeches is part of the furniture of the job, and it shows. Brown takes infinite pains with these set-piece orations, honing them for days before he is satisfied he is saying what he wants to say, and that it is pitched at the right audience.

The defining issue that now emerged was Clause IV of Labour's constitution, which central tenet of faith appeared on every membership card. First drafted by Sidney Webb, the leading Fabian, in 1918 and rewritten twice since, the political objective was spelled out thus: 'To secure for the workers by hand or by brain the full fruits of their industry and the most equitable distribution thereof that may be possible upon the basis of the common ownership of the means of production, ownership and exchange.' The danger words were 'common ownership', which implied a commitment to wholesale nationalisation of industry and services. Labour had not offered the voters any such promises since the disastrous election manifesto of 1983, and a Blair–Brown leadership would never do so. However, Clause IV was tantamount to the Holy Grail of socialism. In 1959, Hugh Gaitskell, Labour's revisionist leader, had tried to ditch it but was overwhelmed by traditionalists in all sections of the party. Even John Smith had shrunk from tampering with it. He had toyed with the idea of printing an expanded statement of aims alongside the sacred text, but his death supervened.

Blair and Brown were determined to grasp the nettle. At their Sedgefield meeting in April 1992 they had discussed abolition of Clause IV among the many modernisations they wanted to make. But it had slipped down the order of priorities in the battle over 'one member, one vote' that consumed Smith's first – and only – leadership year. It was now restored to priority number one. According to Sopel, Blair first disclosed his thinking on the issue to Gordon Brown before they both went off for their summer holidays. Brown shared his new leader's conviction that Clause IV misrepresented what Labour would do when in government, and therefore it should go. It must be a clean break, and they must take John Prescott with them. It was not enough for him to be a reluctant, late convert. He had to be fully on board from the outset, to avoid press speculation about splits in the leadership, and – worse – a concerted counter-attack by traditionalists. 'The vital thing,' said Brown, 'was to deter large numbers of people from hoisting the flag for Clause IV.'[4]

Blair and his shadow chancellor agreed that the nettle should be grasped at the first significant opportunity: the leader's speech at the Blackpool conference in early October, barely ten weeks after the 'coronation'. Nobody could say the new triumvirate of Blair, Prescott and Brown were playing for time. On holiday in France during August, the new leader hired Alastair Campbell, political columnist of the *Today* newspaper, and a secret campaign got under way to get rid of Labour's most hallowed piece of ideological baggage. Prescott was brought into the know only three weeks before the blitzkrieg was mounted at Blackpool, and, while initially reluctant, became a full partner in the enterprise.

In the run-up to conference, Brown set the stage for the advent of New Labour, making it clear that Labour was abandoning the 'old corporatism'. Speaking in East Lothian on 24 September, he described Labour as the true party of economic competence, which would 'redirect existing resources' in public spending, rather than increase expenditure. He was scathing about the Tories' record on spending. Far from achieving their pledge to reduce public expenditure to less than 40 per cent, they had kept it where they found it in 1979, at 44 per cent. Since national income had increased, this represented an extra £73 billion in cash terms. Blair followed up this opening salvo with a speech to a conference on 'New Policies for a Global Economy', three days later, promising that Labour would not spend what the country could not afford. It was unusual for the party's top brass to make such high-profile speeches so close to the annual conference, and those of a sceptical nature began to think that something big was in the wind.

When delegates gathered in the gilded splendour of the Winter Gardens, Blackpool, they could see the first fruits of their party's internal revolution. The theme 'New Labour, New Britain' was emblazoned across a snazzy green stage-set, picked out by theatrical lights. Peter Mandelson's television skills had been put to good use. The whole atmosphere was different. It was as though everyone was taking part in a carefully stage-managed TV extravaganza scheduled to go out during prime time. And indeed they were. New Labour was a show as well as serious politics, and the leaders were addressing a massive television audience as much as (if not more than) the party faithful.

In accordance with the usual schedule, Brown spoke first, in the economic debate on the Monday morning, 3 October of conference. Delegates had before them the party statement, *Building a Strong Economy*, which reflected the transformation in economic thinking that Brown was determined to drive through. First, a deferential nod to history: 'Our new economic approach is founded on the socialist principle that the community must accept its responsibilities for the goals of sustained growth and full employment.' He made a solemn promise to use every instrument of government policy to end mass unemployment, and to set a national minimum wage that would be a memorial to John Smith. He disclosed that the Social Justice Commission, set up by Smith to chart a new way forward on tax, would look at ways of integrating tax and benefits to eliminate means-testing of the elderly. For women, he pledged a national system of child care. To the fat cats of industry, he offered only taxes on their share options.

'The big idea,' Brown added, 'the key to economic success, is people's potential. The big idea is that people have big ideas, huge talents, great and greatly overlooked abilities, and it is by liberating people's potential that we build the dynamic market economy we need.' *Market* economy? Minutes earlier, he had reassured the unions that Labour would halt the privatisation of the railways. Now, he was signalling a conversion to the market, with warnings of 'tough and bold economic decisions' to achieve both economic success and social justice. His speech was a mix of traditional party policy and signposts to a different world. Just how different, the delegates would soon learn. As the shadow chancellor sat down, the chairman warned them to heed the noon deadline for voting in the NEC elections. Brown recovered much ground on his poor showing of the previous year, finishing third.

The other big idea emerged next day in Blair's speech, which was distributed in advance to the media but with the last three pages unaccountably missing. At the end of a long tour d'horizon of New Labour's policies and prospects, the leader said: 'It is time we had a clear up-to-date statement of the objects and objectives of our party. John Prescott and I, as leader and deputy leader, will propose such a statement to the NEC.' It would then be open to debate, he added, and the whole party should get involved in the exercise. As delegates rose to give Blair a standing ovation for his first leader's speech to conference, Labour's spin-doctors fanned round the hall to explain what his words actually meant: the end of Clause IV. The catch-all nationalising commitment had not been specifi-cally mentioned in the text, but that was what it was all about. The lightning raid had paid off. With the exception of miners' leader Arthur Scargill – soon to march off into the political wilderness to form his own party – there was no serious revolt that day. Once reality had sunk in, a mild counter-attack ensued. On the Thursday of conference, delegates voted by the narrowest of margins – 50.9 per cent to 49.1 per cent – re-affirming support for Clause IV. But Brown and Blair chose to regard this as the last gasp of the party's dinosaurs.

Within two months, a timetable for the historic change had been agreed by party leaders, culminating in a national confer-ence in the spring of 1995 to endorse the new statement of aims and objectives. Brown was fully involved in the drafting process, batting texts back and forth with Blair, discreetly ignoring the vote by his own Dunfermline East constituency party to retain the original Clause IV. The new version would be a more general 'mission statement' of Labour's objectives, including social justice, freedom, equality, democracy and solidarity. When he was attacked by Scargill at a Defend Clause Four campaign meeting in mid-November as a 'Clinton clone', bent on turning Labour into a US-style Democratic Party, Brown knew the modernisers were on to a winner. Only two hundred activists, some of them not even party members, turned up to the hard-left rally in a church hall in central London. If that was the true scale of the counter-attack, the battle was over before it had begun.

Throughout the autumn when Labour's internal politics dominated the headlines, the shadow chancellor had been looking for a way to convert popular fury over the second phase of imposing VAT on fuel into a defeat for Major's ailing administration, down to a majority of fourteen in the Commons in the wake of a string of by-election defeats. Uprating of the tax from 8 to 17.5 per cent from April 1995 had been part of Kenneth Clarke's tax-raising, anti-recession budget of 1993, and the government's business managers insisted that there could be no further parliamentary vote on the issue. But Labour's tacticians found a way round the block, allowing Brown to table a procedural motion that could force a vote. His manoeuvre sent ministers into a panic. Tory backbenchers, mindful that VAT on gas and electricity was the most unpopular measure since the poll tax, queued up to assert that they would not be dragooned into supporting the government.

In the debate on the Queen's Speech, Brown argued, 'The VAT rise on fuel is simply wrong. And the excessive pay packages, especially in the privatised utilities, are causing real offence throughout the country.' It was an adroit move to link the two. For many months, Labour had been reaping substantial publicity rewards from a relentless campaign to expose the enormous salaries, bonuses and share options raked in by the 'fat cats' of privatised industry – culminating in a live Cedric the Pig being exhibited with his snout in a trough outside the annual meeting of shareholders of British Gas, chaired by Cedric Brown. Brown was again repeatedly interrupted by Tory MPs, but he got his point across, that the Conservative Party's 'desperate scramble for survival is the only thing that unites it.'[5]

A week later, in the budget debate, he poked fun at Clarke's recent comment that 'the key thing for the party is not to panic'. Brown commented, 'There we have it – the Tory strategy is "Don't panic, don't panic", with the Chancellor as the Corporal Jones of the embattled rerun of *Dad's Army* but without any of the resolve, organisation, leadership or popularity of the original.'[6] He appealed to Conservative MPs to wrestle with their consciences and vote with Labour to defeat the doubling of VAT on fuel.

Enough to them did so to halt the measure, and Chancellor Clarke was forced to make a humiliating return to the despatch box to fill the £5 billion hole left by his shadow's demolition job on VAT. Brown made the most of his second chance to denounce the Conservatives for being out of touch and demand that they should be out of power. His powerful performance boosted his ratings, inside the party and out. The *Sunday Times* noted that Labour MPs who would have preferred his old rival Robin Cook to have been given the Treasury brief in Blair's recent Shadow Cabinet reshuffle must now regard Brown's position as unassailable, in a 'strictly non-Lawsonian sense'. (Mrs Thatcher memorably described her Chancellor Nigel Lawson as unassailable, shortly before sacking him.) The paper added, 'Gordon Brown could eventually become the first Labour chancellor to steer the British economy through a full parliament and pave the way for a second administration.'[7]

The New Year, 1995, opened with another brush-fire. David Blunkett, the shadow education secretary, suggested in newspaper interviews that Labour might charge VAT on private school fees. This was a gift to the Tories. In one fell swoop, Blunkett's casual redefinition of policy cast Labour as the party of VAT, the party of class warfare against middle-class parents wanting to send their children to private schools. Since it was the New Year's Day holiday, the rebuttal machine was slow to react. But by lunchtime Blunkett had his instructions, and he performed a graceless U-turn on Radio 4's *The World at One* – dragging in Gordon Brown. 'The shadow chancellor and the leader of the party think it is helpful to rule out that possibility in order to avoid confusion,' he said. Brown's people were livid at this clear attempt by Blunkett to bolster his leftist credentials, insisting that their man had nothing to do with the charade. They also dismissed suggestions, emanating from

John Prescott, that the shadow chancellor had ruled out VAT on school fees months previously but had failed to inform Blunkett. Charlie Whelan pointed out that the idea was already off the agenda by then anyway, because EU rules would have required VAT to be imposed on university tuition and evening and nursery classes as well. The incident, which provided holiday-season headlines for a week because it turned into a phoney modernisers-versus-traditionalists row, pointed up the tensions never very far below the surface. Brown's vice-like grip across the range of public spending was deeply resented. The incident forced him to abandon a planned press conference on the national minimum wage.

The conference to approve a new constitution was set for 29 April, to avoid Clause IV, Mark II, falling victim to the wrath of activists during the summer, as had happened to John Smith's OMOV reforms. But it first had to clear the hurdle of the Scottish party conference in Inverness. The Campaign for Socialism was strongest north of the border. Jim Mearns, the Glasgow Maryhill delegate to the Blackpool conference – famous for fifteen minutes there for his mimicry of the leader during the nationalisation debate: 'Be tough on capitalism, and tough on the causes of capitalism' – went back home to mobilise. Blair travelled to the Highlands on 10 March to take on the traditionalists, and won by an unexpectedly large margin. Brown and he spent much of the next few days swapping alternative texts for the statement of aims and objectives. During the Inverness conference, full employment was excluded from the final draft, the final rejection of John Smith's support for this consistent plank of party policy since 1945.

Back in the hothouse of Westminster, speculation raged that John Major might be forced to go to the polls a full year before his five-year term expired. Blair put Labour on a war footing in late March. Gordon Brown was put in charge of a new strategy team to handle day-to-day tactics and plan for the election. His team began to meet daily, working on the specifics of a general-election campaign, whether a snap poll materialised or not. The shadow chancellor served notice that he would make a series of keynote speeches during the spring, paving the way for an authoritative policy document at the autumn conference. 'After twenty years of being on the defensive, we are now on the offensive,' he declared. He also promised that, as chancellor, he would not reverse any tax cuts brought in by the Conservatives before the election. Mindful of Labour's pledge to repeal a 2p in the pound tax cut that took effect four weeks before polling day in 1987, his aides said, 'We are not going to fall into that trap again.'

The Methodist Central Hall, Westminster, which had witnessed the adoption of the original Clause IV in 1917, also saw it finally repudiated on 29 April, seventy-eight years later. By a margin of almost two to one, the party conference adopted the new statement of aims and objectives, which laid down that Labour is a democratic socialist party committed to 'a dynamic economy, serving the public interest, in which the enterprise of the market and the rigour of competition are joined with the forces of partnership and co-operation to produce the wealth the nation needs and the opportunity for all to work and prosper, with a thriving private sector and high quality public services, where those undertakings essential to the common good are either owned by the public or accountable to them'. There was a great deal more about the just society, an open democracy and a healthy environment, plus a promise to work with the trade unions. But essentially, the modernisers buried the old left's dream of the British road to socialism to which generations of party members had clung. Now, they had to go out and sell the new vision.

Brown's first big speech of the year, on 1 May 1995, was entitled 'The Dynamic Market Economy'. (In the two days since Labour had embraced its new gospel, 'market' had appeared between 'dynamic' and 'economy'.) Addressing Labour's Finance and Industry Group, which brings together politicians and businessmen, he offered himself as the 'iron chancellor': 'Nobody should doubt my iron commitment to macroeconomic stability and financial prudence.' Britain could not tax, spend and borrow – or devalue – its way to economic success. He put his own seal on the party's radical shift – 'Wholesale nationalisation is not the way to ensure an economy run in the public interest' – and concentrated on competition, offering a fresh political definition of Labour's goal: 'For social-ists, the discipline of competition is an important tool for cre-ating a dynamic economy . . . That is why the new Clause Four commits us to the rigour of competition.' New Labour had a vision of competition more suited to a complex modern econ-omy, he assured his audience. He would adopt a 'prohibitive' approach to anti-competitive practices and abuses of monopoly power. For the consumer, he promised legislation to protect mortgage-buyers and pensioners. On investment, he wanted changes in the corporate tax and financial system to encourage long-term investment. These measures, together with a welfare-to-work programme to end the waste of long-term unemploy-ment, was Labour's way of achieving a dynamic economy.

A little over two weeks later, Brown delivered his thoughts on 'Labour's Macroeconomic Framework' to the same group. He sought to transcend the old divisions between Keynesians and monetarists, recognising that strong and sustained growth and low inflation were necessary responsibilities of government. 'Inflation is an enemy of the poor, the pensioner and the middle-income family. It destroys savings and undermines long-term investment and therefore jobs.' It created instability, and harmed those least able to use sophisticated financial instruments to protect themselves. 'That is why the war on inflation is a Labour war.' Essentially, he was only saying what his predecessors had said. Harold Wilson created an Anti-Inflation Unit at Downing Street in the 1970s, and all previous Labour governments had had perforce to implement counter-inflation policies. But after nearly two decades with no experience of a Labour chancellor, it was only too easy for the Tories to caricature Labour as the 'easy money' party.

In his 17 May speech, the shadow chancellor identified the

three main pillars of his economic policy. First, an explicitly long-term macroeconomic strategy: to raise the trend rate of growth with clear rules for borrowing and public spending, reflecting the need to invest for the future. Second, a tough anti-inflation policy based on 'stable and credible institutional foundations'. Monetary policy had to be accountable, transparent and free from short-term party political manipulation. 'In my view,' he added, 'this requires a careful assessment of the relationship between the government and the Bank of England as well as reform of the Bank to ensure greater accountability.' This was the first serious indication that Chancellor Brown would reform the role of the Bank of England and its relationship with the government. Kenneth Clarke had gone some way towards letting daylight into the relationship, by publishing the minutes of his meetings with Eddie George, the governor of the Bank, in the teeth of right-wing Tory hostility. But against a background of mistrust – a suspicion, later firmed into a conviction, that interest rates were being manipulated for party political advantage – Brown was determined to go much further. The third element of his approach was a commitment 'to rebuild a shared national economic purpose'. This would require greater openness in decision-making, and Brown announced an opening-up of the secretive budget process. A national economic debate, plus a Green Paper spelling out the state of the economy, would precede each budget.

He was equally clear about the limits of government. 'I reject government by unlimited subsidy and government that picks winners,' he said. 'A future Labour government will not attempt to substitute our judgement for the commercial judgement of investors and managers. Second guessing is not the business of government.' His strictures would be put to the test within four months of taking office, when Labour refused to intervene to keep open the privatised 'super-pit' at Asfordby, Leicestershire, opened as recently as 1994 at a cost to the taxpayer of £330 million. RJB Mining, successor to the state-owned British Coal, closed the mine on geological grounds.

Ironically, it had been built substantially at the behest of Nigel Lawson during his chancellorship, as a reward to East Midlands colliers who refused to join the great miners' strike of 1984–5.

The shadow chancellor then showed more of his hand. Labour would have a medium-term growth strategy. Projections for inflation and growth would be published as part of the annual budget statement. In government, Labour would be wise spenders – and wise borrowers, committed to the 'golden rule' of borrowing only to finance public investment and not to fund public consumption. To ensure these commitments were met, he would appoint a panel of independent forecasters with a wide range of economic expertise to give their judgment on Treasury performance. 'Brown's Law is that government will only borrow to invest, public debt will remain stable and the cost effectiveness of public spending must be proved.'

Turning in more detail to the Bank, Brown was scathing about the 'damaging personalisation of the "Ken and Eddie Show"' and proposed a raft of reforms: a new Monetary Policy Committee, to advise the government on monetary policy; expansion of the Court of the Bank, to bring in a wider range of interests from the City, both sides of industry and the regions; and a new statutory framework for the Bank and the other new institutions to make them accountable to Parliament. He hinted that he was attracted to a greater operational role for the Bank, though one that stopped well short of independence for the Old Lady of Threadneedle Street; the government must continue to set the targets for monetary and fiscal policy.[8]

Brown's third speech on 31 May, once again to Labour's Finance and Industry Group, focused on 'Partnerships for Investment'. He pointed out that the total amount of private finance levered into public infrastructure projects in the first twenty-eight months of the Conservatives' Private Finance Initiative was only £500 million – a fraction of the £12 billion of the projects financed from public funds. Reminding his audience of Labour's determination to bring private finance into every area of public activity, including schools and the NHS, Brown argued, 'I believe that so long as we put the battles between public and private behind us, and work together, we can achieve the modernisation of our infrastructure that we all seek.'

These three speeches, running to more than ten thousand words, were Brown's economic credo for government. They were the product of many hours of debate and brainstorming with his own people and outside experts. They betrayed the links between his thinking and that of American economists, but they also make up the most substantial thinking in public by a man who would be chancellor in modern political history. After 31 May, nobody could honestly say (though Conservative Central Office dishonestly did) that the people did not know what Gordon Brown was going to do when he got to the Treasury.

It was an amiable diversion from the cerebral business of inventing the new economics to visit the western Pennines during the hottest days of July. A by-election in the three-way marginal seat of Littleborough and Saddleworth, caused by the death of loquacious Tory MP Geoffrey Dickens, brought Brown to lend his support for Labour's candidate, Phil Woolas. He was in his element, attacking the Liberal Democrats' manifesto: 'Their spending plans would mean large tax increases for the British people.' He could now say this with a straight face, though Labour's monetary rectitude did not sufficiently impress this traditional corner of Lancashire: the constituency was not won until 1997.

Thereafter, it was an even hotter summer – politically speaking – culminating in an entertaining squabble about Labour's pecking order. In mid-September, it emerged that John Prescott, the deputy party leader, had not been invited to a secret summit called seven months previously to discuss the presentation of economic policy. Brown, Blair, Mandelson, Tom Sawyer and Philip Gould, the leader's political consultant, all attended the weekend conference with Labour's advertising agency. Prescott was livid, but masked his rage with a polite statement. His absence spoke volumes about Brown's desire to involve the deputy leader in economic policy.

In the week before the 1995 party conference, Blair formally named Brown as his overall election-strategy chief, erasing any doubt about the importance he attached to this formidable task. Prescott was given the task of winning the battle for marginal seats, and Robin Cook the more amorphous role of campaign policy. This 'A-team' would begin meeting after the conference, though Brown's own campaign team had been meeting regularly for months. The Brighton conference was billed as the conference of the toffs, because on a fine, breezy Sunday, 1 October, Labour for the first time sponsored a racing day at Brighton racecourse. Brown, with Blair and Mo Mowlam, headed for the hospitality boxes, where, according to the *Evening Standard*, 'party fat cats quaffed champagne and smoked salmon in exclusive privacy'. The paper's sketch-writer, betting fiend Peter Oborne, observed members of the Shadow Cabinet emerge blinking into the sunlight to present the prizes to the winners. 'One of the early victims was shadow Chancellor Gordon Brown,' he wrote. 'It can safely be said that Mr Brown is not a racing man. His scowl was deeper than ever as he strode to the winners' enclosure.'[9]

He had already been given plenty to scowl about that morning, when David Frost put him on the spot over child benefit. Blair had suggested that the better-off did not need it, prompting fears that Labour was moving away from the hallowed principle of universal benefit. On BBC 1's *Breakfast With Frost*, Brown pointed out that the Social Justice Commission had suggested that child benefit should be taxed like any other benefit. 'Now that is what we are looking at,' he went on. 'In principle there is a case for looking at taxation, but what Tony also said was that child benefit would remain a universal benefit, paid to all mothers and therefore to all children.' He fought shy of the tax issue, insisting, 'We have got no plans.'[10] In fact, he was working on radical plans, going one stage further than any previous shadow chancellor with the starting-rate of income tax cut to as low as 10p in the pound.

The first day of conference found him in his usual role, seeking approval for yet another strategy statement, *A New Economic Future for Britain*, which brought together policies agreed in the party's machinery and announced in speeches, and an NEC statement, *A National Minimum Wage*. 'Comrades and friends,' he greeted delegates unblushingly, 'we meet here today as a party preparing for power.' He went through the familiar themes: in place of greed, waste and short-termism, the country needed in government a new economic responsibility and moral purpose. There were some good, if slightly laboured, jokes about the Tories and rail privatisation. 'The only connections they care about are the City connections. The only track they want to keep on is the inside track. The only network they want to preserve is the old boys' network and the only train that will always run on schedule is the gravy train.' There was a great deal more about moral purpose, waste and imprudent public spending and a firm pledge to those watching on the City sidelines: 'We will not build the new Jerusalem on a mountain of debt . . . Our programme is costed at £1 billion in its first year, funded, paid for by the windfall levy.'[11] It was not, perhaps, his best conference speech ever, but it was difficult to make the same pitch sound fresh year after year, as Major clung on to office by his fingertips. Brown was rewarded with second place in the NEC elections.

Within weeks, the shadow chancellor was ready to divulge his tax plans. In mid-November, he won Shadow Cabinet approval for a proposal to outflank the Tories by promising a starting rate of tax of 15p in the pound, moving to 10p 'when affordable.' His objectives were leaked in the *Independent on Sunday* ten days before Clarke's tax-cutting budget, though a London cab driver heard them first. Returning from a market-research meeting on the issue, Brown held an animated discussion with his aides in the back of a taxi. As he dropped them off at Westminster, the cabbie volunteered, 'That was interesting.' In fact, the driver was probably one of Brown's target voters. His tax changes were designed to benefit everyone – 'particularly lower and middle income Britain – the decent hard-working majority of this country.' He added, 'Taxation is not some sort of penalty on people who are successful. Labour is against poverty and not against wealth. Nor would we tax to punish people, and there would be no penal rates of taxation under Labour.'[12]

Such was Brown's high profile that Blair had to intervene at the weekly meeting of the Shadow Cabinet on 22 November to give his '101 per cent support' to the 'quite brilliant job' the shadow chancellor was doing. The sniping came from Prescott, increasingly unhappy that his own role as deputy leader appeared diminished, and from Cook, who would cross the road to have a fight with Brown. Cook's complaint was that Brown had failed to consult colleagues (i.e., Cook himself, who was chairman of the National Policy Forum) over his plans to deny benefit payments to young people who refused places on training schemes. Strictly speaking, this was within Brown's welfare-to-work brief, but the more general gripe was that the shadow chancellor wandered at will across the party's policy spectrum, careless of shadow ministerial portfolios. There was some substance in the charge. As head of Labour's election strategy committee, now meeting daily at Westminster, that was his job. But Charlie Whelan ridiculed suggestions that Brown was 'grooming himself as a leader-in-waiting'.

The *Daily Mail* claimed to have discovered another 'whispering campaign' against him, but judging by its impact it too was sotto voce. Brown was involved in a fresh wrangle about welfare-to-work, as Labour backbenchers said it smacked too much of American-style workfare schemes. He agreed that youngsters would lose 40 per cent of their benefit only if they refused places on all four work and training options – including Labour's proposed environmental task force. 'The fifth option, simply remaining unemployed and permanently on benefit, will no longer be an option,' he ruled.

Brown was back on the road in late January 1996, visiting a resource and enterprise centre in South Elmsall, a former mining town in south Yorkshire where another by-election was taking place. This was a safe constituency, even for New Labour, despite the presence of a candidate from Arthur Scargill's new Socialist Labour Party. Nevertheless, the shadow chancellor looked uncomfortable and out of place in a town devastated by pit closures that expected little from the New Economics. He did not see the real 'enterprise' going on in the lane outside, despite winds of Siberian coldness: men bent double, pushing wheelbarrows of small coal they had stolen from the former colliery's tip, destined for sale at £2.50 a bag.

It was clear by late April that the Treasury was preparing for a Labour government, whenever the election came. Senior civil servants began an anodyne redraft of the ministry's 'mission statement' to take account of Brown's economic strategy. Brown drew up his own version, bringing the 1944 White Paper commitment on 'high and stable levels of employment' back into the heart of government policy. The shadow chancellor was pleased by the Ministry's realpolitik but unfazed. 'It would be astonishing if the Treasury were not preparing for a Labour government,' he said. John Prescott was not, however, so prepared. In mid-May, he revived old rancour over Brown's proposal to transform the Treasury into an engine of social and political renewal. He poured scorn on the idea of a 'super-Treasury', and warned against prudence becoming ossified into obstruction.

The interlude was just another scene in the long-running Shadow Cabinet soap opera. More serious was the disclosure that Brown had not spoken to his quondam friend Peter Mandelson for two years, since his betrayal in the Labour leadership campaign. Yet the two would have to work closely together in the election battle. Veteran observers consoled themselves with the knowledge that earlier generations had been just as good haters: overhearing a Labour MP say that

Herbert Morrison, Mandelson's grandfather, was 'his own worst enemy', Ernest Bevin, the foreign secretary, had growled, 'Not while I'm alive he ain't.'

Brown had by this time won the internal feud over ending child benefit for students over sixteen. Initially, his proposal had aroused fears that poorer families would lose money, but he said much of the £700 million saved could be used to set up a system of educational maintenance grants. He faced opposition from within the Shadow Cabinet, but stuck to his guns, arguing, 'Anybody who believes we are going to modernise the welfare state without making tough choices is of course wrong. That is what new Labour is about.'[13] In July, in front of a hundred journalists and ten television crews, he joined Blair and the rest of the Shadow Cabinet for a formal launch of 'The Project', *The Road to the Manifesto*, which was going out to a ballot of all Labour members. Practically everything in it had been well leaked or well trailed for weeks, if not months, but Brown wanted everyone to know that no party in the past had set out its manifesto so far ahead of a general election. Robin Cook was allowed to answer only two questions, the London *Evening Standard* noticed, 'and Blair and Brown had a chat each time he did, which was distracting. The Labour leader uses the same tactic in the Commons when he doesn't like what John Major is saying.'

Blackpool 1996 was the final conference before the general election, which John Major had to call before the following May. As delegates gathered over the weekend, a battle over pensions took place behind the scenes. The shadow chancellor found himself in the firing line, facing two of the Labour Party's most doughty fighters: Baroness Barbara Castle and Jack Jones, former general secretary of the TGWU, both in their 80s. They rebelled over the leadership's refusal to restore the link between the old-age pension and average earnings. It had been broken by Thatcher, who linked pensions to price movements instead, and pensions had fallen steadily behind wages as a result. But Harriet Harman, the shadow social security secretary, calculated that re-establishing the link could cost £5 billion a year, and rejected the proposal. At this point, pensioners' champion Jack Jones – an old adversary of Barbara Castle during the Wilson government years – got into 'dialogue' with Ms Harman. The outcome was a compromise formula, hammered out by Gordon Brown and Jones in a frantic series of telephone calls on 28 September, the day before the national executive met to consider a policy statement on pensions. Brown conceded a standing commission on pensions that would 'advise' a Labour government. It would examine proposals from the Pensioners' Convention, of which Jones was a leading member. However, the statement also reaffirmed the shadow chancellor's ban on commitments to extra spending, and stipulated that measures to help pensioners would be looked at 'in the light of public finances at the time'. Honour and probity were both satisfied by this formula, and the platform won the vote.

Brown was in combative form, exploiting the theme 'You can't trust the Tories' that was to become the bedrock slogan of the election campaign. He invoked what George Orwell once called 'the British genius': 'our inventiveness and creative talents, our adaptability, our belief in education and opportunity – qualities traditionally British, embodying values traditionally Labour. Precisely the qualities that must be recognised and nurtured so that we can succeed as a modern economy. This is a wholly new vision of what can be done by government and people together.' Sounding rather like the Chinese gerontocracy, he called for three modernisations – of industrial policy, of the welfare state and of education. He devoted a special section of his speech to child benefit, arguing that the status quo was not working, and resources should be concentrated on those most in need. Only half the mothers of teenagers aged over sixteen received child benefit 'and I cannot justify the wife of a millionaire receiving child benefit for a teenager over 16 when the mother of an unemployed teenager does not and a total of one million mothers do not. Universal child benefit after 16 there never has been. But universal education – properly financed for the first time for all after 16 – there must be'.[14] Brown's speech at Blackpool was noticeably snappier, more like Blair's: sentences without verbs, 'bullet' points, staccato delivery. Only his happy alighting on Orwell's phrase about the British genius relieved the relentless procession of assertion and withering criticism of the Tories.

Unusually, Brown clashed with one of his predecessors in the run-up to Kenneth Clarke's last budget. Speaking in a Lords debate on European monetary union on 30 October, Denis Healey warned that a single European currency could be 'a disaster economically and politically' that might produce 'riots in the streets'. Labour frontbenchers, particularly the shadow chancellor, fumed at the former chancellor's intervention. Brown observed that Healey was not speaking from the front bench 'and doesn't pretend to do so'. Healey replied with heavy artillery. Gordon, he remarked, had become 'a little too rigid in some respects, and, of course, he's got no government experience'. Brown winced at this lofty put-down, which was scarcely fair, since Labour had been in Opposition ever since he entered Parliament. Healey was just as generous with his apology as with his criticism. 'My comments on Brown were very unfair and I apologised within the hour,' he disclosed later. 'We had a long talk that afternoon. He rang me to say he hadn't put me down. He had said a perfectly sensible thing, as I later saw.' He put his 'foolish' behaviour down to being 'one of the world's champion blurters' and withdrew his comments.[15]

The issue of a European single currency continued to rumble, however. Brown decided to make the party's position crystal-clear, and in November, he went public on a promise that Labour would give the British people a referendum on whether they wanted to go into EMU. That had been decided in principle, he told the *Independent on Sunday*, as 'the appropriate way of securing consent'. The decision followed several months of private talks between Brown and European finance ministers and economic spokesmen of different parties. 'No major decisions will now be made in the European Union until after the general election,' said the shadow chancellor. 'The next summit is not until June 1997. It is now clear we will not know until after the general election whether European Monetary Union will go ahead and on what terms.' A decision should be made in the national interest, at the right time. 'That is why we say we will keep our options open. It also means that if a decision is being considered during the course of the next parliament, then a referendum at that time is the appropriate way of securing consent.'[16]

His decisive move brought to an end an internal policy wrangle at the highest levels in the party. Some (and Brown might have been numbered among them) had wanted to keep open the option of a clear commitment in the election manifesto to join EMU. Indeed, the shadow chancellor would not rule out joining the single currency in the first wave of participating countries. 'We see advantages in the principle of monetary union because of the benefits it could give in terms of greater stability, lower long-term interest rates, reduced speculation and lower currency transaction costs,' he said. But he promised that any decision on EMU would take account of the employment consequences, so graphically described by Denis Healey, before asking the British people to undertake 'an act of consent'. Ed Balls, his economic adviser, said firmly: 'In principle, we want to join EMU. What is becoming apparent is that it will go ahead, and there are substantial costs attached to the UK being left behind.'[17]

Brown's initiative was well received, and it focused attention once again on the continuing divisions over Europe within the Conservative Party, whose official 'wait and see' plus referendum policy did not go far enough for many on the government backbenches. The Europe row raged afresh in December, when Brown clashed with Clarke in the Commons on the eve of an EU summit in Dublin. Brown teased the chancellor about his views on the single currency. He had said he had 'no objection, in principle' to it. Yet many Tory MPs said they would oppose the Euro in principle in their election manifesto. 'Has the

Cabinet agreed a dispensation for them?' he asked mischievously. Clarke sidestepped the question, insisting that the UK
should 'stay at the table'. (In fact, John Major would be forced
a few months later into giving exactly the dispensation that
Brown forecast, such was the weight of Euroscepticism among
his MPs.) The shadow chancellor replied, and had much good
fun with Clarke's recent, well-publicised two-bottle lunch at
which he had confided to a BBC journalist that the source of a
story about the government ruling out a single currency was
'someone close to the Prime Minister'. 'In vino veritas,' scoffed
Brown. 'No wonder his mind was not on the Budget or the
economy. It was on the attempted betrayal, as he saw it, of No
11 Downing Street by No 10.' Clarke leaped to his own
defence. 'Wine played a much smaller part at the lunch than he
believes,' he retorted. In his peroration, Brown was scathing.
'Three years ago,' he said, 'the Chancellor said that the
Conservative Party was in a hole. It still is. It has long ceased to
be able to govern on the vital issue of Europe . . . Its divisions
are damaging the national interest. It is time the national
interest came first; it is time that this government went.'[18]

The countdown to election in the New Year revived the long-
running speculation about divisions in the Shadow Cabinet,
this time with a new twist: Brown was now said to be at odds
with Blair – over tax. The shadow chancellor still hankered after
a top rate of income tax of 50p in the pound for incomes over
£100,000 a year, whereas the leader wanted no change in existing levels and 'what Tony wants, Tony gets'. The row was
largely synthetic, because a new rate at that level would bring
in no more than £1 billion a year, said Brown's supporters.
Another, more machiavellian theory was that the rumour was
self-serving. It showed the shadow chancellor in a good light,
pushing for higher taxes but reined in by his more conservative
leader. Interestingly, a Gallup poll for the *Sunday Telegraph* suggested that 66 per cent of voters believed the Tories were just as
likely as Labour to put up taxes. And 72 per cent favoured the
higher rate of tax. Anthony King, Professor of Politics at Essex

University commented: 'The key development since the last election is not that Labour has lost its reputation as a high tax party, but that the Tories are also seen as a high tax party.'[19]

Brown and Blair finally agreed the shape of the tax package at a secret 'summit' at the leader's home in Islington on 5 January. 'We didn't have to go to Granita's this time,' Blair joked to friends. The leader got his way on the top rate of income tax, while his shadow chancellor won the maximum room for manoeuvre in other areas of revenue-raising. Brown then met Ed Balls and Charlie Whelan five days later, and decreed that the time had come to declare Labour's policy on taxation and the tough spending regime he would impose. Typically, Brown proposed to do it in a series of speeches spread over six weeks, starting with an address to the Labour Finance and Industry Group on 20 January. His strategy was endorsed at a meeting with Blair and his top fixers, and John Prescott was briefed. The Shadow Cabinet was brought into the picture on 15 January, but only on the timing, not the content.

Some broad outlines began to leak out, judiciously, a week before the first speech. Labour would keep the Conservatives' 23 per cent basic rate of income tax, and the 40 per cent top rate. New Labour, no new taxes. But until millions of radio listeners heard the speech, 'Responsibility in Public Finance', delivered at the Queen Elizabeth II centre in Parliament Square, the secret was known to only about half a dozen people. Brown was keen to maximise the element of surprise to keep the Conservatives guessing and make the biggest media impact possible. He succeeded.

In his speech, written by Ed Balls and Ed Miliband, the shadow chancellor said, 'We want to send the clearest possible signal that we want to encourage employment and work, not penalise it. The Conservatives try to claim that Labour will penalise work and success by raising taxes. Nothing could be further from the truth. Because we want to encourage work, and after 22 tax rises since 1992 which have hit hard-working families, I want to make clear that a Labour government will not increase the basic rate of income tax. It is because we understand the importance of work that there will be no return to penal marginal tax rates at the top.'

Brown also confirmed that there would be no new commitments in the manifesto that required additional spending: only the welfare-to-work programme funded by the windfall tax, which would be levied in the first budget, to be delivered within two months of polling day.

He further pledged not to spend more than the Tories in his first two years as chancellor. 'Our first Budget will not reopen overall spending allocations for the 1997/98 financial year,' he declared. Local government allocations would also stand. 'We will hold to the capping limits.' For 1998/99, departmental ministers could re-order spending to meet Labour's priorities, but only within already announced departmental budgets. Moreover, every spending minister would be expected to undertake a full-scale review of his department's spending programme to redirect resources to front-line services. The Cabinet's EDX Committee of high-ranking ministers and a team of Treasury officials would oversee these reviews. The purpose would be 'to put our public spending principles into practice . . . at the centre of which is our commitment to shift resources from welfare to education'.

Press reaction the next day, ranged from the exultant to the sceptical. The pro-Labour *Mirror* described the speech as 'an inspired, workable vision of Britain at the start of the 21st century'. The pro-Tory *Daily Mail* said: 'Gordon Brown's speech was as significant an act of exorcism as we have witnessed in the post-war history of British politics. Impressively, the Shadow Chancellor set about laying to rest the gibbering ghosts of tax and spend that have bedevilled his party's prospects for a generation. What can no longer be denied is that, on the Tories favourite battleground of tax, he is a proving an ever-more formidable adversary.' The equally pro-Tory *Daily Express* said, 'Mr Brown and his colleagues are light years away from traditional policies. That, in itself, deserves a cheer.'

The Times found his determination to stick to Tory spending plans 'encouraging', while the *Guardian* found it a 'frightening admission' that Labour had abandoned the moral and political case for redistribution. The *Daily Telegraph* did not trust Brown, and the *Financial Times* thought his promises owed more to politics than economics. The *Economist* accepted that 'Labour's manoeuvre is a smart one'. Kenneth Clarke thought his promises 'incredible', even though Brown was setting himself the same targets as the chancellor. Generally speaking, Brown was judged to have substantially advanced his party's chances of being elected.

The plaudits had barely faded when Brown hit the headlines again, with his decision that Labour would not fund a £60 million replacement for the Royal yacht, *Britannia*. Michael Portillo, the defence secretary, had announced the government's intention, if re-elected, to buy the Queen a replacement vessel out of public money. But with the Royal Family in turmoil, the public was aghast. Newspaper polls immediately recorded votes of 20:1 against using taxpayers' money in this way, and the shadow chancellor 'let it be known' to Buckingham Palace through the usual channels – a senior civil servant – that in government a new yacht would not figure in his public-spending priorities. The announcement created some grief in Tony Blair's private office, whose staff had not been consulted, but it was a sure-fire winner with voters. During the election campaign proper, his parsimony with the Queen invariably won a round of applause.

It was not long before the Conservatives began picking holes in Brown's spending programme. They pointed out that Labour had a £4 billion 'black hole' in its calculations, caused by a lack of privatisation receipts and plans for students loans repayable through the tax system. Around £1.5 billion was expected in 1998/99 from the sale of the National Air Traffic Service (which Labour opposed) and other, as yet unspecified, privatisations. A further £1 billion arose from the transfer of students loans to the National Insurance system, which

Whitehall officials said was still classified as public spending. Brown's aides talked down the 'black hole' problem, which was no bigger than a bottom-of-the-page item in the *Financial Times*. But it would come back to haunt them.

At the end of January 1996, Brown announced his intention to stand down in October from the NEC, on which he had served since 1992. His departure coincided with another tranche of internal reforms that would, in any event, weaken the powers of the once-mighty executive. Tony Blair was determined to ensure that his chancellor did not share the fate of Denis Healey, who was shouted down by left-wingers on the executive during the IMF financial crisis of 1976. More to the point, he also wanted to rule out any possibility of conflict between Westminster and the party. The NEC would be obliged to support the Cabinet, and the annual conference would become a showcase for its policies, rather than the battleground it had been under previous Labour administrations. Policy motions would come not from affiliated unions and local parties, but from the regional and national policy forums originally set up by Neil Kinnock to bypass the 'unrepresentative' conference. Brown said he was happy to step down, now that the party was implementing reforms to give ordinary members a greater say in its affairs. He completed a busy month by warning public-sector workers that there would be no 'blank cheques' for pay under his iron regime. Labour would not fund inflation-busting awards from independent pay-review bodies for nurses, doctors, teachers and members of the armed forces.

He began in February by announcing a one-year pay freeze for government ministers, MPs, Whitehall mandarins, judges and the military top brass. Brown himself was among a handful of Labour MPs – including Blair – who had refused to accept a 28 per cent pay rise for MPs the previous summer.

An opinion poll in the first week of February jolted Labour's complacency. Sixty per cent of voters in a *Guardian*/ICM poll said they believed a Blair government would increase public spending, while 55 per cent said that Gordon Brown would put up taxes, while only 12 per cent thought he would reduce them. Coming only a fortnight after the shadow chancellor's speech on 'Responsibility in Public Finance', the figures were disappointing, particularly because they were very similar to poll findings ahead of the 1992 election, which Labour lost substantially on the tax issue. Nevertheless, Labour still enjoyed an overall sixteen-point lead over the Tories in voters' intentions, and the *Guardian*/ICM polls consistently undershot other polls.

The prospect of Labour not being in government seemed to excite the media less than the notion that Gordon Brown might refuse to use Dorneywood, the official country residence of senior ministers (initially, the foreign secretary) since it was gifted to the nation by Lord Courtauld-Thomson in 1943. His spokesman, Charlie Whelan, was quoted as saying that Brown would have no use for 'a country house or something ridiculous like that'. The house, near Burnham Beeches, a beauty spot in the Berkshire countryside, is owned by the National Trust. Under the terms of the gift, the chancellor has to buy the food for himself and the guests, but the staff eat free. The Dorneywood affair filled practically a whole page in the *Evening Standard*, whose columnist Anne Applebaum opined that politicians are not ordinary people – for if they were, they wouldn't be doing what they are doing. Quite so. Her advice to the son of the manse was: 'Gordon Brown should drop the tabloid language about fat cats, drop his Calvinist objections to officialdom, move into Dorneywood and grow up.'[20] In fact, three months after the election, he did motor down to have a look at the place. The boycott, if ever it really existed, is unlikely to last.

Brown escaped the increasingly febrile atmosphere of Westminster for a few days in late February to visit the United States. The high spot of his trip was a fund-raising bash with Oscar-winning Glenda Jackson, Labour MP for Hampstead, at the Century Club in Manhattan, known as an old-fashioned bastion of capitalism. Its oil paintings, wood-panelled rooms and lush carpets rather put Dorneywood in the shade. Hobnobbing with the likes of Bianca Jagger and Arthur Schlesinger, historian of the Kennedy family, they raised a reputed $1 million for Labour's election war chest. Next day, 20 February, it was straight down to Washington for talks with US Treasury Secretary Robert Rubin and his deputy, Larry Summers. Brown blew cool on the prospect of Britain joining the first wave of a single European currency, arguing that 1999 looked premature. 'In our judgment, the real obstacles facing Britain and the other European Union countries will be increasingly difficult to overcome by 1999.' He listed five tests that the Euro would have to clear: the likely impact on investment by British and foreign firms; whether UK financial services would benefit; the problem of other EU countries being at different stages in the economic cycle; whether there was enough flexibility in the system; and the impact on jobs. 'Getting it right is more important than getting it quickly,' he emphasised. 'So there is a triple lock: the British opt-out, a vote of the British parliament and a vote of the British people.'[21] It was a more sceptical line than hitherto. Brown was perhaps responding to a perceived shift in mood. The Tories were now openly 'hostile in principle' to a single currency, according to Foreign Secretary Malcolm Rifkind.

On his return, he ran into different kind of hurdle. The Conservatives' diagnosis of a 'black hole' in Labour's economic strategy was worrying the Treasury team more than they cared to reveal. So, press-inspired speculation that Chancellor Brown might privatise the Tote, the state-run monopoly of pooled betting on horseracing set up in 1928 by Winston Churchill to channel funds into the racing industry, was not denied. The story just 'grew and grew', until Robin Cook, a keen racegoer, said it was not party policy and ruled out the sale – which could have netted £400 million. 'We never thought about Cook. It had nothing to do with him,' said a Brown aide. 'We had been quite pleased. We thought, this gets us out of the black hole.

We were furious when Cook intervened.'

The spat was forgotten when Brown gave his third and final speech on economic policy on 26 February, spelling out his plans for independence for the Bank of England. There was not a great deal of new thinking in the speech, much of which had been trailed, as early as May 1995, but it still made front-page news. The *Financial Times* described his plan as 'a half-way house' to independence. The new dimension was Brown's confirmation that Labour would adopt the outgoing government's inflation target of 2.5 per cent or less. He was speaking more and more as a chancellor-in-waiting, and the waiting was drawing to a close. Labour's capture of the hitherto-safe Tory seat of Wirral South on 27 February, with a swing of 17 per cent, was the last writing on the wall. In his speech to the Scottish Labour Party conference in Inverness on 8 March, he told delegates: 'We meet here at most four weeks before the declaration of the general election that will decide which government and which economic and social vision will lead this country into the next century.' It was closer than he thought.

CHAPTER 11

A VERY PRIVATE LIFE

SUE LAWLEY ENTERTAINED GORDON BROWN ON THE BBC'S imaginary desert island on 3 March 1996. It proved to be the most controversial *Desert Island Discs* in the programme's fifty-four-year history, because the show's presenter questioned the shadow chancellor about his private life in such a way that his sexuality was made an issue. She speculated that when a man is middle-aged and unmarried – as Brown is – 'people think you are gay or have a personality flaw'.

The ground is always well prepared for this flagship Radio 4 programme. Researchers spend many hours digging through the files of press cuttings, and talking to those who know the celebrity castaway. They build up a comprehensive picture on which the show is based. Lawley herself is a former newspaper reporter, cast in a very different mould from the show's creator, Roy Plomley, who preferred obscure opera-singers to politicians. Under her, the half-hour interview – condensed from one that takes two or three times longer – has become something of an amiable ordeal, particularly when the castaway is a public figure. There is occasionally the sense that she is still looking for a news 'scoop'.

Given the scale of editorial preparation, it is unlikely that the BBC was unaware that, for several years, rumours about Gordon Brown's sexuality had circulated in the bars and tea-rooms at Westminster. The suggestion that he might be gay was bandied about chiefly by political journalists, often reporters for Scottish newspapers who claimed to be 'in the know' about some dark secret from his years in Edinburgh. Not a shred of evidence was ever produced for these allegations, which those who know him well – and they are few in number – knew perfectly well were false. In a sense, he was a victim of his own reticence. Apart from his unceasing public role, Brown lives a very private life. His taciturnity has counted against him. In the gossipy hothouse of Parliament, invention is the mother of rumour. What the players do not know, they speculate about. Just how vicious the speculation can get was apparent in the suicide of a fellow-Scots Labour MP, Gordon McMaster, who committed suicide in the summer of 1997, citing among his reasons in a letter to Chief Whip Nick Brown unfounded allegations at Westminster that he was gay and had Aids.

Lawley disclosed some days after the programme had gone out that she had contacted political sources prior to her interview. 'I did talk to a Labour colleague and friend of Gordon Brown's about what I should ask him, and he said "I do think you should ask him about not being married." I believe it is true, if not a particularly palatable truth, that people like him are speculated about.'[1]

So Lawley plunged in. After Brown's fourth record – a Gaelic rendition of the twenty-third psalm, which had been sung beautifully at John Smith's funeral – she asked about Labour's new leader, Tony Blair. How important was the fact that he was a family man, and that the electorate on the whole might find that more appealing than the idea of a bachelor prime minister? Brown, who did not know the question was coming but was used to hearing it, replied, 'I'm not married. It just hasn't happened. I hope it does. It may yet. It probably will do . . . I think once you get into Parliament, if you're not married by the time you get there, then you're in a situation where you're living in two places.' Things became more difficult, he explained. 'You don't hear much about MPs getting married, but you hear a lot about them getting divorced.' She pressed him: was that a factor in the leadership decision? No, he didn't think so. 'Not at all . . . never mentioned?' she continued. 'No, it wasn't mentioned,' he confirmed. The conversation moved on to his position as shadow chancellor, and his strong friendship with Blair, before Brown chose Runrigg's version of 'Loch Lomond' for his fifth record.

They talked about tax and the stakeholder economy, and played his sixth choice, 'Cry Freedom', the song of South Africa's strugglers for freedom, before Lawley took the interview back to his private life. 'You're always asked about women and marriage,' she said. 'Does that irritate you?' Not at all, he replied. 'It's a question that, er, I expect and that I've already answered during the course of this interview: that it just hasn't happened and it's one of the things that I suppose I'm surprised hasn't happened . . . but it hasn't.' Lawley was not satisfied. It was interesting, she ventured, that it would probably be less of an issue for Brown if he had been married three times. 'People don't remark on that but they do remark on non-marriage.'

He kept his cool, saying, 'I think that's true, and it certainly appears in all the profiles. I've got some very good friends, obviously, but it just hasn't happened. It's one of those things that may yet happen.' Undeterred, Lawley ploughed on. 'But you do understand people's curiosity. It is something that middle-aged men and women have to put up with: people want to know whether you're gay or whether there's some flaw in your personality that you haven't made a relationship. You may feel . . . "Look, I don't have to answer these questions," but you do perhaps accept that as a public person it's a price you have to pay.'

Brown was patient. 'I don't mind answering the questions. It's something that comes up and certainly I think people are right to know what their politicians do and what their arrangements are. I'm not surprised at that.' She pursued him. 'Do they have the right to know?' It was different in other countries, he observed, 'but I think, yes, people have got a right to know. I'm standing as a candidate at an election. I'm asking people to support me. They want to know what sort of person I am.' Lawley wanted still more. One of Brown's colleagues had said the truth was that in fact he was a loner and actually 'despite the fact that you say you'd like to get married, you rather like life on your own'. He repeated, 'I've always assumed I would be married. I actually don't think of myself as middle-aged and maybe I am, maybe I'm not.' There was more about him being a loner, and more denials before they got on to the 'shambolic mess' in which he was said to live. A relieved Brown pleaded guilty to the charge of untidiness.

The extent of Lawley's questioning about his private life, and its intensity, aroused a great deal of interest, much of it hostile to the presenter. It must be confessed that this author did not help the situation, erroneously attributing the remark 'Look, I don't have to answer these questions' to Brown rather than his inquisitor in the *Independent on Sunday* of 3 March, the day of the lunchtime broadcast of *Desert Island Discs*. I was working from a bootleg typescript copy of the interview, which had no quotation marks. A break in the text appeared to indicate that Brown was getting irritated with this line of investigation – as many men would have done, and with some justification. After hearing the programme, I immediately telephoned Charlie Whelan and asked him to convey my apologies for this unpardonable error to the shadow chancellor. I also apologised to the BBC. But the damage was largely done. Journalists who simply looked up the cuttings used it over and over again, and still do.

However, the hue and cry that ensued cannot be laid simply at my door. Roy Plomley's widow, the actress Diana Wong, was listening to her husband's creation while rushing round her Putney home getting ready to play tennis at the prestigious Hurlingham Club. She told Pauline Peters that she thought the programme 'not very nice'.[2] Sue Lawley was also asked to comment on the Sunday of the broadcast, but declined. Mrs Plomley was more robust in the *Daily Express*. 'I felt the questions were incredibly intrusive. I could tell what she was working towards by asking him why he was not married – she was asking if people thought he was homosexual. Sue has done this before, asking people questions about their very private lives,' she said.[3] In the *Daily Telegraph*, she was equally forthright: 'I did not like all that probing of private and intimate details, I think it is rude.' She thought Lawley hosted the programme well, 'but it is a pity that sometimes she takes what I call a journalistic approach, looking for headlines.'[4]

The BBC had less than a handful of calls when the programme went out, rising to fifty a couple of days later when the publicity reached a wider audience. There were also twelve letters to Radio 4's *Feedback* programme for listeners' complaints, enough for Lawley to have to answer on air criticisms that her questioning had been 'insistent' and 'haranguing'. She insisted, 'It was a perfectly fair and proper piece of interrogation. It would not be responsible, even on a programme like *Desert Island Discs*, to give a politician a simple and easy ride, so that he could present a rose-tinted view of himself.' Afterwards, she told Valerie Grove, 'I replied that we live in the second half of the 1990s; that the programme is fifty-four years old and that it had to gently move along with the times, and, while very aware of the Radio 4 audience, one had sometimes to address issues which they might not find comfortable.'[5] And that the interviewees did not find particularly congenial, she might have added. Lawley argued that *Desert Island Discs* is a biographical interview, and personal relationships are bound to come up. She thought her questioning was not deeply offensive or prurient. 'I do rehearse my questions,' she added. But she would not have asked about the sexuality of another famous political castaway, the former prime minister Edward Heath. 'It's a generational thing.' Not everyone shared Ms Groves's insouciance. In the same paper, Brenda Maddox wrote that 'To ask Gordon Brown, the Shadow Chancellor, to defend himself against charges of homosexuality because he is unmarried at fortysomething is as out of place as if on Newsnight Jeremy Paxman were to ask the Chancellor, Kenneth Clarke, which book he would like to take to a desert island excluding the Bible and Shakespeare which are already there.'[6] Much later, Emma Forrest, a *Guardian* writer observed, 'In Radio 4 speak, she [Lawley] basically was asking: "Are you a fag?" Annoyed, not at the implication, but at the intrusion, he refused to answer yes or no. He showed such certainty in himself that he didn't have to deny it, which for your average heterosexual man, let alone a politician, is a very big deal. And, apparently, he is not remotely gay. The rumours sprung from a case of wishful thinking all round.'[7]

A spokesman for the BBC said the corporation was happy with the interview. 'There is no question of anyone being reprimanded over it. We haven't a problem, and, as far as we know, Mr Brown hasn't.' And there the matter rested. Yet this was a pity, because if Sue Lawley and her researchers had gone more thoroughly into Gordon Brown's very private (though increasingly less so) life, they would have uncovered a fascinating world of relationships down the years. As they say north of the border, he *is* one for the lassies. What does he look for? 'It's obvious,' he once confessed. Girls who are 'attractive, humorous, exciting.'[8]

Social life in his youth in Kirkcaldy revolved, inevitably, around the kirk: the badminton club, the Youth Fellowship and bible classes. Young Gordon played the piano as well as the violin in the school orchestra, but when he reached his teens his interest in music naturally turned to pop. He got himself a guitar, and grew his hair fashionably long. Then around this time, his uncle sold Gordon's stamp collection to a London dealer for more than £20, quite a large sum. He bought a Dansette record-player, one of the type that automatically played one LP after another, and Gordon and his big brother John, the more extrovert of the two, organised dances to the pop hits of the day in the church hall. The Kirkcaldy church hop was probably not the hottest 'nite spot' in Fife. 'My father was always very suspicious of dances in the church hall, and would come along to police them – sometimes with the elders of the kirk,' John recollected. 'But they were very successful dances, especially at Christmas time. We sold quite a lot of tickets.'[9] The money they raised went to a Glasgow boys' charity.

A schoolfriend, Marie Maxwell (now Dewar), remembers the kirk hops with distant affection. 'I knew both Gordon and his brother John well. They were always organising dances and selling tickets. Gordon was always in the thick of things,' she told the *Sunday Mail*. 'He was a lovely boy. The boys and girls didn't mix much at school but we had plenty of fun at the dances. The last couple of years at school were great.' Another member of his class, Fiona Buchan (now Johnstone), also recalled that 'The thing about Gordon was that he was good fun. I remember him always smiling.'[10]

In the family archives, Gordon's 'Address to the Lassies', delivered at a Burns Night supper on 20 January 1967, has been preserved. For a sixteen-year-old boy writing in the 1960s, it is extraordinarily mature: witty, generous and radical. Proposing the toast, he said, 'It strikes me that before the eighteenth century, women would not have been addressed formally in this way. Burns revolutionised this – as he did many other things. But like many men, he found one woman insufficient, a fact quite beyond the female comprehension. He may be termed "man of the world" for the very reason that this term IMPLIES (his capitals) more than one DARE explain tonight. He was to eighteenth century Ayrshire what James Bond has been to our era. Both enjoyed more than their share of amorous adventure, unrestricted excitement and considerable intrigue; but where BOND drove his Aston Martin, BURNS manipulated his plough, where BOND entertained beautiful nondescript blondes, BURNS entertained country servant girls, where BOND encountered enemy agents, Burns encountered mice and where Bond escaped the consequences, Burns had to pay them' (capitals in the original).

From his earliest days, Burns was fascinated by and obsessed with the lassies, and after many years of experiencing 'the exhilaration of love' wrote his first poem, 'O once I lo'ed a Bonie lass'. He was fifteen then, pointed out Brown. 'In a sense therefore he never grew out of his youth. For the rest of his life, as a bachelor and a married man, he was actively involved with women, plural.' The poet had more to offer posterity than children, however. 'Though many of his ideas were too revolutionary for his age, they seem only too relevant for ours. Burns for instance realised that women had a special role to play in society.' At that time, the female was regarded as fit only for the kitchen sink and creating a family to replace her there. 'But Burns first of all saw the advantages of associating the female with some thing or some idea. For example in the "Bonie Lass of Albanie" he uses the female as a symbol for enslaved Scotland.' This method of association was now much exploited. 'Today when you are buying your soap, you are really buying that beautiful girl with the soft skin, when you are buying Fairy Snow, you are buying all the bliss of married life and when you are buying your toothpaste you are buying that gorgeous girl who smiles 50 times a day just for you. Much of the psychology of advertising rests on the appeal of a woman.'

The battle for equality must begin again, he argued. 'You all know the theory of the creation. God created Adam. Adam wasn't satisfied. So God created Eve. Man could not live without woman, but the world would be lost without man. That is why all the spinsters in the Russian city of Ivanovo have been moving out following the redeployment of all the virile men in Siberia.' Gordon joked that Burns realised the mistake of his philosophy. 'Thanks to Miss Snodgrass, I have discovered that Burns's address to the Devil is really an address to the lassies.' This, he said, became perfectly clear upon examining the poem:

Hear me auld hag for a wee
And let poor damned bodies be
I'm sure sma pleasure it canna gie
   Even to a woman
To skelp an' scaud poor dogs like me
   And hear us squeelen

Lorna Snodgrass was a classmate at Kirkcaldy High. Was she his first girlfriend, referred to by Murray Elder, his close friend, who said, 'He had a girl friend at school – Lorna – who lasted a bit longer' (than schooldays)?[11] Thirty years after this Burns Night entertainment Lorna Snodgrass, now Mrs Lorna Harris, a lawyer with the Serious Fraud Office in London, recalled, 'We were great mates and I particularly remember a happy youth fellowship trip to Sweden in our last year at school. I was as close to him as anyone. He was so happy-go-lucky and not dour at all, as some people say he is now. We have kept in touch and I spoke to him only last year when we bumped into each other in London. I wrote to him at the time of John Smith's death.'[12] Alas for romantic fiction, she was not the Lorna of his affections. That honour went to Lorna Henderson, his girl-friend and tennis partner until he was eighteen.

Gordon evidently knew something of the passionate feelings that were Burns's favourite subject, urging 'take away the aspi-rations for and assertions of superiority, and we have left the lassie Burns knew. He experienced all the conceivable emotions and many more – and we cannot fail to share with him the joy and innocence of young love, the hopes and disappointments of adolescence and the security and stability of marriage. The aphorism "If death came from Burns, then the lassies would be immortal" fits him perfectly. Like Burns, we find we cannot live without the lassies.'

The boy who could not live without the lassies praised the quality of his school's female pupils. 'Whether your virtue (if I may use that word, ladies, be in your beauty, personality, intel-ligence or wit, you are the life blood of man. I could, ladies,

compliment you personally, but such a eulogy would be boring
not only to you but to my fellow men, who will have done or
be about to do this anyway. It is in this context that I should
first of all give you Miss Snodgrass's telephone number and secondly report that historically speaking Miss Ednie is well up on
her dates this year.'

He closed with some poetic advice from Burns:

> The bonniest lass that ye meet neist
> Gie her a kiss an a that
> In spite o' ilka parish priest
> Repentin' stool an a that.

He asked them not to take it to heart right away, for they would
find it impossible to leave the hall. 'Gentlemen,' he commanded, 'rise from your seats as a measure of respect and not
inferiority and toast the lassies!' Small wonder that his classmate Marie Maxwell could sigh, 'He was a lovely boy,' three
decades later. Gordon Brown, tall, athletic, rugger first-
fifteener, brilliant debater, long-haired, guitar-strumming Dux
of his school, must have been the pin-up of his year. His shy-
ness would have only made him more attractive to the girls.

Later that summer of 1967, Gordon went on the trip to
Sweden, organised through the church. The mixed-sex party
sailed from Hull, and spent two weeks in Gothenburg and at a
town by the sea in the north of the country. Murray Elder
remembers it well. 'It was great. We had great fun. The Swedes
were very good company. There was much pairing off, and
attempted pairing-off going on.'[13] But with the approach of
autumn, Brown had to tear himself away from these seemingly
innocent pleasures to go up to university, and he had been there
only a few days before the eye injury that was to affect the rest
of his life. He was alternately confined to bed, compelled to lie
on his back as part of the treatment, and catching up on his
history course in his squalid lodgings in the Grassmarket. It was
not a time for girls, though friends recollect the name of May,

a Fife schoolteacher, who later married an American sportsman and emigrated to the USA.

'There were girlfriends, always steady ones,' recalled his friend and occasional flatmate, Jon Wills. 'Gordon is a charmer and sometimes a flirt, but he is not promiscuous. When his parents were visiting Edinburgh, frantic efforts were made to remove all traces of female occupation from the flat. This went on long after he had been elected to Parliament. It's not that Gordon was ashamed of his relationships. He just didn't want to upset his mother, whom he revered.'[14] Sometimes, these efforts were more frantic than thorough. Wilf Stevenson, a close friend from student days, remembers the time when Mrs Brown came to stay at Marchmont Road, and insisted on doing the copious amount of washing. 'She discovered a pair of girl's panties in the wash,' he says. 'They were the resident girlfriend's at the time. They both chose to ignore them. Then, she laid them on top of the pile. Gordon said: "I don't know how they got there. They must have come from the laundry." It was ridiculous. Both knew that the other knew.'[15]

Gordon Brown's first great love, Princess Margarita of Romania, arrived on the scene in 1968. She came to Edinburgh to read for a degree in sociology and politics. He met her at one of the occasional soirées thrown by a Sir John Crofton, a professor of respitorial medicine, who liked to gather budding student politicians round him and spring the question 'What are you going to do to make the world a better place?' Dr Colin Currie, a fellow-student at the university who remains a member of Brown's inner circle of friends, said, 'That was the first time they surfaced. One heard about her, and what she was trying to do, and he was going to be a politician. It was just great fun: this very liberal chap, and a lot of students being very silly. He decided to be sensible and find out about students.'[16] Their paths also crossed in campus student politics. In those days, Gordon smoked a pipe, perhaps to make himself look older (he was still only in his late teens), but he didn't dabble in drugs. 'Like other students, he sometimes got tipsy but he always drank beer or wine and never, to my knowledge, became oblivious like some of us,' remembered Wills. 'I don't recall him ever smoking a joint. Other drugs were out of the question. Gordon is, after all, a son of the manse. And that is the key to understanding what makes him tick.'[17] Another university contemporary, Bill Campbell, head of Edinburgh-based Mainstream Publishing, which has published most of Brown's books, suggests, 'Women were not number-one priority in Gordon's life. He was much more interested in ideas. He was a great social beast at times. He liked nothing better than to go for a few beers, but he always lived in the realm of ideas, making plans – particularly politics. I always got the impression that he was more attractive to women than he ever realised. And he is much more of a charmer to women than he ever realised.'[18]

Princess Margarita is the eldest daughter of the exiled King Michael and the great, great, great granddaughter of Queen Victoria, fifty-third in line to the British throne. When she was born in 1950 the Romanian royal family lived a wandering life. Her home as a child was in the Hertfordshire village of Ayot St Lawrence, where her father supported himself in the 1950s with a market garden and chicken farm. There were homes later in Lausanne, Florence, Denmark and Edinburgh. They had no crown jewels and little money. 'We didn't have a privileged upbringing,' she said later. 'On the contrary, there were a lot of financial problems.'[19] The family now lives comfortably in a large villa beside Lake Geneva. In the late 1960s, feisty, dark-haired Margarita, nicknamed 'the Red Princess', became one of the key figures, along with Gordon, in the movement to elect a student rector. Friends say he partied and drank less than other students, and did not waste his evenings looking for new girlfriends because he always had the same one – Margarita, 'the broad Left beauty'. A friend of the period said, 'She was sweet and gentle and obviously cut out to make somebody a very good wife. She was bright, too, though not like him, but they seemed made for each other. She took a great deal more care of him than he did of himself and he loved her attention.'[20]

She even moved into the flat in Marchmont Road. From time to time, an official car would bring a formal invitation to the door. These occasions, it was noted, coincided with a visit to the city by a member of Britain's royal family, who were, said Margarita, 'always very, very nice to us, and very supportive'.[21] The relationship, about which Brown has never talked (in common with every other relationship), lasted for five years. 'She stayed over in Marchmont Road, though she had her own place,' said Wills. 'They were very much an item. Everybody assumed they would get married as the rest of us did in a rather boring, predictable way.'[22] 'It was a very solid and romantic story,' Margarita subsequently told *Harpers & Queen*. 'I never stopped loving him, but one day it didn't seem right any more. It was politics, politics, politics, and I needed nurturing.'[23]

She did not have to look very far. Friends say she ended the affair with Gordon Brown and took up with Jim Keddie, a firefighter and Labour activist from the working-class district of Leith. 'She left him in some style and went to live with an enormous fireman, a great big bear of a man,' said a close friend of Brown. 'She brought him round the scene. She had decided that if Brown wouldn't marry her . . .' Gordon and his Red Princess were still seen socially together, but the relationship was over. Big Jim, now a stonemason in Shetland, seems to have been bowled over. 'He was probably a bit embarrassed, and probably had no idea when he met her that she was an intimate of Gordon Brown. I think Gordon was very bitter about it. But Jim was jolly good company, attentive and funny – and didn't give up his entire weekends to politics,' says a fellow-activist from the period.

Friends of the couple insist that 'she loved Gordon madly – and probably still does – but he just never had the time to take her out for dinner and all the other things you do when you're courting. He was too busy. He couldn't say "no" to meetings. He was always willing to help out, but at great personal cost.'[24] There was also another consideration. His close friend Dr Currie concedes that the affair with Margarita was 'a hugely important relationship', but believes Gordon also had his sights fixed on Westminster. 'How would a Romanian princess go down with a left-wing selection committee? That is maybe a factor,' he hinted.

Owen Dudley Edwards, reader in history at Edinburgh University, sees it a different way. 'When you're in love with a girl that you can't marry, it must be almost impossible to get over. You have to understand that his anxieties about this friendship were not the result of his being ambitious, but because he is a truly moral character. To him, it was a matter of honour. He had his beliefs, his principles.'[25]

But though Big Jim supplanted him, Gordon and Margarita remained on friendly terms. She helped him during his parliamentary election campaign in 1979, knocking on doors in Edinburgh South, and she was at the polling-night party when he lost. Their friendship has continued down the years. Princess Margarita was present at some of the inner-circle gatherings in London in the early summer of 1994, when Brown was agonising over the Labour leadership. 'She was a good friend of mine, and still is,' he said in 1995.[26] In 1996, Margarita married Radu Duda, a Romanian actor, and the couple live in the family villa, where Princess Margarita's charitable foundation for disabled children in Romania is based.

Friends say that Brown had a 'wee flutter' with the television personality Sheena Macdonald after Margarita. Sheena, dark-haired and engaging, came into the picture as arts editor of *Student* newspaper on the Edinburgh campus in the autumn of 1974, during Brown's second year as rector. She was born in Dunfermline, a daughter of the manse. Her father was a former moderator of the General Assembly of the Church of Scotland. She was educated at the prestigious George Watson's ladies' college in Edinburgh, and after taking an MA at Edinburgh gained a film-studies degree at Bristol University in 1977 before returning to work first for BBC Radio Scotland and then for STV. According to a *Sunday Times* profile, 'At Edinburgh she also dated Gordon Brown, a relationship no contemporary is prepared to discuss.'[27] She was said to be 'fascinated' by him, and attended his parties at Marchmont Road. There is scant likelihood of any relationship between them while he was with his Red Princess, for Gordon is nothing if not loyal. 'He certainly would not have two-timed anybody,' insists Wills. 'He is very strong on loyalty.' But it works both ways. 'Anybody who is seen to have transgressed would have been cut off. I would say he is a serial monogamist. He tries his best, but it's not good enough. He never learned to leave enough time.'[28]

In 1981, Gordon Brown began a relationship with Marion Caldwell, a rising young advocate working in Edinburgh. It was to last for thirteen years, before foundering on the same rocks that had destroyed his first big romance. Marion was the daughter of an engineer from Denistoun in the eastern suburbs of Glasgow. From school, she went to work as a journalist with the DC Thomson group in Dundee, publishers of a wide range of newspapers and magazines from the *Sunday Post* to the *Beano*. From there, she went on to university to study law.

The two hit it off extremely well. Marion, three years younger than Gordon, was very bright, intuitive and sharp. 'Politically sharp,' says Colin Currie. 'More sharp than Gordon gave her credit for, maybe. Certainly, that led to a complementarity about Marion and Gordon. She is a very clever and open-minded person.'[29] Friends saw a likeness to Margarita. The new woman in his life could deal comfortably with people right across the social spectrum. She, too, had a flat in the Marchmont district. Over the years, the two holidayed together in France and the United States. Apart from the obvious attractions of being thirty-something and in love, they shared a passion for books and tennis. According to friends, they even lived together for a time in the barn-like detached house in North Queensferry, overlooking the Firth of Forth, that Brown bought in the late 1980s.

'They were a very steady number,' said a friend of both. 'It got close to marriage. She had a huge regard for Gordon. He agonised in the spirit; in the spirit, and all that. It came to a slow, uncertain and painful end over some years. That was a matter of great distress to people who liked both of them.'[30]

Some find parallels between Marion Caldwell and Cherie Blair: both are dark and pretty. Both have made it to the upper reaches of the legal profession from fairly humble origins. There the resemblance ends. Cherie Booth got her man, and Marion did not. She is, nevertheless, a figure of some substance in the Scottish legal establishment, sitting on prestigious public inquiries such as the Piper Alpha and Orkney child sex-abuse investigations.

In the wake of this second failure, Sheena Macdonald re-emerged. 'She was a theme revisited,' said an unkind friend. But by the early 1990s, she was a successful, sought-after television presenter and interviewer. She hosted the BBC coverage of the Labour Party conference, and was equally at home conducting a high-profile interview with Sinn Fein president Gerry Adams. Gordon was 'still going out with' Sheena, according to one of his inner circle, when Sarah Macaulay arrived in his office at Millbank one bright morning in February 1994. The suggestion that he was in a relationship with Ms Macdonald surprised people at the BBC, where it had been assumed for some that they were 'no longer an item'. It also runs counter to the accepted view of Brown as a 'serial monogamist'. But the break-up of his relationship was chronicled in the *Daily Mail*, which reported, 'Relations with Miss Macdonald ended on a sour note – so much so that after a recent telephone interview between the two, her producer was moved to demand: "What's going on here? Why the naked hostility?" She is said to have snapped: "What do you expect when someone goes out with you for four months and then drops you like that, without even a goodbye?"'[31] It was perhaps, a case of 'Hello, Sarah, goodbye, Sheena'.

Sarah, now 34, a stunningly attractive willowy dark-blonde with blue eyes, is a partner in the Soho-based public affairs consultancy of Hobsbawm Macaulay with Julia Hobsbawm, daughter of the famous Marxist historian Eric Hobsbawm.

Their company employs twelve people (only four men), and specialises in working for good causes, such as the race-relations think tank the Runnymede Trust, the Medical Foundation for the Care of Victims of Torture, and Emily's List, the pressure group that helps women become Labour MPs. But their client list also includes *Vogue*, the *New Statesman*, Mercury Communications, the British Television Advertising Craft Awards and Forward Publishing, owned by the poetry-loving millionaire William Sieghart. They also collaborated with employers and the engineering union AEEU on Manufacturing Matters, a campaign to raise the public profile of the metal-bashing industry. Now, she was working on the Labour Party's celebrity fund-raising bash to be held at the Park Lane Hotel in Mayfair in late spring. Gordon was involved in 'fronting-up' the appeal to businessmen and corporate luvvies who were prepared to pay £500 a head to sit down to dinner with the party leader, John Smith. This was the fateful dinner on 11 May at which Brown's mentor was 'in really good form', before dying a few hours later.

Sarah Macaulay had seen rather more of the world than Gordon had at this age. She was born in Beaconsfield in October 1963, the eldest of three children. Her father, a Scot, was an educational publisher and her mother an infant-school head teacher; they met while studying at Edinburgh University. When she was only two, the family moved to Tanzania, east Africa. She went to school first in Arusha, at the foot of Mount Kilimanjaro, and then at the International School in the capital, Dar-es-Salaam. On their return to the UK, her parents split up. The children, Sarah and her younger brothers Sean and Bruce, lived with their mother in London, but spent their summer holidays with their father in Falkland, Fife. After attending schools in north London, Sarah went to Bristol University, and took an upper-second honours degree in psychology. Even as a student, she began working in the field of events, organising a Contemporary Arts Festival in Bristol for two years. She also did some assignments in London for Lord

Mackintosh, a former Labour leader of the GLC, who had a research consultancy.

Her work brought her back into touch with Julia Hobsbawm, whom she had known since her teens at Camden School for Girls, and who was now organising events – particularly with people in the cultural field – for Labour. After a stint at the design firm Woolf-Olins, Sarah joined Julia in setting up their own 'integrity PR' company in 1993. Sarah brought her knowledge of the business world to complement Julia's wide contacts in the arts and politics. She got to know John Smith and Murray Elder, his chief of staff, and moving in those circles she was bound to meet Gordon Brown sooner or later. Sarah was also friendly with Sue Nye, Brown's chief aide, who had originally worked for Neil Kinnock. She introduced the two over dinner almost a year before Sarah was called in to help with the celebrities' dinner.

Brown was clearly attracted to Sarah Macaulay, and they began dating. Because of his intense dislike of publicity for his personal life, they met most often in the Soho House 'hip club' in Old Compton Street, hard by her office. Though it was frequented by showbiz types, it was unlikely that many of them would recognise the tall, slightly podgy figure sitting in the corner with the PR high-flyer from next door. The relationship was kept secret for more than year, through the tumult of the leadership campaign and the shadow chancellor's long grind towards a new economic policy for Labour. It first surfaced in the *Mail on Sunday* in April 1995. The paper's *Night and Day* magazine reported that Gordon's 'long relationship' with the broadcaster Sheena MacDonald had ended recently, and he was now close to Sarah Macaulay, a business consultant whose company had undertaken PR work on behalf of a number of Labour Party causes. The article added: 'She describes their relationship as "on-off".' As usual, Brown would not discuss it, and his press secretary, Charlie Whelan, ('himself a friend of Ms Macaulay') adamantly denied its very existence.

Perhaps there was not much to deny at that stage. It was

another four months before the now-defunct *Today* newspaper picked up the threads of the story, suggesting that the most eligible bachelor in the political world was considering giving up his solo status. A friend of Sarah's was quoted as saying, 'Gordon is so worried that this will get out that he even takes along his assistant so no one thinks he is romancing Sarah. But he certainly is!'[32] There was also a tormented interview that month in the *Daily Mail*, in which the journalist Steve Poole skewered the shy shadow chancellor. He spun the usual line about 'the fact that I'm not married is just a fact that things didn't work out, or haven't so far' and then, enigmatically, offered: 'Things will change.' The interviewer pounced: 'Do you want to get married? "I think it would be quite good,"' he replied. The writer observed that 'quite good' must be Brownspeak for positively ecstatic, and pressed his point: 'Do you find it hard to fall in love? His face and whole body twitch like a fly that's just been sprayed and is not quite dead. He finds these questions excruciating but says "No, I don't think so at all."' Brown further volunteered that he felt at a turning point. 'I do have a relationship at the moment, but I don't think she'd appreciate me talking about it. I don't try to be secretive, but . . . I think maybe my personal life's been changing quite a bit. I don't think talking about it in interviews particularly helps.'[33] That is the line he still takes. I pressed one of his closest aides on the matter. Does he love Sarah? After some humming and ha-ing, back came the answer, a firm 'Yes.'

However, the flurry of stories at the beginning of 1997 that Gordon and Sarah were to marry were, to say the least, premature. 'Mandrake', the diarist of the *Sunday Telegraph*, said with total assurance that they were secretly engaged, and it was their intention to tie the knot after the general election. For good measure, he 'disclosed' that Sarah had taken rather belated advantage of the 1996 leap year, and had proposed to him at the end of December. An announcement of the engagement was confidently predicted for the summer of 1997. The diarist also claimed (wrongly) that Sarah had 'an unrequited passion' for the playboy Darius Guppy, which prompted an immediate solicitor's letter to the newspaper. The story of the 'engagement' appeared on the same day in the *Express on Sunday*, which also quoted an unnamed Scots Labour MP who had known Brown for twenty years. 'Sarah is a smashing girl and most of us think he will tie the knot eventually.'[34]

This is also the view of his close friend Wilf Stevenson, director of the British Film Institute. 'He has yet to settle down and have a family. These things will happen, I am quite confident. The future Mrs Brown may have a view about that, which he might share,' he hinted. 'He come from a very, very happy and integrated family. Both brothers have children he adores. There have been several eligible women, but somehow it hasn't worked. I think it will work at some point. There is that point in our adult development that the genes tell us to settle down and calm down, and it will happen to him as it does to everybody else.'[35]

Alarm bells rang just before Brown's first budget when he allowed the best-selling *News of the World* to take his photograph with Sarah in a Soho restaurant, Vasco and Piero's Pavilion. The two were pictured at a discreet corner table, with Sarah gazing lovingly at Gordon. He looked rather more reserved, but the picture, taken on 27 June, ran for days in the national press and triggered a fresh bout of speculation. The couple had agreed to have their photograph taken after a tip-off to the *News of the World* and even consented to a second take when the nervous photographer thought he had not got a good enough shot. It was therefore an 'official' picture, a semi-formal acknowledgement of their relationship. A friend of Sarah said he wanted to 'formalise' the relationship so that she could visit him in the flat he occupies in 10 Downing Street 'without ducking and diving out of the back door'. She is, in fact, a frequent visitor.

Sarah is, of course, also a political animal like Brown – she enjoyed Alan Clark's tell-all diaries – but it is not known how much he talks politics to her. The chancellor has a very tightly knit group of friends including Wilf Stevenson and Dr Colin Currie, in whom he confides. However, even they are not as close as his brothers, Andrew and John. For instance, the decision not to contest the Hamilton by-election in 1978 was 'a family issue', said Stevenson, adding, 'There are views that are stronger than [those of] his friends.'[36] Brown consulted his elder brother a great deal in the aftermath of John Smith's death. 'I was keen for him to stand,' said John. 'I believe he could have done it.' He also disclosed that Gordon was upset by Mandelson's private letter during the 'phoney war' period of the Labour leadership campaign, the burden of which was he should stand down for the good of the party.[37]

His closeness to his brothers is matched by his filial devotion to his parents, John and Elizabeth, who live in retirement in a modest bungalow built by the family construction firm on the outskirts of Insch, Aberdeenshire. Even at the height of the general election campaign in 1997, Gordon broke off from the hectic battle to visit his mother and father on their golden wedding celebration on 27 April. His mother says, 'He is a good son to us. Very kind.' The couple have watched the rise and rise of their son with admiration, and not a little bewilderment. 'I am amazed that he does this,' confesses Elizabeth Brown. 'He was the shyest member of the family when he was very young. The other boys were extroverts, but Gordon was the opposite. I'm amazed he does this.'[38]

CHAPTER 12

ELECTION

IN THE EARLY EVENING OF SATURDAY, 15 MARCH 1997, while the Conservative Central Council was winding up its annual gathering in Bath, rumours began to circulate in what used to be called Fleet Street that 'something big' was about to emerge. In the newsrooms of the Sunday papers, there was an air of expectation. Shortly after eight o'clock, it broke. The early edition of the *Sunday Times* splashed across its front page the prediction that Major was to name 1 May. There was to be an emergency Cabinet meeting on Monday, 17 March, after which John Major would go to Buckingham Palace and ask the Queen for a dissolution of Parliament in the week following the Easter holiday. With the last possible date for a general election so close, she could hardly refuse his request.

Unlike so many Sunday newspaper 'flyers' – not least those in the *Sunday Times* – the story was clearly grounded in fact. A similar prediction appeared in the *Express on Sunday*, the nearest thing Conservative Central Office had to a client state. Frantic late-evening telephone calls to Charles Lewington, the Tory party media director (and erstwhile political editor of the *Express on Sunday*) yielded neither confirmation nor denial. His nervousness was palpable. Reticence on this scale was enough for most seasoned political observers. This was it.

Gordon Brown, at home in North Queensferry, was alerted to the rumours as they broke. He declined to comment, but he decided to act. He had a telephone conference with Blair, and flew back to his office in London. Ed Miliband was already there, preparing speeches and discussing how to play a debate with chancellor Ken Clarke – an event that was promptly cancelled. Brown already knew that Rupert Murdoch would take a decision that weekend about his papers' party allegiance during the election campaign. Everything was coming together, if rather more rapidly than expected. Labour Party strategists had already drawn up a four-week 'grid' of steps to be taken in the event of a snap poll announcement. It was agreed that the first two days of this plan would be put into practice. After that, they would play it by ear.

An NOP opinion poll in the *Sunday Times* on 16 March put Labour on 53 per cent. Twenty-five points ahead of the Tories and up three on the previous month. The Tories were down four on 27 per cent, and the Liberal Democrats unchanged on 13 per cent. Most people – 54 per cent – thought Labour was ahead because it was 'time for a change'.

John Major duly called the Cabinet together on 17 March, and announced the election date in Downing Street at 12.35 p.m. It would be a six-and-a-half-week campaign, the longest in modern political history. Flying in the face of the opinion polls, he declared he would win.

Brown went into session with his advisers, planning how to ensure that Major did not. Brown was to chair the daily election briefings for the media in a purpose-built mini-cinema in the Millbank HQ. He would also chair four daily meetings of the top-level election-campaign team, bringing in Whelan, Mandelson and Alistair Campbell. The team would determine which issue they wanted to dominate that day's agenda, and would also assess how the daily Tory briefing – held before Labour's – had played, so as to provide an immediate response. 'The aim was always to set the agenda,' Brown recollected.

'Remember, we had been practising for two and a half years. We had held meetings in my office at 9 o'clock every weekday morning in which we worked on the day's agenda while parliament was sitting. The location and context was different during the election, but we knew what was required.'[1]

Apart from the election announcement itself, the first day of the pre-Easter 'phoney war' was dominated by the defection of the *Sun*, Britain's biggest-selling daily paper, to the Labour cause. This was a devastating blow for Major. Five years previously, when he unexpectedly triumphed over Neil Kinnock, the paper had claimed that 'It Woz The Sun Wot Won It'. Newspapers do not win elections, but they can certainly help to lose them. Brown's first big day, 18 March, was well received. Even the irretrievably Tory *Daily Mail* rated his performance better than Ken Clarke's counter-attack.

Brown announced that, if Labour won, a minister of Cabinet rank would be appointed to oversee his £3 billion 'welfare to work' programme designed to get unemployed young people and the long-term jobless back to work. He created waves by refusing to name the privatised utilities on whose 'excess' profits he would levy the windfall tax to pay for the programme, teasing reporters with a reiteration of his long-standing definition that the tax would be on 'industries regulated and licensed by the state' that had been privatised since 1979. Some interpreted this as meaning that British Telecom and the privatised airports authority, BAA, would be exempted. Clarke heaped scorn on the plan, insisting that 'the real economy out-performs taxing and scheming social democratic policies'. He asked, 'How can you trust a Shadow Chancellor who will not answer a straight question about which companies will pay the tax, when they obviously know who they intend to target?' Indeed, Brown knew precisely how and where the windfall tax would fall, but saw no virtue in giving hostages to fortune to the outgoing chancellor.

Brown had also been watching closely the developments on parliamentary 'sleaze'. Along with the rest of the Shadow

Cabinet, on 19 March he signed a parliamentary motion demanding that the government, 'for the good of our parliamentary system and in the public interest', publish the report by the parliamentary commissioner on standards, Sir Gordon Downey, into allegations of misconduct against a number of MPs. The case against one, Neil Hamilton, Tory MP for the Cheshire constituency of Tatton, included claims that he had taken thousands of pounds for asking parliamentary questions. John Major's move to prorogue Parliament early had scuppered publication of the 'sleazebuster's' verdict, infuriating the Opposition parties, who saw it as a cunning act of censorship. If MPs were not sitting, the Commons Select Committee on Standards could not see the report, and therefore it had to remain under wraps until after the election – effectively lifting the controversy out of the public domain. Brown determined otherwise. He urged the prime minister to adjourn Parliament, rather than insist on prorogation two weeks ahead of dissolution. Major refused, and was promptly accused of a cover-up. Brown then looked for other ways of keeping the gaze of public attention on sleaze, and suggested that an anti-sleaze candidate should be found to stand against Hamilton in Tatton. 'The one thing we hadn't anticipated was sleaze becoming an issue,' Brown said later. 'I felt it was a good idea, having read about anti-corruption candidates standing in the 1920's, for a similar campaign in Tatton.'[2]

On 19 March, the Tories showed their electoral hand. 'Britain is Booming. Don't Let Labour Ruin It' was to be their theme. A big fall – 62,800 – in the official number of people out of work and claiming benefit brought the dole queue down to 1,746,300, or 6.2 per cent, the lowest since October 1990. Labour dismissed the figures as 'not a true reflection of the situation' and switched the spotlight back to sleaze as Major promised to rush out a carefully edited version of the Downey Report. An incandescent Brian Mawhinney, chairman of the Tory party, accused the shadow chancellor of 'looking for a smear to stop the people of Britain focusing on the good news'.

When it came out, the potted version of Downey was only eight paragraphs long. It absolved a number of Tory MPs on minor charges, but failed to address the 'cash for questions' issue and the *Guardian* intensified disquiet by publishing Hamilton's own confidential admissions to the inquiry.[3] Armed with this damning evidence, Brown put out discreet feelers on the prospects of Labour actually withdrawing its own (third-placed) candidate in Tatton in support of an anti-sleaze contender, if the Liberals Democrats agreed to do likewise.

He went on BBC TV's *On the Record* on the morning of 23 March, the first Sunday of the campaign, still playing a straight bat on the windfall tax. A chancellor did not raise taxes on individual firms, he pointed out, only on specified groups of businesses. The liability of any company to pay would be known only after the Treasury decided its profits were excessive. He repeated Labour's pledge to leave undisturbed the 23p in the pound basic rate and 40p top rate of income tax, and promised that VAT on fuel would be cut to 5 per cent. He also let it be known that Labour would for the first time publish a 'business manifesto', and pledged an 'audit of public spending to establish where the Tories have left us' and an immediate review of public spending to prepare for his first budget. The *Herald*, Scotland's leading morning paper, declared that Brown 'dominated the interview by giving John Humphrys little opportunity to pin him down'.[4] This was a tactic that would be more in evidence as the campaign wore on. Brown said he would not repeat the errors of his predecessors in 1964 and 1974 by spending too much in the first two years and then having to cut back in the next three years.

Week two of the campaign found Brown promising to increase the share of national income spent on education, by reducing the share spent on unemployment. 'We will reverse the trend of the Conservative years,' he insisted, at the Tuesday morning media briefing (at which a photographer from the *Independent* snapped him sitting under the word 'failure' on the set backdrop). The manifesto cleared its final hurdle – the

'Clause V' meeting between the Shadow Cabinet and the NEC – on 26 March amid tight security. Copies of the draft were numbered, and had to be handed back in after the meeting. The rump of the left wing on NEC was comprehensively routed, most of Dennis Skinner's amendments not even attracting a seconder. His only success was in ensuring that the document gave an assurance that BBC television and radio would remain in the public sector. The shadow chancellor also ruled out any pretence that Labour would try to buy back Railtrack, the privatised railway system. The £2 billion cost of buying a majority share was too high, he argued, and this was accepted.

The same day, at a press conference, Tony Blair explained why Brown was missing from his usual chair on the platform: he was 'on his way to Basildon to trumpet our plans for a new 10p starting rate of tax to help those on lower incomes'. He arrived in the Essex new town, famous for being the nation's barometer of public opinion, two hours after the oleaginous home secretary, Michael Howard, had left. Brown delivered what the *Independent* called 'a blistering speech on the betrayal of Basildon Man', reminding his audience of John Major's broken promises on tax. He drew gasps from the audience by breaking the news that Sir Tim Smith, one of the Tory grandees named in the Downey Report, had just resigned his parliamentary seat. The audience was impressed by him. Geraldine Evans, 51, landlady of the Barge pub, said, 'I never believed anyone as moderate as myself could vote Labour. But I've looked at their policies and they're closer to my own beliefs.'[5]

On 2 April the Tories published their manifesto. It was more like a Lib-Dem manifesto, making promises it would not have to keep because the party would not be in government. They would spend more on schools, the police and hospitals, but 'virtually eliminate' public borrowing within three years and make Britain 'the best place in the world to live'. The shadow chancellor costed their programme at 'at least £13 billion in a full year', drawing a furious reaction from Kenneth Clarke, who, before Labour had even unveiled its manifesto, accused the party of having a £30 billion spending plan, and a £12 billion hole in expenditure forecasts, even if a Blair government stuck to the Conservatives' forward commitments for the next two years. 'Our tax plans are carefully thought out and costed,' expostulated Tory spokesman Alan Duncan MP. 'It is Gordon Brown who cannot do his sums.'

The charge bounced off Brown, whose constant repetition that he would not spend any more money than Clarke had set out in 1997/98 and 1998/99 was getting home to voters. On 3 April, the pledge was enshrined in Labour's manifesto, published at a press conference that attracted six hundred journalists from home and abroad. 'For the next two years Labour will work within the departmental ceilings for spending already announced.'

That day, the Tories thought they had seized on a Brown glitch. On Radio 4's *World at One*, the chancellor was asked if Labour would privatise the national air-traffic-control system. He replied, 'Well, we have said we will look at this.' Central Office gleefully unearthed the pledge made by transport spokesman Andrew Smith – a Brown protégé – at the 1996 party conference that Labour would do 'everything we can to block this sell-off'. In fact, careful reading of the transcript clearly shows that Brown was talking about privatisation receipts as a whole, not just one sale. In fact, Labour was planning a thoroughgoing review of all state assets, such as land and buildings, to see what could legitimately be disposed of. The 'air-traffic scandal' ran in the papers for a few days, prompting the *Daily Telegraph* to suggest on 5 April that it had drawn 'the most unlikely drop of blood of the campaign so far'. But no wound was visible: Brown was turning into the 'Teflon chancellor' and the scare stories simply did not work.

A more serious criticism was voiced by Peter Riddell, veteran commentator of *The Times*, who argued that Gordon Brown deserved credit for shedding Labour's old tax-and-spending image and ruling out 'most, though not all, uncosted pledges'.

He went on: 'But the manifesto is full of grand-sounding aspirations about improving education and health which cannot be reconciled with Labour's fiscal authority.' He, too, thought there was a £1.5 billion black hole in Labour's programme, bequeathed by the Tories. 'No wonder Mr Brown is keen not to rule out possible privatisations, such as that of the air traffic control system, and I'll bet the Tote will be back on the agenda.'[6] Selling the Tote had been firmly stamped on by Robin Cook. Another idea floated by Brown's staff was the privatisation of the ParcelForce arm of Royal Mail.

By the end of the second week of the campaign, Brown was airing his proposal for an 'urgent review' of the future and saleability of all government services, plus land and buildings – conservatively valued at £122 billion. This proposal was described by that ubiquitous source 'a party insider' as 'the final piece in the jigsaw' of Labour policy on privatisation. 'We will look at everything on a practical, case-by-case basis, not from an ideological point of view,' the source promised. That week also saw Brown and his key aides move, lock, stock and barrel, from his Westminster office to Millbank. They had been frequent visitors to the 'war room' for months; now it became home. Brown had his own high-ceilinged office directly off the main campaign floor. His secretary, Sue Nye, a veteran of two Kinnock campaigns, ran his private office with a rod of iron.

After the Easter break, all eyes were on the first heavyweight public debate of the campaign. Plans for a televised Blair–Major contest had been abandoned amid mutual recriminations between the parties, and it fell to Brown to attack Kenneth Clarke, and to advance Labour's position as the party that had ditched its tax-and-spend image, in a three-way BBC2 programme *The Debate for Chancellor* on Sunday 6 April; the third 'contestant' was Malcolm Bruce, the Liberal Democrats' Treasury spokesman. Peter Jay, broadcaster, former ambassador to the USA and ex-economics editor of *The Times* was in the chair for what turned out to be less a clash of the titans, more a good-mannered exchange of views. Jay promised that 'the gloves were off', but it was scarcely a bare-knuckle fight. Each of the three delivered a short policy speech and then spouted well-prepared responses to debating points raised by Jay on tax, Europe, growth, jobs and interest rates. Bruce, standing on a little platform because he was shorter than the other two, did better than expected. He and Brown each won two rounds of applause. Clarke, who looked as though he had just run a half-marathon in his suit, raised the only laughs. Brown sidestepped pressure from Bruce to declare in favour of making the Bank of England independent – though he was secretly planning to do just that on his first day in office. Brown sustained the image of a serious chancellor-in-waiting, promising not to raise income tax and driving home the slogan 'You can't trust the Tories on tax'. It was a workmanlike performance, which strengthened his image, but showbiz it wasn't. Stephen Glover in the *Daily Telegraph* described it as 'the big fight that never was', while Robert Chote, economics editor of the *Financial Times* said there were 'no fatal gaffes and no killer blows . . . amateurish yet competent. Very British. The stuff of history.' Des Wilson, a former Liberal Democrat campaign manager, judged the contest a draw, but wailed, 'How one yearned for a head to head between Gordon Brown and Kenneth Clarke: it was only in their unprompted exchanges that the argument came alive.'[7] It was a useful exercise rather than a campaign watershed, and in the following day's papers the debate was eclipsed by the announcement that the independent anti-sleaze candidate in Tatton was veteran BBC war correspondent Martin Bell. Brown was not dismayed. Fielding an anti-corruption candidate had been his idea (not Mandelson's, despite him claiming the credit), and it put the Tories on the defensive. 'They just didn't seem to have a strategy,' said Brown. 'Week one was sleaze. Week two was sleaze, and then it was division over Europe. At which point Brian Mawhinney announced everything was going to plan!' Labour had also tightened up its policy on Europe, to reflect the growing mood of scepticism in the electorate. Robin Cook voiced doubt that Labour would join the European single currency during the five-year lifetime of its first government.

The TV debate also overshadowed Brown's involvement in the Scottish campaign. On 6 April, he wrote in *Scotland on Sunday*: 'Devolution matters for me: a Scottish parliament will be the achievement of a goal I have worked for throughout my political life.' He recalled that his first speech to a Labour Party conference, in 1976, had been on the subject of a Scottish Parliament. 'And for the last twenty years my advocacy on this issue has been consistent. It matters to me . . . and it is a clear and personal commitment of Tony Blair.' This was designed to steady Scottish Labour nerves, badly shaken in some cases by Blair's apparently lukewarm attitude to devolution. Brown rejected any notion of U-turns, or watering down party policy, insisting that a referendum would be held by the autumn and the whole Cabinet would be campaigning for two 'yes' votes. 'Let me repeat,' he wrote, 'the referendum was proposed to speed up the process, not slow it down.' Brown confided that he feared a repeat of the five hundred wrecking amendments from the Lords that devolution had faced in the 1970s. But with the popular will expressed in a referendum, the Lords would find it hard to resist – as the Tories had already accepted that devolution 'once done, cannot be undone'. Brown went back to his favourite game for the right metaphor. On the football field, Scotland had far too often snatched defeat from the jaws of victory. Don't make the same mistake on 1 May, he urged.

This was his busiest day so far. Speaking less like a shadow chancellor and more like the real thing, he used BBC Radio 4's *The World This Weekend* to unveil formally his plans for a 'national inventory' of government assets to determine if they were still needed by the state. 'If they are of no further use to the public sector, we will take a decision to get rid of assets that are of no further use to us.' Labour's 'Business Manifesto', due out later that week, would disclose that every government department would have to draw up a comprehensive register of its interests by November. Commentators were quick to point

out that Brown was compelled to make Labour's historic switch
to privatisation because of the 'black hole' – variously estimated
at between £1.5 billion and £12 billion - in his public spending plans. Brown was wheeled out on the *Today* programme on
7 April to face the charge that Labour had performed a U-turn.
It was, he insisted, 'an absolute lie' by the Conservatives,
whipped up by one or two newspapers. Labour, he pointed out,
had ditched its nationalising Clause IV two years previously,
and now espoused a policy of 'the market where possible,
government activity where necessary'. But he was on the defensive about individual privatisations, concluding lamely that 'we
will look at this in government'.

With little more than three weeks to go before polling day,
these two days of hectic policy-pronouncing found Labour –
and Brown – ill at ease with some of the detail. On the issue of
privatising Britain's air-traffic-control system, he lacked conviction. The Tories found some firm ground to stand on with their
accusations of U-turns and 'making policy on the hoof'. There
was one consolation that Monday night, however. Yvette
Cooper, an *Independent* journalist and partner of Brown's chief
economic adviser, Ed Balls, won the selection conference at the
safe Labour seat of Pontefract and Castleford in west Yorkshire,
thrashing Derek Scott, economics adviser to Tony Blair. This
was one in the eye for the old SDP. Scott was rejected by
traditionalists in the mining constituency on the grounds that
he had once stood as an SDP candidate, and that he was too
close to Blair. Another Blair insider, Jack Dromey, national
secretary of the TGWU and husband of Harriet Harman, the
shadow social security secretary, had been eliminated in the first
round. Being close to Gordon Brown was clearly less of an
impediment in traditionalist circles than proximity to the
leader himself.

On 8 April, the day Parliament was dissolved, Brown went
on a one-day whistle-stop tour of East Anglia. With him went
fellow-Fifer John Lloyd of the *Financial Times*, once a man of
the ultra-left and now an arch-moderniser. Lloyd found Brown

'friendly, but not wholly at ease' with a group of teenagers gathered to met him in a Norwich restaurant. Asked about Labour's shift from grants to loans for students, Brown took refuge in a mass of statistics about the need to move to loans when education ceased to be the preserve of the few. Then it was on to Great Yarmouth, where he teamed up with John Prescott for a rally. There was, observed Lloyd, 'no sign of affection' between the two men, but the act was disciplined and vigorous.[8] Brown's promise that 'the long night of Tory rule is drawing to a close' drew applause, and they laughed at his joke – said to be true – about Peter Mandelson. Attending a dinner with Brown, Mandy asked if he could borrow 10p to telephone a friend. 'Here's 20p – phone them all,' shot back the shadow chancellor.

Two days later, on 10 April, Brown paid a flying visit to Manchester, promising to regenerate the economy of north-west England, via a development agency that would draw up a strategy to revive the region's 'dangerously weak' industrial base.

However, the week's 'wobble' over privatisation (and the vague promises of trade-union recognition in Labour's manifesto) contributed to a sharp dip in Labour's poll lead in the *Guardian*'s ICM poll published on 9 April. Blair's lead was cut to twelve points over the Tories – 46 per cent to 34, the Tories' best performance for four years. Moreover, MORI pollsters in *The Times* found that voter confidence in Labour as the best party on taxation and on managing the economy was sliding alarmingly: the Conservatives were rated better on both these key issues.

In *The Times*, Peter Riddell argued that the reason for the wobble was not events over the past ten days but the style of policy-making over the last three years. 'Tony Blair, Gordon Brown and their small group of allies have constituted a Leninist vanguard, operating by coup rather than consensus and fait accompli rather than debate.' The typical pattern was for Gordon Brown ('and it is almost always him') to make a speech that had been perfunctorily cleared with Shadow Cabinet colleagues – often only the night before, on the telephone. Brown's staff gave advance briefings about the shadow chancellor's intentions – sometimes going beyond what the actual speech said – and the initiative was then firmly fixed as policy. This was true of the public-spending and tax proposals, said Riddell. But sometimes the process came unstuck: over the reallocation of child-benefit money for sixteen- to eighteen-year-olds, and over the privatisation of the Tote.[9]

There was much to be said for Riddell's analysis of 'policy-making by briefing and bounce'. That *was* the way it worked in the run-up to the election. Brown, and sometimes Blair, would float a policy shift or declaration in the Sunday broadsheet press – usually the *Sunday Times, Observer* or *Independent on Sunday* – and then encourage the story to gather strength through the Sunday radio and television news and current affairs programmes, before emerging as fact in the Monday press. The system could backfire, though. Labour MPs, including other members of the Shadow Cabinet, were sometimes caught on the hop, unsure of how firm the new policy commitment was. Occasionally, they reacted badly, giving the impression of division, and had to be swiftly brought into line by instructions barked down the telephone. It was not democracy: more like democratic centralism, indeed. But on the whole it worked. Brown subsequently confirmed that that was how things had worked. 'The vital decisions were made a long time ago. In some cases, nearly three years ago. Soon after Tony became leader, we decided that it was not only essential to make constitutional changes to the party, but to make sure the policies were fireproof.'[10]

Events in the real world provided a destabilising backdrop to the campaign juggernaut. Sterling continued to climb sharply, reaching its highest level since 'Black Wednesday', 16 September 1992, and City commentators were unanimous that the incoming chancellor would have to put up interest rates within days of taking office. Speculation also began to mount that Brown would have to raise taxes in his first budget. Cambridge don Dr John Wells, who co-wrote the shadow budget that helped Labour lose the election in 1992, said Brown would need much more than a windfall tax to pay for his programme and predicted cuts in allowances and the phasing out of mortgage tax relief.

Tax and privatisation dominated the daily media conferences chaired by Brown. On tax, he called a special briefing when John Major accused Labour of hypocrisy on 9 April. At issue was a report from the Institute for Fiscal Studies showing that the average family was paying an extra £7 a week more in taxes since the last election, but was £1,110 a year better off because of improvement in the economy. Major claimed the tax burden was 'exactly the same as it was five years ago'. Brown dismissed this as 'a lie'. In truth, they both had a point. Both quietly ignored the main conclusion of the IFS report: that taxes would have to rise even to meet the Conservatives' spending plans, to which Brown had committed a Labour government.

At the close of the fourth week, observers detected jitters at Millbank HQ, despite the restoration of Labour's twenty-plus points lead in the polls. As the top strategist, Brown came under fire. As Ewen MacAskill reported in the *Guardian,* 'Labour's poor performance has started a whispering campaign against the shadow chancellor, Gordon Brown, who is in overall charge of the campaign. One criticism was that he is doing too much and has taken too high-profile a role. An insider blamed the problems at Millbank on internal tensions between Mr Brown and Peter Mandelson, who is in charge of implementing campaign strategy.'[11] That such tensions, stemming from the leadership contest, did exist was indisputable. But Brown spoke to Mandelson several times a day, and 'Mandy' accepted his secondary role – though this did not prevent him claiming credit for the famous victory after it had been won.

Then there was a further 'blip' over the windfall tax. According to reports, Brown and Blair were at odds over the scale of the windfall tax. Blair wanted to keep receipts at the lower end of the scale of £3 billion to £5 billion, while Brown was looking for more: much more – £5 billion to £10 billion. They could not agree, either, on who should bear the brunt of the tax. Blair was keen to hit the water and electricity companies hardest, while Brown's team saw lucrative 'excess profits' ripe for taking at British Telecom and BAA, the airports operator. Naturally, spokesmen for both men played down reports of the dispute as 'preposterous', but there was some substance in them, deriving in part from the chemistry between the two. An anecdote circulating at the time illustrates the point. Blair went into Brown's office, and found him on the telephone. Instead of making his excuses and putting down the telephone to speak to his boss, Brown carried on his conversation and kept Blair waiting until he had finished. An observer was quoted as saying, 'There is not the slightest doubt that Brown regards himself as entirely Tony's equal – there is not a hint of deference in that relationship.'

The issue was settled on 10 April, when Blair and Brown appeared together at the morning briefing. Asked whether the windfall tax would be limited, Brown got in first: 'This is a matter for the Treasury and it's a matter that will be decided in government.' Blair added, 'Absolutely correct. Thank you.' The Labour leader was asked if he wanted to keep the levy below £5 billion. He replied, 'In principle, as Gordon has just said, these are decisions that have to be taken by the chancellor in government. And that is what will happen.' The *Daily Mail* headlined this exchange 'Brown's Victory', though in fact it was no more than a public enunciation of what had already been agreed in private.

Labour's business manifesto, *Equipping Britain for The Future*, launched in the City on 11 April, essentially confirmed the promises of the main manifesto and made more soothing noises in the direction of industry and commerce. It promised to develop and speed up the Private Finance Initiative, the Tory government's instrument for channelling private-sector funds into public projects that had become bogged down in red tape.

The document was generally welcomed by business, though there was some disquiet that it made no concession on Labour's core policies on the windfall tax, the national minimum wage, signing the Social Chapter and bringing in statutory recognition for trade unions. Brown told an invited audience that Labour was now 'the entrepreneurs' champion'. He insisted, 'We want Britain to be a great place to do business. We want business in Britain to succeed and deliver healthy growth, good profits, rising living standards and more jobs.' A far cry, indeed, from the Brown of the *Red Paper*.

Brown, with Blair alongside him, put on show some impressive converts. Gerry Robinson, chairman of Granada, said he had never before voted Labour but would do so this time. He was confident that 'business could do business' with New Labour. Tim Waterstone, founder of the bookshop chain that bears his name, went further: Gordon Brown would be 'one of the very finest Chancellors'. He added, 'I watch his lips and I believe him. I think he has an almost apolitical approach to the need for stability in the economy.'

At the close of that week, Brown seized on an apparent division between two senior members of the Cabinet. At the Saturday-morning briefing at Conservative Central Office, Defence Secretary Michael Portillo was asked if he had been on the same side as John Redwood, arguing for an early exit from the European exchange-rate mechanism, and against the imposition of VAT on fuel. Portillo replied, 'I was rather, and still am indeed, rather a junior member of the Cabinet and didn't get involved in these discussions.' Brown fired off an immediate letter to Portillo repudiating this ludicrous statement, pointing out that Portillo had been chief secretary to the Treasury when these decisions were implemented. The real motive for obfuscation, he argued, was Portillo's desire to 'run away from the wreckage' of the Major administration and position himself to run against Redwood in the Tory leadership election that would undoubtedly follow the general election. 'You should bear in mind that honesty may still count for something among a few Tory MPs,' he admonished. Brown's analysis was correct, but even his powers of prediction did not run to envisaging that Michael Portillo would lose his seat. The defence secretary did not reply: the letter was meant for publication, rather than elucidation.

The Tories were now completely at sea on policy over Europe. In the face of widespread revolt on his 'wait and see policy' over the European single currency, John Major gave his ministers and candidates complete freedom to espouse whatever view they wished. This cave-in was dressed up as democracy – in contrast to Labour's 'Stalinism'. But it fooled few. Brown said the Tories were 'in chaos' on the issue. It was playing into Labour's hands.

Yet the Sunday papers that weekend concentrated more on Labour's jitters than on the Tories' woes. A Gallup poll in the *Sunday Telegraph* cut Labour's lead to 16 points, the lowest this pollster had recorded since Blair became leader. Brown and Mandelson were said to be at loggerheads. The ubiquitous 'insider' was wheeled out to tell the paper, 'There is panic in the air. It's been getting catty between those two.' By this stage of the campaign, many of the political journalists were getting bored with the sameness of it all: the Labour monolith, the divided Tories. Trouble at t'Millbank made good copy.

But it was only a cameo performance. The following week's polls re-established Labour impregnable lead. Not even a fresh fall of 41,000 in the number of people claiming unemployment benefit on 16 April disturbed the trend, amid further signs of Tory trouble on Europe. To appease his rebels, John Major offered a free Commons vote on the European single currency. Brown retorted that the Conservatives had descended into complete chaos and confusion. However, this was an issue that gave him too some concern. A MORI poll for *The Times* on 17 April put support for staying in the EU on only 40 per cent, with those in favour of withdrawal on the same figure and the rest undecided. As one of the most pro-European members of the Shadow Cabinet he was nervous about where the Tory strategy was taking the nation. 'The Conservatives managed to unite the country in an anti-European feeling,' he said later, 'while fatally exposing their own divisions. The mood of the country was inevitably affected by the way the Tories fought the campaign. But the basis of our position towards Europe was not changed.'[12]

The Tories declared the fifth week of the campaign, ending on 19 April, 'a golden week for the economy'. Factory-gate prices up only 1 per cent a year. Retail sales increased by just under 3 per cent. Unemployment down. Public borrowing down. The Conservatives 'firmly on target' to balance the budget by the year 2000. Inflation at 2.6 per cent – in line to achieve Kenneth Clarke's target of 2.5 per cent by the end of the current Parliament. Clarke was bullish. 'In your pockets, you know Tory economics works,' he told the Saturday-morning press conference. But the media ignored the positive message and seized on his gaffe about the 'paranoid nonsense' of hostility to the European Union. He told reporters, in a barely coded challenge to the party's right wing, 'The European Union is not a threat. Leading European politicians are not a threat.'

That weekend, the talking-point was pensions. The government was furious beyond measure about Labour's charge that a fifth-term Tory administration would end the basic state pension. At the Saturday-morning briefing on 19 April, Brown pointed out that the Conservative manifesto proposed 'a costly, risky scheme' involving privatisation of the basic state pension as well as SERPS (the state earnings-related pension scheme) for younger workers. This scheme, he argued, would cost £300 billion in the years to 2040, yet the government had no idea how to fund it. His message was, 'If the Conservatives win again, what is to stop them privatising the basic state pension for more than just the young?' Hidden in the small print of the Tory proposals, he went on, 'it says, and I quote: "The proposal assumes that the scheme would cover future people entering work and those who are aged up to their early twenties when the scheme begins. But it might be possible to bring older people into the scheme if the public finances permitted. The great majority of older people would, of course, also like those in the new scheme, be accruing rights in occupational or personal pensions." ' Brown argued, 'This clearly opens the door to the wholesale privatisation of the basic state pension all round. And the Conservatives' record on pensions suggests that if they were elected again they would stop at nothing, including the complete privatisation of the basic state pension.'

Nothing that Brown said during the campaign, or before it, provoked such uproar. The Conservatives were beside themselves with rage at what they saw as the biggest lie of the election. They saw that on the doorstep this carefully crafted formula would simply translate itself to millions of pensioners as 'The Tories will take your pension away.' Indeed, Brown himself said as much: 'Your pension is not safe with the Tories.' In the face of red-faced Tory outrage, and more thoughtful media criticism of this strategic sally, Brown was unmoved.

The increasingly desperate Tories decided to intensify their attacks on tax. Labour's plans to increase spending on education, they said, were another 'black hole': this time £10 billion deep. Brown's spokesman dismissed the charge as 'propagandist nonsense', adding, 'I take it with a pinch of salt and so will the British public.' But Andrew Dilnot of the Institute for Fiscal Studies gave some weight to the Tories' arithmetic. For a Labour government to keep its pledge to 'increase spending on education as a proportion of national income' during its first Parliament would require extra resources over and above the limits laid down by Kenneth Clarke – and adopted for the ensuing two years by Gordon Brown.[13] In fact, Brown was not even two months into his chancellorship before he, too, in the weeks before his first budget, discovered a convenient 'black hole', allowing speculation to gather that taxes would have to rise. At this stage in the campaign, however, he was cheered by an opportune world prosperity league table from the Organization for Economic Co-operation and Development

(OECD) showing that the UK has slumped to twenty-first place, behind Ireland and Finland. This news, he said, boosted Labour's case for investment in business.

Week six continued with a novel intervention. Jacques Santer, the President of the European Commission, launched an attack on Eurosceptic 'doom merchants' in Britain who wanted to halt the integrationist drive and make the EU revert to a simple trading arrangement. Brown, despite being a strong European, was obliged to slap him down. 'Mr Santer should be in no doubt that a Labour government will make decisions based on British needs in the British interest,' he declared.

In the face of the Tories' leaking of Labour's confidential 'election war book', which dealt frankly with some of the party's shortcomings, Brown launched his party's last big policy initiative: the switch of £200 million of National Lottery money every year to boost health and education spending. The cash would be available for schemes that might not otherwise qualify for Whitehall cash, such as after-school 'homework clubs', training teachers in information technology, a chain of health and fitness centres and a National Endowment for Science and the Arts. Celebrities joined Brown and Blair on the podium: the athlete Steve Cram, Anthony Minghella, director of *The English Patient* and television personality Dr Miriam Stoppard. The timing of the announcement was driven not by the Conservatives' disclosure of the war book, which was largely a restatement of familiar themes (like 'smarmy Tony'), but by a timetable laid down months previously. 'When it became clear it would be a long campaign we knew we had to pace ourselves, said Brown. 'We only had a limited number of new announcements and we decided to let the manifesto be centre-stage the first week and the business manifesto in the second. We were going to make the announcement on funding from the Lottery in the first week, but realised that we needed to hold back some initiatives to sustain momentum. All other announcements were kept back until the second half of the campaign.'[14] By this stage of the campaign, Labour's lead over the Conservatives had hardened to between nineteen and twenty-one points, except for a 'rogue' poll lead of only 5 per cent in the *Guardian*.

By 23 April, the government was talking as though a Labour government was a fact. John Major had privately told his aides that the game was up. Publicly, he issued a statement about 'Labour's emergency budget' in July, which Brown had just promised. This was a manifesto commitment, but one man's promise is another man's threat. Major told his morning news conference, 'Gordon Brown has threatened us with an emergency budget for July. Why does Labour need a budget? Because it wants to spend more. They would put up taxes, like they always do.' The broad outline of Labour's first budget was already in place. Brown and Blair now turned their energies to discussing who should be in the first Labour cabinet for eighteen years.

As the last full week of campaigning drew to a close, the Conservatives could not contain their ire over pensions, accusing Labour of 'barefaced lies' and contemptible smears. Brown responded with a letter to the prime minister on 25 April, asking him to confirm that the state pension was to be replaced by 'privately purchased provision' and that the scheme might eventually be extended to include older people, as the small print of the Tory proposal had suggested. Turning the knife, he added, 'Instead of the bluff and bluster we have heard from you today, it is time for answers.' Answers came there none, but there was more good news from Rupert Murdoch. His mass-circulation Sunday paper the *News of the World*, came out in favour of Labour on 26 April. Together with the *Sun*, this meant Labour now had the support of papers selling 20 million copies by polling day. The other News International title, the broadsheet *Sunday Times* came out in favour of the Tories 'warts and all'.

By then Brown clearly believed that, despite continuing warnings against complacency, the contest was as good as over. 'There is,' he told the *Independent on Sunday*, 'a settled view among a very large section of the population that they do not want another Conservative government. As someone put it to me, it's not that the Conservatives don't deserve another five years - they don't deserve another five minutes.' The people's conviction was unmistakable. 'They have made up their minds.' He conceded that Labour had suffered a 'wobbly week' when its policies on the economy, privatisation and the unions were put under the microscope, but said with a grin, 'I don't think any party goes through an election without the odd interesting incident. But the general strategy has been right.'[15]

The last few days of the campaign were characterised by what Brown called 'panic and desperation' in the Tory camp. The last polls showed Labour's lead running at between ten and twenty points, and Brown, heading off to Dunfermline East appealed to the electorate: 'Don't hope for change. Vote for change.'

Brown spent polling day, 1 May, at his home in North Queensferry. It was evident from the polls that government was only hours away. At lunchtime, he spent a long time on the phone to Tony Blair at his Sedgefield home, discussing the arrangements for the morrow, determining his Treasury team and debating the general shape of the government. They also decided to go ahead with the most radical decision of their first week in Downing Street – transfer of the power to fix interest rates from the Treasury to the Bank of England. There was some discussion about staff, too. Blair was not happy that Brown was taking his entire 'inner cabinet' of Ed Balls, Charlie Whelan, Ed Miliband and Sue Nye into government.

In accordance with custom, Brown toured a few polling stations in his constituency. The scale of Labour's victory was already becoming clear. Whelan had been privately given the figures of the BBC's nationwide exit poll two hours before it was broadcast. 'We still didn't believe it,' he confessed. Confirmation came just before Brown made his victory speech at Lochgelly Town Hall. Bill Bush, head of the BBC Political Research Unit, predicted a landslide for Labour. Whelan, listening on an earpiece, broke the news. 'I told Gordon just before his speech that we had a majority of 170. Bush had said so – and he's reliable.' Brown did a few interviews, and read out a prepared text in which he said, 'This result is not just a verdict against Conservative rule. It is a clear and positive endorsement of the desire of the people of this country for new politics. For eighteen years, the people of this constituency and the people of Britain have yearned for a government which is on their side. And if the verdict of the people is as it looks around the country this evening, then I believe under Tony Blair's magnificent leadership the Labour Party is now ready to rebuild the bond of trust between the people and their government.'

Brown and his closest advisers then drove over the Firth of Forth to Edinburgh airport, from where a private plane took them to London. As they flew south, the tide of results signalled a defeat of historic proportions for the Conservatives, their worst since 1906. In the most dramatic election night since Attlee's triumph of 1945, Labour could scarcely believe the political carnage in what were regarded as safe Tory seats. Brown's party went straight to the Festival Hall, on the South Bank, where the biggest celebration in Labour's history was under way. The atmosphere was 'sensational'. Brown arrived before Blair, and stayed for the triumphal speeches before leaving at 7.30 a.m. To his surprise, the chancellor-in-waiting was mobbed outside by delighted supporters. It was a taste of things to come.

He and his friends went to Geoffrey Robinson's eighth-floor penthouse flat at the Grosvenor House Hotel overlooking Hyde Park. He had a couple of hours' sleep, before getting up at ten to breakfast and fix the day ahead. 'We were knackered, but we had to plan how to tell the Treasury about the Bank of England,' said an aide. Whelan went to Whitehall to organise a photo-call on the steps of the Treasury. The timing of Blair's trip to Buckingham Palace to accept the Queen's invitation to form a government had been arranged in advance. So had the call to Brown confirming him as chancellor. Brown was so tired he went back to bed while this momentous event took place. He was woken at around 3.30 p.m. by Sue Nye to say the summons had come from Number 10. Brown himself never actually got the call. He was driven to the gates of Downing Street, and walked through the cheering crowd to the prime minister's residence. The cheers were not accidental, but they were genuine. Labour had brought in hundreds of party workers who contributed to the famous victory, and this was their hour of satisfaction.

Chancellor Brown spent three-quarters of an hour with Prime Minister Blair. 'We knew it would be a long meeting because of the Bank business,' said a member of his staff. At the appointed time, Brown walked round the corner to the Treasury. His staff had not been prepared for the noisy welcome from normally reserved civil servants. 'That was completely spontaneous,' insists Whelan, not usually one to miss a trick. 'If I'd known, I'd have had a camera crew in there. All we had was Scottish Television.' Brown went up to his office on the second floor, and told his private office people, 'Let's get down to business.'

CHAPTER 13

REALISING THE VISION

SHORTLY BEFORE FIVE O'CLOCK ON THE UNSEASONABLY HOT afternoon of Friday 2 May 1997, James Gordon Brown stood on the steps of Her Majesty's Treasury in Whitehall and smiled broadly for the cameras. On this occasion, they could not accuse him of dourness. He was greeted on the steps by Sir Terry Burns, his permanent secretary, and shook hands. Then he waved, grinned, and strode in to take direction of the nation's economy. Around two hundred civil servants lined the grand central staircase to welcome the new chancellor, at 46 the youngest in recent memory. Many officials applauded. They, too, had been waiting for this day, when two decades of Tory rule would come to an end. One civil servant enthused, 'He got a pop star welcome, with people shaking his hands and kissing him. It was a bit like a street party.'

Similar scenes had been enacted a few hours earlier in Downing Street, when Tony Blair, the man who had once sat at the feet of Gordon Brown, took over the premiership from a defeated John Major. The two Labour politicians had worked together for fourteen years to reach this goal, their close relationship surviving a bruising passage of arms in the battle for the party leadership. Together, they had reformed their party. Now, they would transform the country. As Blair said outside Number 10, 'Today, enough of talking – it is time to do.'

Brown called in Sir Terry Burns, who had served Kenneth Clarke, on Friday afternoon, before the final result of the election had been declared. He was determined, in the downmarket phrase of his press secretary, to 'hit the ground running'. He gave Burns a copy of a three-page letter he proposed to send to the governor of the Bank of England. It gave details of how Labour proposed to give a very substantial measure of independence to the Bank, giving it, in concert with a Monetary Policy Committee appointed by the chancellor, responsibility for setting interest rates. This bold step was designed to implement the manifesto pledge 'to ensure that decision-making on monetary policy is more effective, open, accountable and free from short-term manipulation'. The letter had been prepared well in advance by Brown, Ed Balls and Geoffrey Robinson, a former industry minister, who was returning from the political wilderness to take up a senior role in the Treasury team. Nevertheless, it took the Treasury mandarins by surprise that Brown was acting with such speed, before Parliament was even sworn in.

A close-knit group of around ten top civil servants were brought into the operation, amid tight secrecy. 'We were desperate that it didn't leak out. We wanted an element of surprise,' said an aide. 'We thought that was important.' The Treasury people wanted to delay the announcement, for a day at least, but gave way in the face of Brown's determination. They worked on the operation right through the weekend, and it was ready late on Sunday, 4 May. Brown went round to Blair's Islington house that night, where the two went over it together. The new prime minister was already aware of his chancellor's intentions: they had talked it over during their meeting at Downing Street on Friday night.

In fact, there had been broad agreement between the two on this issue for several months, following earlier discussions after

Brown's talks in the USA with Alan Greenspan, head of the Federal Reserve Bank. An arrangement similar to that now proposed for the Bank of England worked very well in the USA, and Brown was determined to emulate it. It was obvious, he argued in public and private, that UK interest rates were being decided for political rather than economic reasons. Kenneth Clarke and Eddie George had batted forward and back on interest-rate decisions in a way Brown found distasteful, and he was determined there would be no 'Gordon and Eddie Show'.

On Monday morning, which was the May Day bank holiday, Brown called in Eddie George and gave him the letter personally. George was delighted, and came out of the chancellor's office beaming. 'He may not have realised that it was "take it or leave it",' disclosed a member of Brown's staff. 'He did want to make some changes in the letter. But they only made textual alterations.' The Bank had had an intelligent idea of what to expect, from Brown's policy speeches in recent months, but did not expect it all to happen so quickly. The Treasury people loved it, according to insiders. Brown's decision was popular, because it was not only decisive but correct politically and economically.

Not a sniff of the radical reform leaked out to the media. Over the weekend, the newspapers were obsessed about the prospect of higher interest rates that week, following the chancellor's scheduled 'first' meeting with the governor on Wednesday, 7 May. Most City commentators agreed that rates should rise – and would have gone up earlier if the Conservatives had not been fighting for their political lives. The economy had grown by 1 per cent in the first three months of 1997, driven by consumer spending that was about to be accelerated by windfall gains from building societies converting into banks. Some observers, like Alex Brummer in the *Guardian*, thought Brown might be wary of early action on interest rates, waiting until his new Monetary Policy Committee was in place before acting. 'Better act now,' he argued, 'before the Tory inspired boom has run out of control

and even bigger rate rises become necessary.'[1] Little did he
know that Brown was preparing not only to increase rates, but
also to ensure that this would be the last time a British chancellor did so.

At the start of the first full week of Labour government, public attention was focused on the living arrangements of Blair
and his chancellor. Cherie Blair had already inspected the
accommodation at Number 10 and declared the 'flat over the
shop' totally inadequate for a couple with three growing
children. Brown volunteered his own, much larger, flat inside
Number 11, the Chancellor's official residence, if he could have
the smaller flat inside Number 10.

It was a fair swap, and not as inconvenient as might sound.
The two houses are inter-connected by doors on all three levels,
which lock from the prime minister's side. Past chancellors who
have been at odds with their prime ministers have often found
the doors locked, but this was unlikely to happen with Brown
and Blair. The chancellor would keep the use of Number 11's
ground-floor study, the stately dining-room where finance
ministers and bankers are traditionally entertained and the
first-floor drawing-room for receptions. He was also anxious to
have access to the kitchen in the flat, which mystified some
aides, as Brown is not exactly Marco Pierre White. The ironic
potential of the new arrangements was not lost on observers.
Brown, who had given way to Blair in the race for Number 10,
would now be living there. In fact, he was still living in his flat
hard by Westminster.

Early on Tuesday, 6 May, the media plan was put into action.
Charlie Whelan rang Reuter's news agency at 7.58 a.m. to tell
them to expect an important announcement. Michael
Brunson, political editor of ITN, also got a call telling him to
prepare for something big. Brown's staff decided on a
'presidential-style' press conference to announce the Bank
reforms. They wanted it to be carried live to readers of all the
City screens. They had already arranged an exclusive interview
with the *Financial Times* whose otherwise astute staff didn't

'clock' what was in the wind. 'We were slightly nervous. We didn't know what the reaction would be,' said an aide. 'We had a fair idea that most of the papers would back us. The slight worry was the European dimension: would what we were doing make us more likely to rejoin the exchange rate-mechanism? But we got the most amazing reaction.'

As a courtesy, and perhaps also to allay subsequent criticism, Brown phoned all the recent chancellors, Tory and Labour, to tell them what he was doing. They were very much taken by the approach. Nigel Lawson agreed with the reform, as did Denis Healey and Lord Callaghan, though Kenneth Clarke, when he was finally tracked down, said he would have to criticise the move as 'rushed' because he was a candidate for the Tory party leadership. He was still shadow chancellor, and it was his job to oppose. The one chancellor whom Brown's private office did not phone was John Major: everyone forgot his brief period at the Treasury, though it was he who took Britain into the ERM.

Speaking on a raised podium at his first press conference as chancellor, Brown announced his 'revolution at the Bank' moments after putting up the Bank's base rate for the first (and last) time by a quarter of 1 per cent to 6.25 per cent. Interest rates had to go up, he argued, to stop inflation overshooting the government's 2.5 per cent inflation target for 1998. Then he dropped his bombshell. 'This is the time to take the tough decisions we need for the long-term interests and prosperity of the country. We will not shrink from the tough decisions needed to deliver stability for long-term growth. I have therefore decided to give the Bank of England operational responsibility for setting interest rates, with immediate effect.' He vigorously denied that the move marked the first stage in rejoining the ERM or signing up to the European single currency, insisting that it was 'a British solution to meet British needs'. Interest rates would be set by the governor of the Bank, acting with a nine-strong Monetary Policy Committee made up of five top-level Bank officials and four outside appointees nominated by the chancellor. Only in exceptional circumstances – like the outbreak of war – could the chancellor override the Bank. A run on the pound, the event traditionally most feared by Labour chancellors, would be handled by the Bank. Tony Blair described the announcement as 'the biggest step in economic policy-making in Britain since World War Two'.

Brown's boldness delighted the City. The stock market and the pound soared to new highs: the FT–SE index breaking through 4,500 for the first time, and the pound closing at a post-ERM record of DM 2.8202. Press comment was ecstatic. *The Times* said the new chancellor had 'hit the ground not so much running as sprinting' The *Sun* headlined 'Brown's "brilliant" bid to defy Lefties.' Columnist Donald Macintyre in the *Independent* found the dynamism of 'Flash Gordon' electrifying, claiming, 'At a stroke, Labour has laid a historic claim to the high ground of economic virtue.'[2] The *Economist* called it 'an astonishingly bold start'.

And so the encomiums went on. The *Financial Times* called his decision 'unexpected, but welcome', saying it should have been taken by the Tories and Brown was to be congratulated on taking it himself instead. In an *FT* interview, the chancellor defended the precipitate nature of his move, and springing it on Eddie George. 'Once we had decided it was right in principle to go ahead, it was right to implement it as quickly as possible.' Brown was clearly in his element in the chancellor's grand office. He joked with *FT*'s four-strong inquisitorial team about how much more fun it was to make decisions than to talk about them. But he made clear that he was just beginning, and everything he did must been seen in the context of the long term. It was clear, *FT* recorded, that Brown had plans for the Treasury that went far beyond its traditional role as keeper of the public purse. He might have handed control of monetary policy to the Bank 'but his ambitions elsewhere are likely to see the Treasury regain the influence it last enjoyed in the mid-1980s under Nigel Lawson'. The chancellor gave one pointer to his long-term aims: 'The present welfare state is in need of radical reform. I want to rebuild it around what I have sometimes called the work ethic.'[3] In an article in the *Sun* on 7 May, Brown himself wrote: 'I am cutting the politicians and the politics, out of setting interest rates.' Alongside was a table setting out the mortgage-bill increases triggered by his hike in the base rate.

Naturally, there were dissenters from the general welcome. From the right, Anatole Kaletsky in *The Times* compared him to previous Labour chancellors - including the archetypal 'iron chancellor', Philip Snowden – in trying to stave off the innate hostility of the financial markets by 'locking the pound in a golden casket and throwing away the key'. He predicted that hostile economic conditions would test the reform 'perhaps to destruction', and likened the announcement to John Major's equally unexpected and 'irreversible' decision to join the exchange rate mechanism.[4] From the left came equally trenchant criticism. Ken Livingstone MP, spokesman for the Campaign Group of MPs at Westminster, heaped scorn on expectations that the reform would insulate monetary policy from short-term manipulation as the height of naivety. 'It assumes that central bankers do not have politics – which is ridiculous.' The policy must have been thought through months in advance, he correctly divined. But it was not in the manifesto, and it had never been agreed by the party conference, the national executive or even the Shadow Cabinet. Brown had not even waited twenty-four hours to consult the parliamentary Labour Party. All true, though it is difficult to see any Labour chancellor 'consulting' the PLP.

'We were never sure the Bank business would go down so well,' explained an aide. 'The first week was better than any expectations. We were slightly concerned about the party. Gordon held two receptions, and met every new Labour MP.' These parties at Number 11, where the chancellor dispensed wine he paid for himself, helped allay the very real sense among some that the parliamentary party had been 'bounced'. There was also a genuine sense of comradeship. Brown remembered when he first became an MP fourteen years previously, in very different circumstances. The new boys then had had nowhere to go, and certainly no ministers to welcome them.

As an operation, however, the Bank revolution was a brilliant success. Few noticed that the chancellor had said nothing about reappointing Eddie George to a second term at the Bank when his current five-year incumbency expired in 1998. Brown's resolve embodied the sense of urgency and 'can-do, will-do' that characterised Labour's first week in office. Robin Cook, the foreign secretary and Brown's great rival in Cabinet, out-lined a new mission for British foreign policy, bringing human rights much more into play. Douglas Henderson, the new min-ister for Europe and a confidant of Brown, was despatched to Brussels to commit the UK to signing the Social Chapter as part of a more constructive line on Europe. There was more to come. When the Cabinet met for the first time on 8 May, ministers were told they would have to follow the example set by Blair and Brown, and forgo until April the £16,000-a-year pay rises promised by a salaries review body.

Looking around the Cabinet table, Brown could take satis-faction that the choice of Harriet Harman (a former member of his Treasury team in Opposition) at Social Security and of Margaret Beckett at Trade and Industry had been accepted by the prime minister. His political influence would spread far and wide beyond the Treasury, and not simply through control of spending. His close ally Geoffrey Robinson was appointed paymaster-general at the Treasury, responsible for reviving the faltering Private Finance Initiative. Almost his first act was to sack Alastair Ross Goobey, chief executive of Hermes, BT and the Post Office Pension Fund and a 'committed Conservative', from his post as chairman of the Private Finance Panel. To com-plete his ministerial team, he appointed Alastair Darling, a sharp Edinburgh advocate, chief financial secretary, Dawn Primarolo, an articulate figure on the left, financial secretary – both had been with him for the last three years of Opposition – and Helen Liddell, former general secretary of the Scottish Labour Party, economic secretary to the Treasury, with responsibility for financial regulation.

The chancellor continued his assault on the quiet life by letting it be known that he would be wearing a lounge suit, not evening dress of stiff collar, white waistcoat, bow tie and tails, when he explained more of his economic thinking in the Mansion House speech on 12 June. Informality of this kind was unknown at the City's most prestigious annual bash for the barons of capital. The ubiquitous Treasury 'source' said it was 'a sign of the times'. Kenneth Clarke only had the nerve to downgrade the occasion from white tie to black tie, and the City grandees still wore gilded ceremonial dress.

While the commentators got into a lather over this fresh break with orthodoxy, Brown 'opened the books' that had been left by the outgoing administration. 'That exercise just confirmed what we already expected: that if action was not taken, inflation would go above 3.5 per cent a year in 1998,' said an insider. Then there was the question of the windfall tax. 'He just handed it over to them.' Brown was keeping to a punishing schedule: into the office at 7.30 a.m., and back to the Grosvenor House flat in time to watch BBC's *Newsnight* fifteen hours later. He also pleased the civil servants by eating in the Treasury's top-floor staff canteen, though he was not the first chancellor to do that. There was some mandarin displeasure about 'hair-shirtism' in the Treasury, stemming in part from a memo sent round by Brown asking them to put their home telephone numbers on any papers they submitted. The reason, they claimed, was that the chancellor liked to study papers between 6 a.m. and 8 a.m. when all sane people were having their breakfast. The hair shirt was plainly a good fit. Commentator Robert Peston noted, 'Brown is thriving on this punishing regime. The bags under his eyes have shrunk, and his normal pallor has been replaced by a rude glow. Meanwhile, officials who previously moaned that Ken Clarke was never known to read a document from cover to cover are showing signs of nostalgia for the whiff of his cigar smoke.'[5]

Work on the budget was also under way. Aides said other

incoming governments had done things in their first hundred days, but 'We're doing it in ten days.' Speculation mounted in the press than Brown would present Labour's first budget for eighteen years several weeks earlier than expected, on 10 June. There seems to have been some factual basis for this inspired conjecture, though insiders insist they were always working to 2 July – and had told Treasury officials so three weeks before the election. However, this date conflicted with Blair's trip to Hong Kong for the hand-over of the colony to China. Most other dates were ruled out by other overseas meetings. Peter Mandelson, the minister without portfolio, promised it would introduce the biggest welfare changes for fifty years.

Brown, attending his first meeting of European finance ministers in Brussels on 12 May, was giving little away, though he did chalk up his first victory over the European Commission by forcing officials to concede he could keep his election promise to cut VAT on fuel from 8 per cent to 5 per cent. Initially, they said it would be contrary to the spirit of Community legislation and threatened to take the UK to the European Court. Brown stuck to his guns, retorting, 'Our proposal to cut VAT on fuel is legally watertight and it is my intention to go ahead in the Budget.' The EU officials backed down. The *Daily Telegraph* hailed this development as 'a symbolic, but important victory for the government' building on its promise of a fresh start in Europe. Rare praise, from such a quarter.

The Queen's Speech on 14 May contained proposals for twenty-six Bills, but few surprises. The government promised a windfall tax, a national minimum wage, the gradual and 'appropriate' release of £5 billion from the sale of council houses currently frozen in bank accounts, in a wide-ranging package of reforms covering law and order, devolution, the regions, health, gun control and the National Lottery. The Bank revolution merited only a mention in passing: the biggest change in the Bank's 300-year history would be accommodated in a short Bill amending the 1946 Bank of England Act. It would put the Monetary Policy Committee on a statutory footing, and make changes in the Bank's Court of Directors so that it became representative of the whole of the United Kingdom. The legislation would give the government power to suspend the Bank's independence 'if, in extreme economic circumstances, the natural interest demands it'. The Queen's Speech further underlined Brown's commitment to the 'golden rule' that the government would borrow only to invest, rather than to fund current expenditure when the economy got into a mess. Businessmen also welcomed the Statutory Right to Interest on Debts Bill, which gave small firms the right to claim interest on the late payment of business debts. In the crowded Lords where the Queen outlined the government's plans, the television cameras picked up Gordon Brown chatting animatedly to Robin Cook.

It was all going according to plan. But suddenly, the windfall tax triggered the first business revolt against the chancellor. Soon after announcing company pre-tax profits of £3.2 billion for the year to 31 March, Sir Iain Vallance, chairman of BT, threatened to take the government to the European Court over the tax. His convoluted threat stemmed from legal advice that levying the tax on BT might constitute discrimination under EU rules, because its main rival, Mercury, would not face the levy. Sir Iain thought he had a secret pre-election understanding with Tony Blair that BT would not be hit by the windfall tax, or would at least be let off lightly. 'I wouldn't have voted Labour or put this government into power if BT had been mentioned in the manifesto,' he whined. 'If the tax is open to legal challenge, we would be failing in our fiduciary duty to shareholders not to challenge it.'[6] Brown had consistently said that Labour would levy the tax on all privatised companies 'licensed and regulated by the state' – a clear indication that BT would fall within the net.

One utility adviser questioned the wisdom of BT's hitting the headlines in this way, only hours after announcing profits equivalent to £100 every second, adding, 'It doesn't look very clever. And there is another thing companies should bear in mind – Gordon Brown does not react well to threats.' In this case, he did not react at all. He did not need to. In his desk was *that letter* from Sir Iain Vallance, in which he recognised that Labour had won an electoral mandate for the windfall tax – and that BT would be liable to pay it.

The six contenders for the Tory party leadership found common cause in this squalid little argument. They all signed a round-robin letter to *The Times* claiming Brown was about to open a Pandora's box of ills. A windfall tax would put up utility prices, wipe millions of pounds off shares and thus hit pension funds, affect investment programmes and threaten jobs. 'Labour's big idea is coming unstuck as we write,' they wrote, seemingly oblivious of the election result.

At the start of his third week in office, Brown ordered the National Audit Office to conduct an independent scrutiny of the Treasury economic forecasts he had inherited from the Conservatives. The clear inference was that he suspected they had been cooking the books. The assumptions behind the forecasts looked too 'rosy'. His announcement of the investigation was trailed the day ahead of his appearance at the despatch box to debate the Queen's Speech on 20 May. But when he got to his feet in the House, he stunned MPs with another groundbreaking announcement. Henceforth, the Bank of England would lose its supervisory powers over other banks and financial institutions to a revamped, enhanced Securities and Investment Board. The old system of self-regulation and supervision by the Bank would be abolished in favour of a new watchdog with statutory powers of scrutiny and enforcement. Having given to Eddie George with one hand, he was now taking away with the other.

This was another Brown coup. Much thought and planning had gone into how it might work. The man to take over 'Super-SIB' as it became known, was Howard Davies, currently deputy governor at the Bank. He had the right credentials – ex-director-general of the CBI, former head of the Audit Commission, high-flyer in Whitehall as special adviser to Nigel

Lawson. The chancellor and his closest circle worked on the plan all weekend. Davies was out of the country, in Buenos Aires. Brown telephoned him and offered him the post. He accepted immediately. At lunchtime on Monday, Brown called Eddie George to the Treasury to tell him what he proposed to announce the next day. This time, George was not so pleased. 'He didn't look happy; his face was pretty ashen. But he realised there was nothing he could do to stop it,' revealed the aide. 'We just said we were doing it. Obviously, he thought we would spend years discussing it with the Bank, not that we would simply announce it the next day. They thought they could try to block it.' In fact, the governor had been told two weeks previously, at his first interview, that Brown intended to look also at banking regulation. But, crucially, he had not been told when.

George was on a difficult wicket. The collapse of Bank of Credit and Commerce International, the failure of the old-established Barings Bank at the hands of rogue trader Nick Leeson in Singapore, the Maxwell pensions scandal, the mis-selling of personal pensions and other financial outrages had created a public climate of distrust that made the Bank ripe for shaking. In the Commons, the chancellor said, 'The distinctions between different types of financial institution – banks, securities firms and insurance companies – are becoming increasingly blurred. Many of today's financial institutions are regulated by a plethora of different supervisors. This increases the cost and reduces the effectiveness of supervision.' The success of Britain's financial services in the twenty-first century could not be ensured without modernising arrangements for the protection of investors. The current system had not worked, and he would replace it by one that put the public interest first and increased public confidence. 'The new arrangements, taken together, will enhance significantly the credibility of UK monetary policy and improve the workings of the financial markets.'[7] In turn, that would bring lower long-term interest rates and higher growth and investment, in line with Brown's vision.

Kenneth Clarke, robbed of an opportunity to make a fuss about the Bank's new powers over interest rates because there was now a fresh issue up and running, could only bleat about the chancellor's ' failure to consult'. Could Brown stop acting like a chancellor in a hurry? he asked. There was no prospect of that. He was not 'acting like' a chancellor in a hurry: he was one. There was a brief battle of sound-bites that day. Clarke accused the government of behaving 'like 18-year-olds in the saloon bar trying every bottle on the shelves'. Brown shot back that Clarke himself had wanted to make the changes. 'I have had the courage of his convictions,' he said, to the delight of Labour backbenchers.[8]

Once again, expert opinion was with Brown. Peter Ellwood, chief executive of the Lloyds TSB group said, 'We are supportive of this move.' Sir Peter Davis, head of the Prudential, said, 'We welcome this news.' So did the Association of British Insurers, and the Consumers' Association. The city editor of *The Times* commented that the Bank deserved to be shorn of its responsibility for prudent supervision of banks, because the public had clearly lost faith in what had become 'a poor relation in the Old Lady's family of priorities'.

The wrath of 'Steady Eddie' George was still to come. Initially, he supported the chancellor, saying that what mattered was not the Bank's position but the whole structure of bank regulation 'and what is best both for the depositor, investor and policy-holder protection on the one hand, and systematic stability on the other'. So far, so obfuscatory. The next day, he lit the blue touch-paper. In an interview with BBC radio, he admitted that Brown had give him an outline of his intentions on Bank Holiday Monday. 'It was the timing that was a surprise.' The surprise he had for the chancellor was his further comment. Asked if he had considered resigning over being kept substantially in the dark over such an important strategic development, the governor replied that he had 'never seriously considered it'. 'All sorts of things go through your mind,' he added, but the thought of resigning 'went away very quickly'. George was clearly irritated that his powers had been trimmed, arguing that the point had not been reached where a 'mega-regulator' was required.

On the face of things, an admission that the thought of resignation over an issue of this nature has crossed one's mind does not rank high in the excitement index. But when the point of issue is between the Conservative-appointed governor of the Bank of England and the chancellor of a newly elected Labour government, then, in the governor's words, it is 'mega'. It made front-page headlines in the papers of Thursday, 22 May. Commentators noted the first signs of tension between Brown and the governor, which might preclude George getting his second five-year term of office. The *Daily Mail* bellowed about a 'dangerous rift' opening up, with the Governor 'spitting blood' and almost resigning on the spot, 'a move that would have cataclysmic consequences in the City'. He felt stitched up because Brown had offered the 'Super-SIB' role to his deputy. All good pot-boiling, tabloid stuff.

Much more dangerous was the disclosure in the *Financial Times* that an unnamed senior minister who wanted the government to replace George had said the governor's criticism 'played into our hands'. The spin was getting dangerously out of control. The anonymous minister's reported comments rallied the City behind the governor. Brown's people went out to spread the word: 'Any idea that Mr George has not got the support of the Chancellor is nonsense.' He would still be the Governor 'this time next year'.[9] Sceptics pointed out that George's term expired in just over a year. They directed atten- tion to Gavyn Davies, chief international economist at the merchant bank Goldman Sachs, who was reputedly in line to take over from Eddie George. Davies is a multi-millionaire Labour loyalist and husband of Sue Nye, Gordon Brown's most trusted aide. City traders muttered darkly about the emergence of a Soviet-style 'Labour *nomenklatura*' at the top. In fact, insiders argued, 'It would be extremely unlikely that the

Governorship would go to someone so close to Labour.'

It was a damaging, if brief, interlude – the first fleck of blood drawn from Gordon Brown, chancellor. One commentator said the 'orchestrated humiliation' of Eddie George showed that power had gone to his head. Brown put the brouhaha behind him, naming 6 June as the date for the first Bank of England decision on interest rates, even though only four of the nine Monetary Policy Committee members had been named: Eddie George, Howard Davies and two executive directors of the Bank, Mervyn King and Ian Plenderleith. Interest was still focused on the date of the budget. Brown let it be known that he would await the outcome of the National Audit Office inquiry before naming the day. He already knew, of course, that it would be 2 July. What he sought from the NAO investigation was independent 'proof' that the national accounts were in worse shape than suggested in Clarke's final budget the previous November. Charlie Whelan told the media: 'There is widespread suspicion that improper assumptions were made about privatisation receipts and revenues from "spend to save" [the clampdown on benefit fraud]. We now want an open and accountable system with no cooking of the books.'[10]

The chancellor was already getting plenty of advice what he should do in his Budget. The TUC argued for higher taxes, not interest rates, forgetting the latter were no longer in his power. The CBI called for a £3 billion rise in personal taxes. There was much institutionalised lobbying. The National Institute of Economic and Social Research proposed a £6 billion tax hike. The Institute of Directors told him to cut public spending and phase out mortgage tax interest relief. The left-leaning Institute for Public Policy and Research demanded a 'greening' of the tax system. The Institute for Fiscal Studies and Goldman Sachs released a joint report saying there was no immediate need to raise taxes at all. Gavyn Davies identified himself with its findings and said publicly, 'There is quite a lot of fiscal restraint in the pipelines.' Brown's staff begged him not to say any more. Robert Reich, the former US labor secretary, urged the chancellor, 'Don't overdo the austerity.'

After the Bank of England drama, it was a quieter time: not exactly the old-fashioned purdah – seclusion and silence – of chancellors in times past, but a less turbulent period. On 30 May, President Bill Clinton made a whistle-stop visit to Downing Street for his first meeting with Tony Blair. The two heads of government announced that Britain would host a special conference of the Group of Eight industrialised nations (G7, plus Russia) to draw up programmes for boosting employment without undermining social cohesion. Apart from the prime minister, Gordon Brown was the only Cabinet minister who met the US president. They talked for about forty minutes, and Clinton expressed pleasure that employment was going quite well in the UK. Brown explained how the jobless figures had been massaged by successive Conservative governments. The president was 'quite shocked'. The chancellor's main decision that week was that a woman would be made one of the two deputy governors he was planning for the Bank of England.

On 2 June, in the Commons, Brown finally announced the date of the budget: Wednesday, 2 July. It would be the first Wednesday budget since 1980, when Sir Geoffrey Howe's first choice clashed with the enthronement of the Archbishop of Canterbury. Brown was going back to an earlier tradition: Stafford Cripps and Reginald Maudling also favoured mid-week budgets. Wednesday, the new day for Prime Minister's Question Time, was rapidly becoming the pivotal day of the parliamentary week.

The chancellor also named his four appointees to the Monetary Policy Committee: Ms DeAnne Julius, chief economist with British Airways, a US citizen with experience of working for Shell and the World Bank; Professor Charles Goodhart, professor of banking and finance at the London School of Economics, said by his peers to be 'the best monetary economist in the country' and a former senior adviser to the Bank; Professor Willem Buiter, professor of international macroeconomics at Cambridge University, formerly of Yale and Princeton; and Sir Alan Budd, chief economic adviser to the Treasury since 1991. They began work immediately, holding their first two-day meeting on Thursday and Friday that week.

Using its new powers for the first time, on 6 June the Bank increased interest rates by 0.25 per cent to 6.5 per cent, explaining that its timely action offered 'the best chance of achieving continued growth in output and employment at a sustainable pace'. Building societies and banks responded with a 0.35 per cent hike in mortgage rates. The chancellor made no comment. He had scant reason to do so. A post-election Gallup survey for the *Daily Telegraph* published the same day found the public's love affair with the Labour government still growing. No fewer than 82 per cent of voters were satisfied with the prime minister – a post-war record. On the economic front, the news was also encouraging: 78 per cent agreed with the national minimum wage, 73 per cent approved of Brown's decision to introduce a single banking regulator, 59 per cent agreed with giving the Bank of England freedom to set interest rates, and 48 per cent agreed with the UK signing the European Social Chapter (36 per cent against).

While it scored the lowest rating, public approval of the Social Chapter was particularly welcome, considering the ferocious political onslaught on this issue mounted by the Conservative government over several years. It chimed well with a fresh European initiative on jobs. Chancellor Brown wrote to EU finance ministers ahead of the 9 June meeting in Luxembourg to win their support for a 'Get Europe to Work' programme. The plan called for series of measures to cut bureaucracy, increase trade and investment and promote welfare-to-work in the EU. Europe had 18 million out of work, and had created only 5 million jobs in twenty years, compared with 36 million generated in the USA.

'We know the problems in the European economy. It's now time for the British government to influence the solutions,' said Brown. 'We believe we are changing the terms of the European economic debate. Jobs, getting Europe to work, creating employability and labour market flexibility will be the major themes on the economic side of the UK presidency next year.'[11] He was, however, cool on a proposal to extend the Social Chapter's provisions for company works councils from firms with two thousand workers to those with just fifty. Not everyone was impressed by the Euro-initiative. Peter Riddell, wise old owl of *The Times*, argued that 'the grandly titled Action Plan' was not a plan at all, merely 'a defence of the Blair–Brown approach by encouraging employability and flexible markets'. Chancellor Brown duly secured the support of European finance ministers for his package of ideas, and voiced the government's reserve over a single European currency. In what was seen as a side-swipe at the German chancellor, Helmut Kohl, he argued, 'Unless you take action on jobs, there will be no public support to move ahead on other issues.'

While Brown was trumpeting the virtues of his action plan, at home the leader of Britain's biggest union warned the chancellor that, if he really did stick to Conservative spending plans, jobs would be lost in the public services. Rodney Bickerstaffe, general secretary of the 1.3 million-strong public-service union Unison, told delegates to the union's annual conference to expect 'severe budgetary pressures' in the NHS and local government by the autumn. 'If the government is set to stay within these public expenditure parameters, it is going to be very, very tight.' Jobs found for young people under the welfare-to-work programme would be offset by job losses in the cash-strapped public sector. 'My own view is that they are going to have to increase public spending.'[12] Bickerstaffe, who is also chairman of the TUC's Economic Committee, had urged these views on the chancellor when the unions made their pre-budget submissions. It was an issue that would come back to haunt Gordon Brown.

Brown's role in the heart of government was confirmed when the full list of Cabinet committees was published on his return from Luxembourg. In addition to the chancellor's usual chair-

manship of the Economic Affairs and Public Expenditure committees, which gave him virtually untrammelled freedom to
shape economic policy, he was to sit on eight more: Defence,
Constitution, Intelligence, Ulster, Home and Social, Environment, Local Government and Europe.

Chancellor Brown appeared at the despatch box on 12 June
for Treasury Questions for the first time. Tory MP David Prior,
son of Lord Prior, the former Northern Ireland secretary,
bowled him a straight ball, asking if the windfall tax was indeed
to be a one-off levy. Brown pointed out that the precedent had
been set by the Conservative government in the 1980s, when
the banks had been taxed in the same way. 'That windfall tax
was imposed on the banks to deal with the costs of failure.'
Labour was tackling a problems that Tory MPs should be concerned about. 'Indeed, they should be ashamed that the previous government did not act to tackle youth and long-term
unemployment.' He quoted a new report showing that half a
million long-term unemployed people needed proper skills and
training to get back to work. 'People will be asking why the
Conservative Party is defending the utilities instead of the long-
term unemployed.' After all, James Rogers, co-owner of
Midlands Electricity had recently said, 'A windfall tax would
require us to deal with the sins of those before us. A one-off tax
is not inconsistent with that.'

It was vintage Brown: lots of references to the unemployed,
the long term, Tory shame – and sin thrown in for good
measure. He also gave short shrift to a new Conservative MP,
Julie Kirkbride, who was asking awkward questions about the
impact of the national minimum wage on the public sector.
Welcoming Ms Kirkbride – daughter of a Halifax lorry-driver,
former girlfriend of Stephen Milligan the Tory MP who died
during an obscure sex-ritual – to the House, he quipped, 'She
was a distinguished parliamentary correspondent and is now a
member of Parliament, having moved from a larger
Conservative institution – the *Daily Telegraph* – to a smaller
one, the parliamentary Conservative Party.' Pointing out that

Winston Churchill, Harold Macmillan and Sir Edward Heath
had all supported a minimum wage, he argued, 'It is about time
the Conservative Party joined the modern world.' This apparent non sequitur led to a friendly question from Labour left-
winger Dennis Skinner, much shouting from the Opposition
and then an interruption from Madam Speaker to shut them
up. Kenneth Clarke, the shadow chancellor, picked up Ms
Kirkbride's point – essentially the same as the fears voiced by
Rodney Bickerstaffe two day previously – and claimed that
either the minimum wage would be set at a level so low that it
made no difference to public-sector pay, or else it would affect
public services. 'If he sticks to his commitment not to raise
public spending, the National Health service and others will
face a choice between cutting services and cutting jobs.' Brown
taunted Clarke, a contender for the Tory Party leadership, over
his bid to re-establish 'one-nation' traditions in the Conservative Party, and tried to link one-nation Conservativism to
the virtues of a minimum wage. The conceit did not quite
come off. The best clue to his generosity was in his remark that
'All these questions will be taken into account in settling the
minimum wage'. This hint was taken by union leaders to mean
that they should not expect too much from the Low Pay
Commission and the national minimum wage. The TUC's target was £4.42 an hour. The word at Westminster was that
£3.65 would be as far as the government would go.

The chancellor also announced a major change in inflation-
accounting. He told MPs he would hold the governor of the
Bank and the Monetary Policy Committee accountable if they
failed to meet the government's inflation target. Labour's
election manifesto had promised: 'We will match the current
target for low and stable inflation of 2.5 per cent or less.' But
now, he said, each time inflation was 1 per cent above or below
that target, the governor would have to write a letter to the
chancellor explaining why it had been missed, what action the
Bank proposed to take to correct it and when inflation would
return to the proper range. This formula allowed Brown to

appear tougher on inflation than the Conservatives, but also gave lee-room for inflation to nudge up to 3.5 per cent before the political flak started.

His announcement coincided with the publication of new official figures showing that underlying inflation was indeed 2.5 per cent, in line with the previous government's objective. But the next day, 13 June, Quentin Letts observed in the *Daily Telegraph* that 'Mr Brown had just privatised inflation, or rather, he had just privatised the blame for inflation.' Nor were the City and the Opposition taken in. Liberal Democrat Treasury spokesman Malcolm Bruce charged: 'You are setting a range of 1.5 per cent to 3.5 per cent, beginning a serious relaxation of bearing down on inflation.' Ken Clarke derided the move as a loosening of the criteria for controlling inflation. Brown sought to clarify the situation in a letter to Eddie George. 'The thresholds do not define a target range. Their function is to define the points at which I expect an explanatory letter from you because the actual inflation rate is appreciably away from its target.'

The press was obsessed with what Brown would wear for his keynote speech at the Mansion House. He entered the great hall with Roger Cork, the lord mayor, and Eddie George, dressed in his usual business suit and a slightly more adventurous tie than usual, to the accompaniment of the march from Handel's opera *Scipio*, to be greeted with the traditional slow handclap from the 350 guests drawn from the City. They ate cold soup, smoked salmon with potted shrimps, followed by roast beef and Yorkshire pudding and blackcurrant pudding, all washed down with 1995 Chardonnay, 1986 claret, 1980 Fonseca port and Courvoisier.

As the band switched to *Oklahoma!*, Brown drank, without much enthusiasm, from a loving-cup passed round the top table, then rose to speak. He argued the need for stability in monetary and fiscal policymaking and preached the virtues of 'long-termism', insisting that his new 'rigorous, precise and open procedures' would allow the Bank to deliver on inflation in the long term. 'If we succeed in strengthening the ability of the British economy to sustain growth with low inflation, and if international conditions permit, I would hope to lower the inflation target,' the Chancellor told a somewhat sceptical audience.

Brown travelled to Amsterdam for the summit of European Union leaders early the following week, eager to ensure that finance ministers kept control of the £700 million EU plan to tackle the jobs crisis. At a breakfast with the French finance minister, Dominique Strauss-Kahn, he joked that expenditure on that scale had to be kept out of the hands of social-affairs ministers. His advisers were taken aback by an apparent leak of a key element in the budget in the *Financial Times* on 15 June. The paper reported that the chancellor was planning a contro-versial raid on pension funds' income, by abolishing the 20 per cent tax credits on dividend payouts. This move, which would cost pension funds up to £5 billion a year, was the Treasury's preferred option for raising extra revenue, said the *FT*. Indeed, it was, despite powerful lobbying from the National Association of Pension Funds and the insurance companies. The system worked as follows: when companies paid out a dividend, they also paid advance corporation tax (ACT). Shareholders received an equivalent tax credit, and tax-exempt shareholders such as pension funds could claim a repayment. Some described this as a 'victimless' tax hike, but pension-fund managers claimed it would reduce sharply the value of com-panies on the stock exchange. In the heat and glare of the Amsterdam summit, where a compromise was reached on jobs and the progress of monetary union, Brown's people managed to put the lid on speculation about ACT, but the cat was out of the bag. Immediately after Amsterdam, the pound surged to a new high of DM2.8647, amid speculation in the money mar-kets that the Bank would be forced to increase interest rates again.

The National Audit Office report on assumptions about the future ordered by Chancellor Brown was published on 19 June.

(That was also the day of the final round of the Conservative Party leadership election which saw Brown's old rival Kenneth Clarke consigned to the backbenches after he lost to William Hague, at 36 some twenty years his junior.) The report, prepared by Sir John Bourn, the comptroller and auditor-general, supported Brown's new public spending sums: 'While the assumptions adopted by the Chancellor are not the only ones which could be reconciled with the evidence, in my opinion they have been arrived at systematically on the basis of the available data and by methods which interpret it in a reasonable way.' This cautious endorsement was greeted by Brown as 'independent backing for my new assumptions about public spending'. The key new forecast was to revise downwards the rate of economic growth from Clarke's figure of 2.5 per cent to 2.25 per cent, which would add £3.75 billion to the public sector borrowing requirement (PSBR) in the next financial year, £4 billion in 1999/2000, £5.5 billion in 2000/01 and £7 billion in 2001/02, a total shortfall over the life of the government of £20.75 billion. The shortfall in public finances in 1997/98 was £500 million. This '£20 billion black hole' bequeathed by the Tories made the headlines and gave the chancellor a useful propaganda argument for raising taxes. Preoccupied with the leadership contest, the Conservatives failed to challenge Brown. But the Liberal Democrats were scathing. Malcolm Bruce described the report as 'bizarre and politically inspired' and accused Brown of cooking the books. 'His aim is to worsen the Budget forecasts to justify higher taxes, and in my view he is abusing the independence of the Audit Office,' he said. 'Instead of the NAO independently reviewing Ken Clarke's Budget figures, which was always our understanding, they have in fact been used just to rubber-stamp Gordon Brown's own assumptions.'[13] The *Economist* was more inclined to give the chancellor the benefit of the doubt, arguing that the new assumptions did not make tax increases essential, and noting that, by promising to ask the Audit Office to vet any future changes to budget-forecast figures, Brown had surrendered the chance to fiddle the numbers for political advantage. 'For that, he deserves much credit.'[14]

Before he could unveil his budget, there was yet more summitry: on 22 June the Group of Eight industrialised nations met in Denver. Brown and his party travelled by Concorde to the USA, though they had to fly subsonic on the last leg over American soil. In the last few days before his budget, Brown's pace did not falter. On 25 June, he held a breakfast summit of businessmen at 11 Downing Street, telling them that the business community was vital to the success of welfare-to-work. He disclosed to the thirty-eight chairmen and chief executives gathered over the coffee and croissants that the £3 billion, five-year scheme would be launched nationwide in April 1998. It would, as promised, be funded by the windfall tax on privatised utilities. Pilot projects would start as early as January 1998, in fifteen areas covering 10 per cent of the country.

Paymaster-General Geoffrey Robinson had assembled an impressive round-table of business chiefs, including David Sainsbury, chairman of J. Sainsbury (who had once supported the SDP); Ian McAllister, chairman of Ford UK; Brian Moffat, chairman and chief executive of British Steel; Sir Richard Greenbury, chairman of Marks & Spencer; Peter Birch, chief executive of Abbey National; Sir Ian Prosser, chairman and chief executive of Bass; and George Bull, chairman of Grand Metropolitan. Allan Leighton of Asda, Terry Leahy, boss of Tesco and Lord Blyth of Boots were there too – as were John Monks, general secretary of the TUC, and his economic affairs secretary, Bill Callaghan.

The chancellor put his cards on the table. 'Past schemes failed because they did not properly engage the business community. I am determined that government and business should work closely together to deliver these benefits.' David Blunkett, the education and employment secretary, backed him up. 'This is not a government programme. It is a partnership with business,' he insisted. Sir Peter Davis, chief executive of the Prudential, would head a Treasury task group to oversee the

introduction of the scheme. Brown assured the assembled cap-
tains of capital that they would choose who they wished to
recruit, and their companies would also determine wages and
other terms of employment. In the meantime, the public
employment service would carry out a 'gateway' programme to
prepare the young long-term jobless for their entry into the
world of work.

Essentially, Brown was putting business on the spot: they
could make or break welfare-to-work. McAllister immediately
promised that Ford would take on a hundred extra young
people, under the 'new deal' that gave employers a £60-a-week
subsidy for six months for each unemployed youngster hired
for quality training and work experience. Sir Richard
Greenbury asked for further talks with the chancellor on Marks
& Spencer's role. None of the business leaders expressed opposition. All handed over written pledges after the breakfast
promising to participate in what the *Financial Times* called 'this
giant experiment'.

As budget fever intensified, the weekend papers talked up
Brown's toughness and radicalism. He would come down hard
on consumer spending to prevent the boom getting out of control. He would take up to £5 billion out of the economy. He
would increase National Insurance rates. He would tax, and tax
again, the company car. He would make us all healthier by
jacking up alcohol and tobacco duties. The *Independent on
Sunday* predicted that Brown would continue his predecessor's
gradual phasing-out of the mortgage interest subsidy given to
home-buyers.

Another first for many years was for the Labour conference
to be addressed by an actual serving chancellor. After the long
summer recess, in his first speech as chancellor to a Labour
Party conference on 29 September 1997, Brown said Labour
was 'Not triumphalist but humbled by the great trust placed in
us by the British people, challenged by the scale of the problems we have inherited. Determined to keep faith with the millions of British people who put their faith in us on May 1st. A

modern Party ready to modernise Britain.'

He reminded delegates of his warning two years previous: 'You cannot build the New Jerusalem on a mountain of debt.

'That is why with our deficit reduction plan for public borrowing, with our tough reforms at the Bank of England, with the interest rate rises made necessary by Conservative mistakes, Britain has begun to break from Tory short-termism – and I am now more optimistic that the economy can be back on track next year,' he said. 'And I tell you we have learned from past mistakes. Just as you cannot spend your way out of recession, you cannot, in a global economy, simply spend your way through a recovery either.'

The chancellor added: 'In place of irresponsible Tory short-termism there will be no risks with inflation, no irresponsible fine tuning, no massaging of the figures, no short term dashes for growth but a long-term strategy for our public finances, the encouragement of investment for the future, and, in place of boom and bust, stability.' These policies would revive Labour's old goal of full employment. 'The essential platform for high and sustainable levels of growth and employment, the aims of the 1945 government reaffirmed in 1997.

'We are in power today and in a position to empower people because we had the courage to change and modernise our Party,' the chancellor went on. 'But modernisation of our Party was for a purpose – a greater national purpose – to make possible the second modernisation. The modernisation of our country to equip all our people for the future. We must modernise remote and unreformed institutions and bring power closer to the people. We must modernise our role in the world, and lead anew in Europe and round the globe.

'This root and branch modernisation of our economy with a new welfare state is the modern way, the only way, the New Labour way to achieve what we have always sought and what I affirm as our goal today: employment opportunity for all in every part of Britain. Full employment for the twenty-first century. The ambition of decent-minded people everywhere.

And this party should tolerate no irresponsible demands that put these historic national goals at risk. A government can be credible without being radical, and end up changing nothing – but we are the Party that has always stood for progress. A government can be radical without being credible, but we are the Party that rightly rejects idle posturing. I say: only by being radical and credible can we in government, turn our ambitions into achievements.'

Brown invoked Labour's past heroes in his defence. 'It was because a century ago Keir Hardie looked at the world as it was and saw what a new world could be that he broke with the old order, set politics on a new, modern path and founded the Labour Party,' he argued. 'It was because fifty years ago Aneurin Bevan looked at the old world of disease and deprivation, and saw what a new world could be, that he broke with the private healthcare of the past and established a National Health Service that still serves us today. And so now for our time, let the message go out. We govern and we seek to serve as a new political generation.

'Since May 1st, we have seen the relief and optimism expressed in people's faces. We have heard the hope in people's voices. We have seen an outpouring of compassion from people's hearts. We have seen a glimpse of what Britain has in itself to become. No more a nation divided against itself but a nation united. No longer fearful of the future but hopeful and confident. No more the rich man in his castle, the poor man at the gate. No more the barriers of privilege dividing us, but a society where opportunity is open to all. No longer us and them but we the people. From now on, a Britain where everyone of us has a contribution to make. These are our values. Values we share with the people of Britain. We are the People's Party. Now delivering the people's priorities. As once more the people's government.'

Political commentators were surprised that Brown did not get a standing ovation for his speech. Lord Roy Hattersley considered it the best he had heard 'for a very long time' at a party conference. In *The Times*, Peter Riddell linked the chancellor's performance with the defeat of his one-time political ally, Peter Mandelson, the minister without portfolio. Mandelson failed to win the seat on the party's ruling national executive committee vacated by Brown. It went to Ken Livingstone from the party's left. Riddell pointed out that 'Gordon Brown knows how to bridge old and new Labour whereas Mandelson could, but does not wish to.' That is the critical difference between Brown and many of his fellow-modernisers. He has a gut instinct for the party he has reformed, and might yet lead.

CHAPTER 14

SOCIAL-JUSTICE CHANCELLOR

DR COLIN CURRIE, THE EDINBURGH CONSULTANT IN geriatric medicine who is one of Gordon Brown's closest friends, is (unlike the chancellor) an organised man. He carries around on a clipboard a list of things he has to do. Buried at the bottom of these 'must' items is a print-out of his favourite quotation from the writer and philosopher Isaiah Berlin. It is a description of what Berlin called 'the gift', which entails 'a capacity for integrating a vast amalgam of constantly changing, multi-coloured, evanescent, perpetually overlapping data, too many, too swift, too intermingled to be caught and pinned down and labelled like so many butterflies'. Such a capacity enables one to see the data as 'elements in a single pattern, with their implications, to see them as symptoms of past and future possibilities, to see them pragmatically – that is, in terms of what you or others can or will do to them, and what they can or will do to others or to you'. Berlin defines this capacity as 'practical wisdom, practical reason, perhaps, a sense of what will "work" and what will not. It is a capacity, in the first place, for synthesis, rather than analysis.'[1]

Currie believes that Gordon Brown has Berlin's 'capacity' in abundance. He looks at a chaotic, unfair society and seeks to reorder it in a fairer and more comprehensible manner. His politics have a moral purpose, as well as an economic goal. Prosperity is not the be-all and end-all, only the means by which people can secure and enjoy a fulfilling life. It is not a lazy world picture. Work plays a central role. The chancellor may be an infrequent church-attender, but he holds fast to the Protestant work ethic: that work is dignifying in itself, as well as wealth-creative. Hence, his constantly repeated theme, 'I have seen the future, and it is work.' There are almost echoes of Karl Marx's slogan (lifted from Bakunin) 'From each according to his ability, to each according to his needs' in his outlook. It is idealist, inspiring almost. But will it work?

Brown set out his political philosophy in early 1997 in a Fabian Society/*Economist* lecture marking the twentieth anniversary of the death of Anthony Crosland, whose book *The Future of Socialism*, published in 1956, had been an intellectual watershed in the post-war history of the Labour Party.[2] He took as his theme the basic premise of equality, the fundamental value dividing Labour from the Conservatives. He declared that the case for equality must be argued again from first principles, after the New Right ideology, which worshipped inequality, had dominated the political landscape for twenty years.

'We argue for equality not just because of our belief in social justice but also because of our view of what is required for economic success,' he said. 'The starting point is a fundamental belief in the worth of every human being. We all have an equal claim to social consideration by virtue of being human. And if every person is to be regarded as of equal worth, all deserve to be given an equal chance in life to fulfil the potential with which they were born.'

Crosland had proposed a democratic view of equality, one that sought to prevent the permanent entrenchment of privilege, from whatever source it came. This demanding concept, he thought, had 'revolutionary connotations'. Brown offered his own definition of democratic equality in the 1990s –

inevitably, a little list. First, it required employment opportunity for all, 'because work is central not just to economic prosperity for Britain, but to individual fulfilment'. There must be a permanent duty on government to pursue this objective relentlessly. Second, there had to be continuing, lifelong educational opportunity for all – second, third and even fourth chances so that people were not written off if they failed at school. Were there echoes here of his scorching criticism of the academic experiment at his High School? Third, lifelong opportunity had to be comprehensive, extending beyond education and employment, involving genuine access to culture and, most importantly, a redistribution of power that offered people real control over the decisions that affect their lives. 'The issue for socialists is not so much what the state can do for you, but about what the state can enable you to do for yourself.'

Even in today's global marketplace, proponents of democratic equality have to address wealth and income inequalities, Brown insisted. They must tackle the biggest source of poverty and inequality: unemployment. His commitment to this issue has been consistent over the years. He represents a constituency that has witnessed the savage decline of the coal industry and the rundown of Rosyth, and his own convictions were reinforced by the political teachings of James Maxton. Brown argued that employment opportunity for all was hollow when one working family in five – 19 per cent – had no one earning a wage. 'When I see the levels of worklessness, particularly youth unemployment, in our inner cities, I fear for what will happen in our country,' he said. 'We face a rising tide of alienation among disenfranchised young people, not simply unemployed, but second-generation unemployed who have no experience of work in their family . . . We cannot duck the central importance of work – and the work ethic. For this is the major challenge facing those who believe in equality and indeed anyone who is concerned about social cohesion.'

Brown's answer, set forth in his first budget, was to give new hope to this 'abandoned and forgotten generation'. From the

beginning of 1998, employers are offered a tax rebate of £60 a
week for every jobless young person they take on, and £75 a
week for every person who has been unemployed for more than
two years. This welfare-to-work programme, funded by the
windfall tax on the privatised utilities, is the start of his
modernisation of the welfare state – 'restoring work and the
work ethic to its core', as he put it in his Crosland Lecture.
Linked to a reform of the tax and benefit system designed to
ensure that work always pays, it is a characteristic Calvinist
blend of opportunity and duty. The chancellor has faith that it
will succeed. 'It will take time,' he conceded. 'But it is important to realise that we have thought this through. It starts in the
school. It goes right through the labour market and the reforms
we will make,' he said soon after the election.[3]

Even his greatest admirers have their reservations. Richard
Layard, professor of economics at the London School of
Economics and one of the leading thinkers influencing Labour,
thinks it will work, though 'things don't always work out
exactly as you expect them to'. His enthusiasm warming, he
said, 'There is plenty of hard evidence on which the policies are
based that they will make a difference. It's very difficult. You
have to proceed step by step. It will probably be more difficult
to find solutions for men in their forties – but that will have to
be attempted in due course . . . I don't think there can be any
abject failure, but there are bound to be some disappointments.
This is one of the arguments for a second term.'[4]

To achieve what he wants, Brown has to get the economy
right. Looking at what politicians like to call the big picture,
the man he succeeded is both generous and critical on this
score. Ex-chancellor Kenneth Clarke, now on the backbenches
he last occupied almost two decades ago, says, 'Gordon Brown
has dominated the first months of government. He is the one
minister who hit the ground running, and has actually taken a
whole lot of decisions. But the important thing is to get the
decisions right. We will wait to see whether the country celebrates the millennium with a recession. If so, I shall argue that

some of Gordon's early mistakes were the cause of that. He should not have loaded huge taxation on business. The windfall tax makes no economic sense. It was a bloody good speech in Opposition to exploit the "fat-cat issue" – but as a piece of taxation policy, useless. This is just Opposition sloganising turned into a £5 billion tax. I never hit the corporate sector with that kind of tax.'[5]

The so-called raid on pension funds Clarke dismisses as 'unacceptable'. He adds, 'Gordon Brown has a problem. The tax receipts are flowing in, far ahead of Treasury forecasts. The economy is booming. People are talking about how to slow it down. I agree with all of that. You have to take decisions quietly and sensibly to calm it down. What you don't do is panic. He hasn't panicked. But what he is doing to slow it down will really hit in a year's time. He will slow down the economy savagely – too much. I think he has overdone it. He will have a serious slow-down, not necessarily a recession, but a big slow-down, bigger than he wants, in 1999/2000. He ought to bear the blame for that.'[6]

Few in the government, and, judging by the opinion polls, few in the country, share his pessimism. Giles Radice, Labour chairman of the Commons Treasury Select Committee, claims that Brown is 'potentially the most radical of post-war Labour chancellors'. He looks down the roll. Hugh Dalton nationalised the Bank of England. Stafford Cripps introduced austerity. Hugh Gaitskell only had one budget. Roy Jenkins was 'quite successful': he successfully devalued the pound but didn't win the election. James Callaghan was 'not really' a success, and Denis Healey simply muddled along and was overwhelmed by events.

'What is good about Gordon is his concentration on the long term, the fact that he thought very carefully about what he is doing. For example, partial independence for the Bank. That is about creating a stable framework. We need stability more than the Tories. They can get by flying by the seat of their pants. We cannot. Gordon Brown understands that extremely well. He is running a tight ship, because he remembers only too well the experience of previous Labour chancellors, who gave out money at the beginning and had to cut back later.' Radice agrees there are pitfalls ahead. 'Like all Chancellors, he will be undermined by events,' he predicts. 'It is very difficult steering a medium-sized European economy, particularly one which has such a reputation for instability.'[7]

There is also the big issue of Europe itself, and the single currency. Gordon Brown took the chair of EcoFin, the committee of EU finance ministers, for Britain's six-month presidency of Europe from January to June 1998. He is inextricably bound up with preparations for the Euro, while compelled to reserve the UK's position. The chancellor is widely thought to favour the principle of a single currency, and would take the pound in if he could satisfy the 'Washington conditions' of British self-interest. Monetary union provided Brown with his first real crisis less than six months after taking office. On 26 September, the normally-reliable *Financial Times* led its front page with a story headlined: 'Cabinet Shifts Towards Emu', predicting that the government would soon signal its intention to hold a referendum on UK entry into the European single currency. The paper cited unnamed ministers as its source. It was a quiet Friday. The City went overboard. Shares soared, and the pound plummeted on the back of fears of lower interest rates. The Treasury was taken by surprise. The chancellor was not available in Whitehall to deny the report, which was incorrect. His press secretary, Charlie Whelan, was inundated with calls from the media. He did his best to damp down the speculation, telling the *Independent* with characteristic frankness that it was 'bollocks'. But the fever refused to abate. Two days later, and even more incorrectly, the *Sunday Telegraph* took the story a stage further, promising a virtually imminent plebiscite on the Euro. That same day the *Independent on Sunday* led its business pages with a flatly contradictory story, saying that the government would not join the single currency in 1999 and moreover would almost certainly not hold a referendum until after the general election. In effect, it argued, monetary union would be shelved for the duration of Blair's first parliament.

However, speculation continued to rage. The *Independent* suggested that Brown was trying to 'bounce' Blair into joining the Euro. Ewen MacAskill, the *Guardian's* political correspondent, thought this could be right. Or it might not. 'In politics, it does not always matter if something is true or not,' he observed. 'Perception can matter as much.' (The *Guardian* 20 October 1997). Quite so. Brown counter-attacked by giving an interview to *The Times* for Saturday 18 October, but he could not quite bring himself to say 'No' to the Euro. He talked instead of Britain needing a period of stability after monetary union began on 1 January 1999. Conjecture merely intensified when his trusty spin-doctor, Whelan, firmed up the line for the paper. It did mean no, he insisted, speaking on behalf of the chancellor. Alastair Campbell, the prime minister's press secretary, privately briefed other correspondents along the same lines. Whelan, a clubable man who often spent his Friday evenings in the Red Lion in Whitehall, opposite the Treasury, was overheard briefing the newspapers on his portable telephone, adding to the sense of drama – though he was only responding to frantic press inquiries.

The newspapers cannot resist intrigue, and often see it where it does not exist. The story now became a Whitehall farce of 'government by spin', with nobody really knowing the chancellor's precise intentions. Scenting a political opportunity, the shadow chancellor Peter Lilley demanded a recall of Parliament (MPs were not due back at Westminster until 26 October) and a ministerial statement on the issue. On Sunday evening, 19 October, Brown invited the TV news cameras round to his London flat to put an end to the speculation. He had little choice. The next day, 20 October, was not only the tenth anniversary of 'Black Monday', the great stock market crash of 1987, but also the date for the introduction of computerised trading on the Stock Exchange, and Brown was to inaugurate the new system. He told the nation: 'We are not going to make the same mistakes the Conservatives made over the ERM where indecisiveness caused speculation and damaged our national interest.' He promised a statement to Parliament soon after it reassembled, adding: 'I have already said that entry in 1999 is highly unlikely. Economic cycles have been out of line with our European partners. If we do not join in 1999, then we will need a period of stability, without continuing speculation, while Britain endeavours to meet the five economic tests.' These were: the impact on jobs, the impact on investment, the impact on financial services, the flexibility of the economies and the convergence of the business cycles. This 'period of stability' would be several years, officials confirmed, meaning that UK entry into the Euro would not take place in the life-time of the current Parliament.

His words, repeated in the Stock Exchange as he pressed the button to start up computerised trading, did not prevent mild panic gripping the markets. Initially, the FT-SE 100 Index plunged 120 points, wiping billions off the value of shares, but later in the day the markets rallied, and closed only sixty points down – little over one per cent and not dramatically out of line with a volatile day's trading. 'A mere blip' commented the *Guardian*. City men dubbed it 'Brown Monday', a conscious skit on 'Black Monday' ten years previously. Kenneth Clarke described the chancellor's performance 'an unimpressive display'. Liberal Democrat Treasury spokesman Malcolm Bruce called it 'muddled Monday'. Peter Lilley demanded that Charlie Whelan be sacked, thereby securing his position. But Brown had ridden out his first crisis.

On 27 October 1997, Chancellor Brown made a historic statement on monetary union to a packed House of Commons. The question of a single currency was 'probably the most important question that this country is likely to face in our generation,' he told MPs. He dealt in turn with the issue of principle, the constitutional implications and the economic tests. 'If it works economically, it is, in our view, worth doing,' he said, while recognising that a common monetary policy would inevitably mean 'a major pooling of economic sovereignty.' But if a single currency was good for British jobs, business and prosperity, 'it is right in principle to join' – subject to a Yes vote in a referendum of the British people. He reiterated the Treasury's five economic tests for the Euro to be successful, and concluded that the UK would need a period of stability lasting 'a period of years' to allow European economies to converge. Brown ruled out joining EMU in the first wave of countries on 1 January 1999. He went further, arguing that making a decision in the lifetime of the current parliament was 'not realistic' and the government would therefore not do it.

However, the Chancellor held out the prospect of joining monetary union early in the next parliament, and announced a series of preparatory measures to ensure that Britain would be ready when the time came. Work would begin immediately on the transition arrangements for the possible introduction of the Euro, including notes and coins. A new standing committee on EMU bringing together ministers and business leaders was already being set up, he told MPs.

'To give ourselves a genuine choice in the future, it is essential that the government and business prepare intensively during this parliament so that Britain will be in a position to join a single currency, should we wish to, early in the next parliament,' he said. 'On Europe, the time of indecision is over. The period for practical preparation has begun. Today, we begin to build a new consensus – modern and outward-looking – for a country that throughout its history has looked outward to the world. We are the first British government to declare for the principle of monetary union, the first to state that there is no overriding constitutional bar to membership, the first to make clear and umambiguous economic benefit to this country the decisive test, the first to offer strong and constructive support to our European partners to create more employment and more prosperity.' (Hansard 27 October 1997 cols 583-588)

However, the issue is likely to bring into the open the tension between Brown and Foreign Secretary Robin Cook, for whom he pounded the streets as a canvasser some thirty years ago. Cook is much more sceptical about the virtues of a single currency. Furthermore, he has made no secret of his desire to be chancellor, and Brown is equally determined that he will not get the job. 'They are both pretty good haters,' said a senior party source. 'Cook is very jealous of Brown, and Gordon can be very difficult if you are not on his side. The combination is pretty combustible. It is one of [Tony Blair's] great achievements to keep them in the same operation.'

No one can actually pinpoint the occasion of the disagreement between Brown and Cook, but equally no one in the Labour leadership disputes the existence of sharp rivalry. They began as friends, as far back as 1970 when a teenage Brown knocked on doors for Cook in Edinburgh North. And Brown long believed that, since his erstwhile friend got into parliament ten years before him, he himself would never make up the lost political ground. Yet he has, and therein may lie the explanation.

Cook was already an MP when Brown, still without a winnable seat, made his bid to become chairman of the Scottish Labour Party, which would enhance his prospects of securing a constituency. To do so, he needed as broad a coalition of support as possible. Early in 1982, the year his campaign for the chairmanship was launched (he had to win the vice-chairmanship first), Brown travelled to Westminster to drum up backing from Scots MPs. At the Commons, he met Murray Elder, then working as chief of staff in the leader's office. Brown, Elder and Cook all went for a Chinese meal in Soho. Brown set out his strategy. He needed Cook's support, and he asked for it. Cook replied, 'I am sure you will do very well, Gordon.' Brown asked again, and got the same equivocal answer. It was clear that he could not count on Cook.

There is even a risk that Euro-policy could drive a wedge between Brown and Blair. Kenneth Clarke is mischievous: 'Blair is politically more nervous. I always say, expect no heroics from him. It will be a real test of leadership to seek to sell to the country the advantages of a single currency. I would expect Brown to have the bottle to have a go. Whether he can persuade Tony Blair, we will have to wait and see.'[8]

Getting on with Number 10 is of paramount importance. Previous chancellors agree that the most important single thing is the relationship with the prime minister. If he withdraws his support, the chancellor is finished. The two keep in close touch, meeting at least once a week, more often if there is a crisis. Past chancellors have discovered that they swiftly become surplus to requirements if they get the relationship wrong. In fact, half the chancellors since 1945 either have been sacked or have resigned. In the words of James Callaghan, 'You can leave in good time, or in disgrace.'

Denis Healey jovially likens the role of the two top ministers to a police inquisition. 'The chancellor is the bad policeman, and the prime minister is the good policeman. But of course they work very closely together, if the thing is to work at all.' It is, however, a rather isolated position. Chancellors do not have many friends among their fellow Cabinet members. Nor do they usually command affection among the people. It is sometimes said that if a chancellor is doing his job properly, he must be unpopular, a truism that prompted Norman Lamont to exclaim, 'Then I must be the most successful chancellor there has ever been!'

It is to their mutual advantage that Brown and Blair remain firm friends. They are so close that they are sometimes seen in the back garden of Downing Street, pacing the tiny lawn together, deep in discussion on policy. Ministerial sources say they deliberately choose this location to avoid their conversations being bugged, but their demeanour also bears testament to a friendship that endures.

Looking to the future, the question arises: could Gordon Brown become leader of the Labour Party and prime minister of his country? Before the election, the Conservatives tried to make political capital out of the Labour team's youth and inexperience, in contrast to their own maturity and statesmanship. The voters gave their verdict on that false prospectus in no uncertain manner. And, since Labour's landslide victory at the polls, Brown has emerged as second only to the prime minister in the onerous business of government: more, indeed, of an *alter ego* than a number two. In less than a year, he has proved capable of taking the reins of high office. He has stamped his authority on the Treasury, taking decisions – such as the independence of the Bank of England – that previous chancellors evaded. His is the dominant voice, after Blair's, in the Cabinet, far beyond the range of his economic brief. His influence shows in the choice of key spending ministers. They all report to him on the expenditure reviews of their departments, geared to shift the spending priorities from the Tory legacy to Labour's vision of a 'third way' between untrammelled markets and old-style socialism.

Brown sees himself as playing the long game. The long term is not just for his budgets, but for him too. How far will he go, and how long will he last? 'As far as I can, and as long as I can,' he insisted in an interview on the way to Heathrow for his first post-election holiday in early August 1997. 'My policies are for the long term. The changes I want to make will take many years. I'm young enough to be around for a lot of them. I don't feel old and I am pretty fit. If this is what the Labour Party can achieve in its first eighteen weeks, think what we can do in eighteen years – with the will of the people.' The suggestion that Brown would like to see Labour in power in the year 2015 – which would involve matching the Conservative record of four successive election victories – is extraordinary. Even Tony Blair has only talked of two terms as prime minister. If he stood down towards the end of his second term in, say, the year 2005, Brown would still only be 54 – the same age that Margaret Thatcher was when first elected prime minister in 1979. And, unlike her, he would have almost a decade of top-level ministerial performance under his belt.

Even his predecessor, Kenneth Clarke, concedes that Brown could do what he failed to do, and make it all the way to the top. 'He is "*papabile*",' said the ex-chancellor, borrowing the

Italian phrase for a cardinal who could become Pope. 'He is a serious contender. The key judgment is whether he would be sufficiently people-friendly. Tony Blair can really attract votes. Could this isolated, politically withdrawn, rather dour figure be attractive to the public? Yes, if he has been a successful chancellor – and certainly not if we have had a recession and he is as guilty as Blair. I think I can say that, if you wish to be prime minister, being chancellor is not the best political base, as all history demonstrates. Gordon has one thing in common with me: he will not go out of his way to be popular with his colleagues. You cannot afford to do that. You have to be tough with colleagues if you are to run the country properly. As Norman Lamont said, hardly anyone leaves the Treasury with his political reputation enhanced, though there have been exceptions: look at Roy Jenkins and Geoffrey Howe.'[9] Neither of them of course, became prime minister. Clarke sees beyond the superficial image of a dour Scot. 'As a man, I like him,' he said. 'I find he is more relaxed and friendly than his public image would suggest. I find him quite genial. I happen to have strong criticism of some of his decisions, but I don't have any lack of respect for his judgment. I like his approach to politics. He does take his politics seriously.'[10]

Is he still a socialist? As the philosopher would say, 'it all depends what you mean by . . .' Ken Livingstone MP, the authentic mouthpiece of the rump of Labour's parliamentary left-wing, respects his socialist instincts. Brown himself believes he is in the mainstream of Croslandite democratic socialism, and, unlike Blair, he does not make the rather phoney distinction of labelling his credo 'social-ism'. Naturally, his political enemies like to make much of the way Brown's outlook has developed. Michael Russell, chief executive of the SNP, launched a biting attack during the general election. 'I remember Gordon Brown at Edinburgh University the darling of the Hard Left and the champion of the Socialist confrontation,' he said. 'Now he is the poodle of the British establishment and the most eager of the Blairite proto-Tories. He is a Ramsay

Macdonald in the making, who will soon be "dancing with duchesses" while the people of his country continue to suffer.'[11]

Plainly, Brown's views have evolved since the heady days of the *Red Paper*, but he considers that he has stayed true to his principles, and the final assessment must be that that is how he would wish to be judged. His father, John E. Brown, reflects, 'I don't think he has changed greatly. His outlook is much the same. He is probably rather more intellectual about it now, but I think the basics are just the same. I am quite pleased. It was a basic Christian upbringing, and he values fairness. I like that. He wants to be fair to people, and not take advantage of anybody.'[12]

Murray Elder, who has watched the chancellor's evolution since infancy, is clear on this score. 'I have no doubt that the person with the real strategic view of the way the party is going is Gordon. He is in a class of his own. He has a genuinely first-class mind, and a tremendous capacity for new ideas. But I don't think he has changed from the social-justice agenda with which John Smith was associated.'[13] There was more than a hint of orthodoxy from the beginning. Bill Campbell, who worked with him on *Student*, points out, 'Others flirted with the International Socialists and anarchism. Gordon never had these flights of fancy. He always saw the way through a mainstream political party.'[14]

His friend Colin Currie prefers a nautical image. 'If you can imagine an Edwardian cruise liner, the SS *Great Britain*, there is a charming captain, and deep down in the ship there is a hard Scots engineer who understands all the bits and pieces of the machinery and can wield a spanner in order to persuade people to do the right thing. I think that is really it. He is willing to do the difficult things. It may be better that the person who has to do the difficult things is in the job where really difficult things have to be done.' But he too identifies a moral dimension to Brown's politics. 'He sees politics as a vehicle for doing good in a non-naive, New Testament kind of way. There is a genuine pastoral concern about the excluded, the disadvantaged, that drives all the things he takes on.'[15]

Alf Young, economics columnist on the Glasgow-based *Herald*, who worked alongside Brown in Keir Hardie House, concurs. 'Gordon's always been a curious mix of willingness to compromise while keeping his eye on the big picture. His budget takes the long term very seriously. This is all of a piece with the guy I knew twenty and thirty years ago. It is arguable that he has had to make some pretty hefty sacrifices along the way in terms of change, but there is still the big, long-term objective there that is really about quite fundamental changes in British society. They are not about Clause IV, but they are about Brown's Presbyterian past, about making life better for people.' He also finds a tougher man at the Treasury. 'He has got harder. There is more hardness there than before. I suppose that was inevitable. You develop a carapace.'[16] The chancellor's closest friends and aides concur that Brown is a long-haul politician. Even his mother comments, 'I think he will always want to keep going.'

But Alf Young finds a down-side to this devotion to work. 'Politics have so much dominated his life, I don't think he could give it up.' And if the project failed, if the changes he sought were still as distant in, say, ten years' time, 'Will he feel that his life has been a failure?' Young asks. He notes, 'There is a great streak of self-doubt about Gordon.'[17] Others have made a similar point, on a deep-background basis, though, in a man whose springs of action were forged in such a religious setting, it is perhaps not surprising that there should be theological-style doubts from time to time. Set against those misgivings is the enormous intellectual effort he puts into making up his mind before he acts. Brown, his friends and aides agree, takes a very long time to reach decisions – but once there, it is virtually impossible to shift him.

Professor Richard Layard observes of Brown's political outlook, 'It has a moral basis, springing from a basic instinct for equality as a fundamental component of socialism. I don't mind the word "socialist", if it means an attempt to include everybody in society, and make sure that everybody is able to make a contribution and get a share of the goods that society produced. He has the most extraordinary energy and ability to worry away at the detail of things without losing sight of the wood for the trees. His determination and commitment to having an active Treasury that is pursuing major economic and social goals will be of great benefit to the country.

'It is quite remarkable that even in a situation in which there is an unusually acute shortage of money, there is an optimistic atmosphere in the country, that things will be done, and this reflects the feeling that priorities are being changed against a background of realism. People will feel that they have something to offer to society, and will be willing to participate in society. This *is* a long haul. Tony and Gordon do think their job is to change the country, and make it a more decent, fairer and more prosperous place. I don't see why they should not do all three.'[18]

Layard identifies the long gestation of policy that preceded Brown's accession to the Treasury as the key factor in the new economics. 'The three years of policy development which he did before the election marked a real break in the history of the Labour Party, in shifting priorities towards the development of people as a central focus, and in working out in some detail what was required to be done to help people make the most of their lives. One can say that the Labour Party have never gone into an election with such a well-worked-out and coherent programme of what it wanted to achieve in office, and Gordon was very central to that. I think he has done a lot to break down the artificial distinction that used to exist between economic and social policy, simply because he has emphasised that on the one side everybody has resources and on the other side, the purpose of the economy is to satisfy the wants of individuals.'[19]

Why did Brown, the teenager who sold his mother's homemade toffee for charity, the student who was first seen as a Don Quixote figure, tilting at the windmills of authority, come to choose the greasy pole of politics? He falls back on a familiar theme. 'I was always concerned about issues of social justice, and I always felt that politics was the way to get them sorted out. My upbringing taught me to see things in terms of right and wrong, and the social conditions that appalled me have got to be sorted out.'[20] Perhaps the real clue lies in the judgment of the old socialist Fenner Brockway on James Maxton, Brown's hero, quoted in Brown's book. Maxton, said Brockway, seemed to have got nearest to the solution of life's problems. He always lived his own life, yet he accepted everyone on equal terms. He was friendly to everyone, without being subservient. 'I think the secret of Maxton's conduct was an inherent sense of human equality,' he concluded.[21] Invoking this quality, Brown is more succinct. 'I am a good guy,' he says.

NOTES

CHAPTER 1 – FIRST BUDGET

1 All extracts from Brown's budget speech are from *Hansard*, 2 July 1997, cols 303–90.
2 *On the Record*, BBC TV, 23 February 1992; quoted in John Rentoul, *Tony Blair* (London: Little, Brown, 1995), p. 270.
3 Nicholas Comfort, *Brewer's Politics. A Phrase and Fable Dictionary* (London: Cassell, 1993), p. 226.
4 Malcolm Bruce, statement on the budget, 2 July 1997.
5 *Daily Telegraph*, 5 July 1997.
6 *Sunday Telegraph*, 6 July 1997.
7 *Yorkshire Post*, 15 July 1997.
8 Minutes of the Treasury Select Committee hearing, 21 July 1997.
9 *Financial Times*, 22 July 1997.
10 Dr John E. Brown, *A Time to Serve* (Edinburgh: Mainstream, 1994), p. 60.

CHAPTER 2 – FIFE CHILDHOOD

1 Dr John E. Brown, *A Time to Serve* (Edinburgh: Mainstream, 1994), p. 7.
2 John E. Brown, interview, 13 August 1997.
3 Andrew Brown, written statement to the author, 26 June 1997.
4 Daniel Defoe, *A Tour through the Whole Island of Great Britain*

(London: Penguin, November 1971).

5 Gordon Brown, interview, 20 April 1997.
6 Elizabeth Brown, interview, 13 August 1997.
7 Gordon Brown, interview, 20 April 1997.
8 *Daily Telegraph*, 10 July 1995.
9 *The Times*, 15 May 1993.
10 *Daily Telegraph*, 10 July 1995.
11 *The Times*, 15 May 1993.
12 Murray Elder, interview, 13 August 1997.
13 *The Times*, 15 May 1993.
14 Gordon Brown, interview, 20 April 1997.
15 *The Times*, 15 May 1993.
16 Andrew Brown, statement, 26 June 1997.
17 *The Times*, 15 May 1993.
18 Gordon Brown, interview, 20 April 1997.
19 Ibid.
20 Elder, interview, 31 July 1997.
21 Andrew Brown, interview, 21 June 1997.
22 *Scottish Daily Express*, 28 June 1997.
23 Gordon Brown, interview, 20 April 1997.
24 *Sunday Mail*, 29 June 1997.

CHAPTER 3 – RADICAL STUDENT

1 Gordon Brown, interview, 20 April 1997.
2 *The Times*, 15 May 1993.
3 Gordon Brown, interview, 20 April 1997.
4 Henry Drucker, interview, 16 April 1997.
5 Jonathan Wills, written statement to the author, 10 May 1997.
6 Ibid.
7 *Student*, 25 April 1968.
8 *Student*, April 1969.
9 Drucker, interview, 16 April 1997.
10 *Sunday Times* Scotland, 26 November 1995.
11 Wills, statement, 10 May 1997.
12 Tim Dawson, *Sunday Times* Scotland, 26 November 1995.
13 Gordon Brown, interview, 20 April 1997.
14 *Student*, 25 February 1971.
15 Ibid.
16 *Student*, 29 April 1971.
17 Ibid.
18 *Student*, 13 May 1971.

19 John Campbell, *Edward Heath* (London: Cape, 1993), p. 371.
20 *Student*, 20 October 1971.
21 *Student*, 4 November 1971.
22 *Student*, 9 November 1972.
23 Ibid.
24 *Student*, 30 November 1972.
25 Drucker, interview, 16 April 1997.
26 Ibid.
27 Dawson, *Sunday Times* Scotland, 26 November 1995.
28 *The Times*, 15 May 1993.
29 Gordon Brown, interview, 20 May 1997.

CHAPTER 4 – THE MAN FOR MORNINGSIDE

1 Downing Street meeting held on 28 November 1993.
2 Gordon Brown, interview, 20 April 1997.
3 Gordon Brown, interview, 19 July 1997.
4 *Scotland on Sunday*, 2 October 1994.
5 Gordon Brown, interview, 19 July 1997.
6 Gordon Brown, 'Introduction', *The Red Paper on Scotland* (Edinburgh: Edinburgh University Student Publications Board, 1975), p. 7ff.
7 Ibid.
8 Ibid.
9 Ibid.
10 Henry Drucker, interview, 16 April 1997.
11 Brown, *The Red Paper*.
12 Ibid.
13 Ibid.
14 Ibid.
15 Ibid.
16 Gordon Brown, *James Maxton* (Edinburgh: Mainstream, 1986), p. 36.
17 Brown, *The Red Paper*.
18 Drucker, interview, 16 April 1997.
19 Jim Sillars, interview, 2 June 1997.
20 Gordon Brown, interview, 5 June 1997.
21 Glasgow *Herald*, 28 February 1983.
22 Ibid.
23 Jimmy Allison, interview, 6 February 1997.
24 Gordon Brown, interview, 19 July 1997.
25 Alf Young, interview, 8 July 1997.
26 *Edinburgh Evening News*, 12 February 1979.

27 Cited in Andrew Marr, *The Battle for Scotland* (London: Penguin, 1992).
28 Young, interview, 8 July 1997.
29 Ibid.
30 *Edinburgh Evening News*, 8 January 1979.
31 Marr, *The Battle for Scotland*, p. 160.
32 *Edinburgh Evening News*, 26 February 1979.
33 *Edinburgh Evening News*, 26 March 1979.
34 Gordon Brown, interview, 19 July 1997.
35 *Edinburgh Evening News*, 17 April 1979.
36 Ibid.
37 Ibid.
38 Ibid.
39 Glasgow *Herald*, 28 February 1983.

CHAPTER 5 – VICTORY AND DISASTER

1 Tony Benn, *Conflicts of Interest - Diaries 1977–80* (London: Hutchinson, 1990), p. 499.
2 Gordon Brown, interview, 5 June 1997.
3 Ibid.
4 Jimmy Allison, *Guilty by Suspicion* (Glendaruel: Argyll Publishing, 1995), p. 119.
5 Jim Sillars, interview, 2 June 1997.
6 Glasgow *Herald*, 28 February 1983.
7 Allison, *Guilty by Suspicion*, 'Appendix I: Confidential Minutes of Meeting between Scottish Executive Committee and Michael Foot'.
8 Willie Hamilton, *Blood on the Walls* (London: Bloomsbury, 1992), p. 51.
9 David Stoddart, interview, 25 March 1997.
10 Ibid.
11 Alex Falconer, written statement to the author, 2 June 1997.
12 *Dunfermline Press*, 29 April 1983.
13 Jonathan Wills, written statement to the author, 10 May 1997.
14 Ibid.
15 Alex Kitson, interview, 9 July 1997.
16 Falconer, statement, 2 June 1997.
17 Wills, statement, 10 May 1997.
18 Ibid.
19 Stoddart, interview, 25 March 1997.
20 *Scotsman*, 4 June 1983.
21 Ibid.

22 *Scotsman,* 7 June 1983.
23 Wills, statement, 10 May 1997.

CHAPTER 6 – AMBITIOUS BACKBENCHER

 1 Jon Sopel, *Tony Blair: The Moderniser* (London: Michael Joseph, 1995), p. 74.
 2 Andrew Brown, interview, 21 June 1997.
 3 *Sunday Times,* 17 July 1992.
 4 All quotes from Gordon Brown's speech and Alan Haselhurst's reply are from *Hansard,* 27 July 1983, cols 1226–44.
 5 Rhodes Boyson, *Speaking My Mind* (London: Peter Owen, 1995), p. 186.
 6 *Dunfermline Press,* 3 February 1984.
 7 Alan Clark, *Diaries* (London: Phoenix, 1993), p. 53.
 8 Gordon Brown, 'Introduction', in Gordon Brown and Robin Cook, eds, *Scotland: The Real Divide. Poverty and Deprivation in Scotland* (Edinburgh: Mainstream, 1983), p. 10.
 9 Ibid.
10 Ibid., p. 20.
11 Ibid.
12 Gordon Brown, interview, 28 July 1997.
13 Jonathan Wills, written statement to the author, 10 May 1997.
14 *Dunfermline Press,* 18 May 1984.
15 *Hansard,* 26 November 1984, cols 472–4.
16 David Stoddart, interview, 25 March 1997.
17 Wills, statement, 10 May 1997.
18 Ibid.
19 *Hansard,* 12 November 1984, cols 472–4.
20 Ibid.
21 Gordon Brown, interview, 5 June 1997.
22 *Hansard,* 13 February 1985, cols 454–8.
23 *Dunfermline Press,* 15 November 1985.
24 Andy McSmith, *John Smith* (London: Verso, 1993), p. 110.
25 Quoted in Sopel, *Tony Blair,* p. 83.
26 *Dunfermline Press.*
27 Gordon Brown, *James Maxton* (Edinburgh: Mainstream, 1986), pp. 20–21.
28 Ibid., p. 309.

CHAPTER 7 – SHADOW CABINET

1 Gordon Brown, interview, 28 July 1997.
2 Nick Brown, interview, 7 August 1997.
3 Andy McSmith, *John Smith* (London: Verso, 1993), p. 119.
4 Bryan Gould, *Goodbye to All That* (London: Macmillan, 1995), p. 205.
5 Ibid., p. 209.
6 *Hansard*, 21 March 1987, cols 100–107.
7 Ibid.
8 Ibid.
9 Gould, *Goodbye to All That*, p. 217.
10 Gordon Brown, interview, 28 July 1997.
11 Ibid.
12 All quotes from Brown's speech are from *Hansard*, 1 November 1988, cols 821–6.
13 Nick Brown, interview, 7 August 1997.
14 *Dunfermline Press*, 29 November 1988.
15 *Sunday Express*, 26 January 1989.
16 *Hansard*, 31 October 1989, cols 261–8.
17 Ibid.
18 Gould, *Goodbye to All That*, p. 221.
19 Ibid, p. 235.
20 Labour Party Annual Report 1991, pp. 39–41.
21 Ibid.

CHAPTER 8 – TWO STURDY OXEN

1 John Brown, interview, 11 August 1997.
2 Nick Brown, interview, 7 August 1997.
3 Gordon Brown, interview, 28 July 1997.
4 *Daily Mirror*, 13 April 1992.
5 Ibid.
6 Gordon Brown, interview, 28 July 1997.
7 Quoted in John Rentoul, *Tony Blair* (London: Little, Brown, 1995), p. 255.
8 Nick Brown, interview, 7 August 1997.
9 Ibid.
10 Ibid.
11 Gordon Brown, interview, 28 July 1997.
12 Ibid.
13 Ibid.

14 London *Evening Standard*, 28 July 1992.
15 Ibid.
16 *Guardian*, 15 September 1992.
17 *Hansard*, 24 September 1992, cols 93–108.
18 Rentoul, *Tony Blair*, p. 266.
19 Speech of 29 September 1992, published in Labour Party annual report 1992, pp 18–20.
20 Ibid., p. 24.
21 *Mail on Sunday*, 5 October 1992.
22 Gordon Brown, interview, 28 July 1997.
23 *Hansard*.
24 Rentoul, *Tony Blair*, p. 274.
25 London *Evening Standard*, 15 March 1993.
26 Philip Stephens, *Politics and the Pound* (London: Macmillan, 1996), p. 287.
27 *Hansard*, 9 June 1993, cols 359–74.
28 *Observer*, 11 July 1993.
29 Labour Party Annual Report 1993, pp. 35–7.
30 *Sunday Times*, 3 October 1993.
31 *Hansard*, 25 November 1993, cols 591-606.
32 *Daily Mirror*, 11 January 1994.
33 *Independent on Sunday*, 23 January 1994.
34 *Independent on Sunday*, 20 February 1994.

CHAPTER 9 – DEATH OF A HERO

1 Jon Sopel, *Tony Blair: The Moderniser* (London: Michael Joseph, 1995), p. 174.
2 *Daily Mail*, 22 April 1997.
3 Ibid.
4 *Spectator*, 26 April 1997.
5 John Rentoul, *Tony Blair* (London: Little, Brown, 1995), p. 356.
6 Ibid.
7 Charlie Whelan, interview, 25 July 1997.
8 London *Evening Standard*, 12 May 1994.
9 London *Evening Standard*, 28 July 1992.
10 *The Times*, 13 May 1994.
11 *Sunday Times*, 15 May 1994.
12 Colin Currie, interview, 8 July 1997.
13 John Brown, interview, 11 August 1997.
14 *Telegraph Magazine*, 26 April 1997, p. 26.
15 *Daily Mirror*, 2 June 1994.

CHAPTER 10 – A NEW TREASURY

1 *Independent*, 27 August 1994
2 Ed Balls, interview, 2 August 1997
3 Ibid.
4 Jon Sopel, *Tony Blair: The Moderniser* (London: Michael Joseph, 1995), p. 272.
5 *Hansard*, 23 November 1994, col. 612.
6 *Hansard*, 30 November 1994, col. 1232.
7 *Sunday Times*, 11 December 1994.
8 Speech to Labour Party's Finance and Industry Group, 17 May 1995.
9 London *Evening Standard*, 2 October 1995.
10 *The Times*, 2 October 1995.
11 Labour Party Conference Report 1995, pp. 8–12.
12 *Independent on Sunday*, 19 November 1995.
13 *Daily Telegraph*, 7 May 1996.
14 Speech to Labour Party conference, Blackpool, 30 September 1996.
15 *New Statesman*, 8 November 1996.
16 *Independent on Sunday*, 17 November 1996.
17 Ibid.
18 *Hansard*, 11 December 1996, cols 290–313.
19 *Sunday Telegraph*, 5 January 1997.
20 London *Evening Standard*, 11 February 1997.
21 Labour Party press release, 20 February 1997.

CHAPTER 11 – A VERY PRIVATE LIFE

1 *The Times*, 15 March 1996.
2 Profile of Diana Wong, *Daily Mail*, 11 May 1996.
3 *Daily Express*, 11 March 1996.
4 *Daily Telegraph*, 11 March 1996.
5 *The Times*, 15 March 1996.
6 *The Times*, 13 March 1996.
7 *Guardian*, 3 June 1997.
8 *Daily Mail*, 5 August 1995.
9 John Brown, interview, 11 August 1997.
10 *Sunday Mail*, 29 June 1997.
11 Murray Elder, interview, 31 July 1997.
12 *Sunday Mail*, 29 June 1997.
13 Elder, interview, 31 July 1997.
14 Jonathan Wills, written statement to the author, 10 May 1997.
15 Wilf Stevenson, interview, 28 July 1997.

16 Colin Currie, interview, 8 July 1997.
17 Wills, statement, 10 May 1997.
18 Bill Campbell, interview, 9 July 1997.
19 *Scotland on Sunday*, 18 February 1990.
20 *Daily Mail*, 14 March 1995.
21 *Scotland on Sunday*, 18 February 1990.
22 Wills, telephone interview, 26 August 1997.
23 *Harpers & Queen*, August 1992.
24 Private interviews.
25 *Daily Mail*, 14 March 1995.
26 *Daily Mail*, 5 August 1995.
27 *Sunday Times*, 9 October 1994.
28 Wills, telephone interview, 26 August 1997.
29 Currie, interview, 8 July 1997.
30 Private interview.
31 *Daily Mail*, 30 June 1997.
32 *Today*, 31 August 1995.
33 *Daily Mail*, 5 August 1995.
34 *Sunday Telegraph*, 12 January 1997; *Sunday Express*, 12 January 1997.
35 Stevenson, interview, 28 July 1997.
36 Ibid.
37 John Brown, interview, 11 August 1997.
38 Elizabeth Brown, interview, 12 August 1997.

CHAPTER 12 – ELECTION

1 *New Statesman*, May 1997 Special Edition.
2 Ibid.
3 *Guardian*, 21 March 1997.
4 Glasgow *Herald*, 24 March 1997.
5 *Independent*, 27 March 1997.
6 *The Times*, 4 April 1997.
7 *New Statesman*, 11 April 1997.
8 *Financial Times*, 12 April 1997.
9 *The Times*, 11 April 1997.
10 *New Statesman*, May 1997 Special Edition.
11 *Guardian*, 11 April 1997.
12 *New Statesman*, May 1997 Special Edition.
13 *Sunday Times*, 20 April 1997.
14 *New Statesman*, May 1997 Special Edition.
15 *Independent on Sunday*, 27 April 1997.

CHAPTER 13 – REALISING THE VISION

1 *Guardian*, 3 May 1997.
2 *Independent*, 7 May 1997.
3 *Financial Times*, 7 May 1997.
4 *The Times*, 7 May 1997.
5 *Financial Times*, 12 June 1997.
6 *Daily Telegraph*, 16 May 1997.
7 *Hansard*, 20 May 1997, cols 507–24.
8 Ibid.
9 *Financial Times*, 24 May 1997.
10 *Financial Times*, 26 May 1997.
11 *Daily Telegraph*, 5 June 1997.
12 *Financial Times*, 10 June 1997.
13 Liberal Democrat Party press release, 19 June 1997.
14 *Economist*, 21 June 1997, p. 34.

CHAPTER 14 – SOCIAL-JUSTICE CHANCELLOR

1 Isaiah Berlin, quoted by Dr. Currie.
2 The Anthony Crosland Memorial Lecture, 13 February 1997.
3 *Today*, BBC Radio 4, 14 May 1997.
4 Richard Layard, interview, 27 August 1997.
5 Kenneth Clarke, interview, 30 July 1997.
6 Ibid.
7 Giles Radice, interview, 23 July 1997.
8 Clarke, interview, 30 July 1997.
9 Ibid.
10 Ibid.
11 *Independent*, Scotland, 7 March 1997.
12 John E. Brown, interview, 12 August 1997.
13 Murray Elder, interview, 31 July 1997.
14 Bill Campbell, interview, 9 July 1997.
15 Colin Currie, interview, 8 July 1997.
16 Alf Young, interview, 8 July 1997.
17 Ibid.
18 Layard, interview, 27 August 1997.
19 Ibid.
20 Gordon Brown, interview, 20 April 1997.
21 Gordon Brown, *James Maxton* (Edinburgh: Mainstream, 1986), p. 315.

PICTURE PERMISSIONS

With thanks to the Brown family for kind use of personal photographs.

Copyright on other pictures used as follows:
As a Student: © Scotsman Publications Ltd
Labour PPC for South Edinburgh: © UPPA Ltd
Gordon Brown and Tony Blair: © "PA" News/David Giles
Brown, Blair and Prescott: © Marlow Peter/Magnum Photos
'Believe me': © The Independent/Brian Harris
With Treasury team: © The Guardian/Martin Argles
'The amazing Mr Brown': © Chris Riddell
'Pain at the top': © The Independent/Tom Pilsten
With the Lord Mayor: © Times Newspapers Limited/Alan Weller
With Bank of England: © "PA" News/Michael Stephens
Breakfast at Downing Street: © "PA" News/David Giles
With Sarah Macaulay: © News Group Newspapers/ Chris Ball
Charlie Whelan: © Treasury Office
'The Jaw is Dropping': © Steve Bell 1997 – 1015. 21.10.97/ The Guardian

INDEX